"Sara Moore has return...
before, the critical role that Germany has played in international affairs from the nineteenth century onwards. This book extends the coverage to the present day. In a tremendous sweep, drawing on a huge literature, she has produced a highly readable account of the key political and economic events of the last 100 years. She writes with conviction and reaches unequivocal conclusions on Germany's machinations in pursuit of European domination. It is a highly persuasive account that deserves a wide readership."
Professor Forrest Capie, Emeritus Professor of Economic History at the Cass Business School.

"This astonishingly different view of German political and economic history, from 1870 till the present day, deserves wide attention. The book makes seemingly wild assertions, that Germany started both world wars and was responsible for both the 1929 stock market crash and the Great Depression. It asserts that it was Germany, rather than France, which originally had the idea of the European Union and draws parallels between the Lehman crash and its aftermath and the Great Depression. The book forces us to take its assertions seriously as between half and three quarters of all its sources are German."
Professor Black, Professor of History, University of Exeter.

"I agree with you about a great deal that you report. I am glad that you still uphold the (Fritz) Fischer thesis on the origins of World War I ... You have a wonderful eye for detail."
Professor Stephen A Schuker, William W Corcoran Professor of History at Virginia University, Author of *What Historians Get Wrong About World War I.*

ABOUT THE AUTHOR

Sara Moore is an independent historian, whose initial book, *Peace without Victory for the Allies, 1918-1932* (1994) has recently been receiving increasing recognition and acclaim. Her new book *The Fourth Reich?* takes a broader sweep of history from Bismarck to the Lehman crash. Sara lives in London and Shropshire with her husband and has two daughters and a son.

JOLLIES PUBLISHING

First published in 2016

Print ISBN: 978-0-9954660-0-5
E pub ISBN: 978-0-9954660-1-2

Typeset by Born Group
Printed and bound in Great Britain by Clays, St Ives plc

For my father Lt. Frank Bury who was killed in action while serving in the No 4 Commandos in July 1944.

For the 600,000 old men and boys of the Volkssturm who died after the armaments makers decided that the war was lost but the country must fight on whilst they put their money abroad.

For the slaves at the underground Dora-Nordhausen concentration camp, hanged in March 1945 for sabotaging the construction of the V-1 buzz bomb, V-2 rocket and the A 10 missile destined for New York.

Crucially, for the sufferers from German economic warfare during the 1929 stock market crash and the Great Depression, and the victims of the Lehman Crash.

Finally for my loving family who have waited so patiently whilst I finished this book.

The Fourth Reich?

by Sara Moore

Edited by Charles Lambert
and
Ronan Daly

CONTENTS

Introduction   1

Prologue   4   Setting the Record Straight

Chapter 1   7   Bismarck: Unifier or Conqueror of Germany?

Chapter 2   34   The Coming War

Chapter 3   56   Bismarck's Responsibility for the First World War

Chapter 4   80   Who Won the War?

Chapter 5   111   Peace without Victory

Chapter 6   129   Germany's Great Inflation

Chapter 7   153   The 1929 Wall Street Crash

Chapter 8   170   The Pan-Germans Pave the Way for Hitler and War

Chapter 9   196   Germany and America's Aims at the End of the Second World War

Chapter 10   218   Who Won the Peace after the Second World War?

Chapter 11   246   How Reunification was Achieved

Chapter 12   267   Germany and the Lehman Brothers Crash

Conclusions   291

Notes   305

Bibliography   327

Index   335

Introduction

In the early 1970s I was at a dinner party in Gstaad and sat next to a German called Kurt. It was that conversation which ignited my passion to write this book and started me on my long trail of investigation. We chatted about the differences between life in England and Germany, all the usual dinner party talk, but what struck me as odd were the comments he made about the England he had experienced on his first visit in 1951, when he was just thirteen years old.

Instead of the victorious, thriving nation he had been expecting, Kurt found a war-torn, impoverished country. To the eyes of the young German boy, England felt like it had been vanquished rather than victorious. In 1951 Britons were still heavily rationed whereas in Germany rationing had ended. He thought it ridiculous that Britain hadn't managed to rid itself of its debts in the same way he and his friends had, by creating inflation and washing out the currency completely in order 'to teach the people how to work'.

Those innocuous comments set my mind racing, like a gun going off in my head. If what he was saying was accurate there was something wrong with the way I had been brought up to view Europe's recent history. I went to my son's history books to check on the facts about Germany's Great Inflations after both world wars. They only served to confirm what I had always thought. Kurt was wrong. The books told me that Germany was a vanquished nation, on its knees. It was a fading, dying eagle, slayed by the hand of St George (with the help of the Allies and the Americans, of course). But I didn't leave it there. I became fascinated and searched for more books on the subject. The more I read, the more I realised there might be something in what Kurt had said after all. There might be more than the official story I had been fed in the newspapers and newsreels at the time, the same story my children were being fed at school in the 1970s.

I kept catching glimpses of a very different historical truth but I couldn't find a book which told the whole story in a clear, concise way, rather than all the stodgy, dense and difficult prose I was having to plough through. The information was all out there, but it was hard to find, and it was not a great read.

So, here it is: the book that I have been looking for all these years. This is the book I wish I'd been given at school. This is the story that I feel I should have been told. This is the truth of our history since Bismarck's time, rather than the whitewashed stories of our childhood.

I come from a generation which was taught to be patriotic, and by and large we accepted what we were told without question. I am also reluctant to admit that the British are bad at doing anything. So my discoveries have at times been quite shocking and quite uncomfortable to write, but I want to set the record straight.

There are a number of different narratives about who started the First World War, but I hope to show that there is really no place for uncertainty when we look at the history of German economic and military policy. It was while I was researching this point that some other trends started to emerge. They stretched back to before Bismarck, to the Prussian princes of the eighteenth century, and they are the same policies which I believe the Germans adopted in the 2008 crash – I find these trends impossible to ignore.

So my focus with this book has diverged. Not only will it explore the causes of the First and Second World Wars, but, in addition, it will look at them within the last 150 years of German economic policy in order to arrive at its unsettling conclusion. I want to examine the commonly held notions, the official story and the contents of the popular history books we have used to, fill the minds of this country's youth for the last eighty years. Cut against this I will examine a very different story that historians are unearthing today. Why were we told what we were told at the time? Why have the British people been lied to and why have we been forced to bring up our children on a diet of fantasy and historical untruths?

As we follow the path of the German leadership's economic policy over the last 150 years we will pass many arresting landmarks along the way. Three of those landmarks will begin to seem surprisingly familiar, namely, the economic crashes of 1873, 1929 and 2008.

From the hubbub of the European orchestra, with each country playing a different melody, there is one ruthlessly determined Teutonic drum that has been beating the same rhythm for the past century and a half. Combined with the crushing white noise from across the Atlantic, it has now reached a stage where it is impossible to make out any of the individual European anthems any longer. Through the clever manipulation of American muscle, Germany is now beating the drum for all of Europe. And this is the story of how it happened.

PROLOGUE:

Setting the Record Straight

With a plethora of documentaries, articles and books on the First World War, the British media has been quick to jump on the bandwagon created by all the centenaries of the Great War which raged in Europe between 1914 and 1918. They sit happily alongside all the histories of Hitler and the rise and fall of the Third Reich which have been produced over the years to satisfy the public's seemingly insatiable appetite for this period.

Each one promises some new information on why Europe, in the early part of the twentieth century, became a charnel house. It has always been a gripping subject and as time passes it slips further into history and becomes 'safe'. We view it from an unchallenged, comfortable world. We view it as we might view the barbarism of the Romans or the Middle Ages, or indeed the worst excesses of the imperial empires of the nineteenth century. We view it as a period which is dead and gone, something that could never happen again in our apparently enlightened times. We also view it through the propaganda of the years, but that's okay, for we all know that it is the victors who get to write the history of any war, not the vanquished. But did the victors on the battlefield write our history? Did we, the British (along with our Allies), really win the First and Second World Wars? Just imagine, for one mad moment, that we didn't. If that was the case, then where on earth did the narratives we have all come to believe about those periods come from?

On our journey over the last one hundred or so years, there seem to be nine awkward, embarrassing and uncomfortable historical 'truths' that this book will focus on. Are they actually true? If we can fully understand our own history and stop blaming ourselves for everything that has gone wrong over the last hundred years, we will be in a much stronger position in the future.

We have been told the following facts as if they are indisputable, and we continue to pass them on to our children in the same way:

1. The 'Grand Old Man of Europe', Otto von Bismarck, unified his country and preserved the peace of Europe.
2. Europe just slid into the First World War in 1914.
3. Germany was vanquished in 1918 and the Allies won.
4. Germany was charged huge and iniquitous reparations by the Allies after the First World War, which led to its Great Inflation in 1923, to its subsequent poverty and high levels of unemployment in the Great Depression and to the rise of Hitler.
5. The 1929 Wall Street Crash was caused by the economic bubble in the States and the failure of the capitalist system. Without America's loans Germany could no longer pay the reparations.
6. Chancellor Heinrich Brüning (nicknamed the *Hungerkanzler*), imposed a deflationary policy of austerity on Germany in 1930 in order to return to a policy of sound money and to be able to pay the reparations.
7. Hitler came to power from humble beginnings through the force of his personality.

8. After the Second World War the European Union was conceived to prevent the squabbling European nations from ever going to war with each other again.
9. The Lehman crash in 2008 is too recent an event for our children's history books to comment upon. Germany's *Die Welt* newspaper, however, gives its opinion that the Lehman crash was due to the failures of the open-market capitalist system: 'Greed and stupidity have plunged the market into chaos ... Any economics student in his first semester could have concluded that the American model is not tenable.' While *Die Zeit* newspaper poses the question: 'Is finance-capitalism finished?' and predicts 'the end of world domination by the Anglo-Saxon finance industry.'

So, did the victors really write the history? And if not, who did?

CHAPTER ONE

Bismarck: Unifier or Conqueror of Germany?

In the eighteenth century, Europe bade farewell to the medieval world and embraced the Enlightenment: a new world in which 'The Rights of Man' were declared, and Newton discovered gravity. At this time, when the world looked to France for fashion, manners and taste, a state on the edge of Eastern Europe, called Prussia, was creating a modern Sparta, idolising the virtues of war.

The popular vision of Germany, before the First World War, was of a nation that had produced some of western culture's greatest music, literature and thinkers. It was seen as a nation whose only concern was in becoming unified, a feat accomplished by the Prussian, Bismarck. He was the 'great unifier and social reformer' who tried to lay the foundations for the future peace of Europe – or so we are led to believe.

The emphasis of this chapter, and indeed this book, is to focus on Prussia. It will show that the militarist state of Prussia fought and dominated Germany. From 1871 it dragged along behind it the 'united' (or conquered) German states. Prussian warmongering led to the First World War and today Germany beats the Prussian drum as it fiscally conquers Europe.

Historically, the Prussian nobility regarded themselves as the descendants of the Teutonic Knights, who conquered the land of the Pruzzis in the thirteenth century in the name of Christianity. The Teutonic Knights built a great empire in what is now the territory of Poland. At the centre of their empire stood the castle of Marienburg, which the Polish now call Malbork. At the height of its power, Marienburg Castle housed three thousand knights and is still the largest castle in the world by surface area. Later, the Prussians lost their influence in the region, but in the eighteenth century the Hohenzollern kings built the state of Prussia up into a soldier state, whose citizens, like the warrior knights of old, believed in 'blind obedience' to their King – and in their King's right to invade his neighbours' territory.

In the seventeenth century the Great Elector, Frederick William, built up a sizeable army and used it to enlarge Prussia. The Great Elector's grandson, King Frederick Wilhelm I, created a huge army in Prussia in the early eighteenth century, recruiting 10 per cent of the entire population. Frederick William's son, Frederick II, who became known as Frederick the Great, invaded Austria's richest province, Silesia, as soon as he came to the throne.

Frederick the Great was admired for his intellect and his religious tolerance, yet his influence was pernicious. He advised his successors to accumulate a mighty war chest and then invade their neighbours. 'Money is like a sorcerer's wand,' he declared.[1]

Prussia's General Gebhard von Blücher brought two corps to join the Duke of Wellington at Waterloo, arriving at a crucial time at the battle in the late afternoon. His intervention led to a decisive victory against Napoleon. Blücher became the highest-decorated Prussian soldier in history, and

The first Imperial German Chancellor, Otto von Bismarck.
(1815-1898).

the Congress of Vienna (1814–5), rewarded Prussia by giving it not only large parts of Saxony and Westphalia, but also the Rhineland with its rich seams of coal, which would help bring it immense wealth and power.

The modern consensus of opinion seems to be that the Congress of Vienna was a great settlement, which brought peace to Europe for one hundred years. However, after the Second World War, German Chancellor Konrad Adenauer disagreed, declaring that the greatest mistake the British had made was 'at the Congress of Vienna, when you foolishly put Prussia on the Rhine as a safeguard against France and another Napoleon' and that 'Prussianism in its turn culminated in National Socialism'.

The Congress of Vienna decided that the new German Confederation, comprising twenty-six states of varying sizes, should agree upon a collective policy for trade, transport and customs duties. Prussia was by far the largest state in the new Confederation, and it was determined that the 'collective policy' should be under Prussian rather than Austrian control. By 1834 it managed to create a *Zollverein* free trade zone of the twenty-six states: a microcosm, in a purely Germanic way, of the European Economic Community over a hundred years later. However, Austria was not invited to become a member.

Otto von Bismarck was born in 1815, at the time of Napoleon's defeat. He was eleven years younger than Disraeli and six years younger than Gladstone. Although he was a younger son of a Prussian Junker aristocrat, he was still entitled to call himself 'von', in contrast to the system in England, where only the first-born has the privilege of a title. Many of the Junker aristocracy owned large estates, but Bismarck's family estate was relatively small. Even on small estates, however, fifty years after serfdom had been abolished, the Junkers were the lords and masters and the workers knew their lowly place.

10

Bismarck was a clever but bellicose youth who fought twenty-five duels at university. Initially viewed with the greatest suspicion by the conservative Prussian hierarchy, his marriage to a woman called Johanna von Puttkamer, from a strictly religious Protestant circle, alleviated their suspicions.

Bismarck resisted going into the army, found the civil service constricting and the management of the family's farmland dull. He eventually found the sort of challenge he relished when he became a member of the first Prussian Parliament.

King Frederick Wilhelm IV once refused to employ him, declaring that 'Bismarck (was) only to be used when the bayonet rules unrestrictedly'. However, he made many useful friends during the 1850s, including General Albrecht von Roon.

By the time King Wilhelm I acceded to the throne in 1861, Prussia, with its great seams of coal, was prospering, and so were the independent states of Saxony, Bavaria and Hanover. Otto von Bismarck, who the great historian and liberal politician Theodor Mommson, asserted 'enlarged Germany and reduced the Germans', had yet to become Chancellor.

One of the first things Wilhelm I did on becoming King was to invite Bismarck's friend, General von Roon, to prepare a report on the army. Von Roon's father had died during the French occupation following Prussia's disastrous war with France in 1806. He proposed that the King should enforce conscription for three years and more than double the size of Germany's standing army.

Frederick the Great had lauded the discipline of the Prussian army in his political testament, declaring, 'Military discipline ... makes blindly obedient, the soldier to his officer, the officer to his colonel, the colonel to his general, and the generals to the commander-in-chief.'[2] The backbone of the Prussian army had always been the Officer Corps, which was recruited from the sons of the Junker landowners.

In England, officers used to be recruited from the landed gentry and it was regarded as noble to die for one's country. The Junkers performed the same function in Germany. However, whereas in England army officers were always servants of the government, in Prussia soldiers were responsible only to the King.[3]

According to the Prussian military code, for a civilian to insult an officer was an offence to his uniform, for which it was his duty, without a moment's hesitation, to draw his sword. If a member of the Prussian Officer Corps committed a serious crime like murder, he was not subject to civilian law in peacetime, but was tried by a military court, where he might be 'honourably acquitted', whereas under English law he would have certainly been sentenced to death. In war, therefore, opponents could expect no mercy. Indeed, the Prussian military theorist, von Clausewitz, begged his pupils to avoid a 'benevolent spirit towards a stricken foe and denounced moderation as an absurdity'. The General Staff manual expressly warned the Officer Corps to be on its guard against 'humanitarian notions' and the NCOs were expected to use their fists to discipline the men under their charge. Prussian soldiers therefore were far more terrified of their own officers than they were of the enemy.[4] No soldier would dare disobey the order of an officer to fire upon a crowd, even if it was peaceful. 'Blind obedience' was the diktat in the Prussian army. Countless of Prussia's unfortunate citizens had already become used to 'blind obedience' as Prussia had instituted the principle of universal military service between 1807 and 1813.

King Wilhelm asked the Landstag for the money to implement von Roon's proposals to expand the size of the standing army and enforce three-year conscription. The Liberal government was annoyed at being asked to raise taxes to increase the army's size at a time when Prussia was not under threat. The issue threatened to become a constitutional crisis because

Prussia's civilians were adamantly opposed to the proposals. In the May 1862 elections, the King's conservative supporters were all but wiped out while the Progressive Party received a huge increase in votes. However, the old King remained obdurate. In the end he found the one man who was happy to ignore the wishes of the people, Otto von Bismarck.

Bismarck was tall and powerfully built. He had thinning auburn hair, sported a red-blond moustache and enjoyed dispensing malice towards his opponents. He had always been candid about his disdain for parliament, declaring: 'I am no democrat and cannot be one', and 'We shall bring honour and glory to the name of Junkerdom.' He caused further dismay by declaring: 'The great questions of the time will not be resolved by speeches and majority decisions ... but by blood and iron.'[5] His victory over parliament was complete when the King offered him the opportunity to not only become Minister President but also to be in charge of foreign affairs.

Bismarck assured King Wilhelm that as the economy was in such good shape he could implement von Roon's plans to expand and modernise the army without having to ask parliament to raise taxes. The country was awash with coal and the armaments maker, Krupp, was making a fortune from his patented method of producing train wheels for the fast expanding European railways. Sensing an economic opportunity, Krupp promised to help finance the army's expansion.[6]

In January 1863 a rising broke out in the Russian part of Poland and public opinion throughout Europe expressed sympathy for the heroic downtrodden Poles. However, Bismarck's Prussian predecessor, Frederick the Great, advocated allying Prussia with Russia, stating 'thus we have our back free as long as the alliance lasts'.[7] Bismarck agreed. He had plans for the future and felt that he needed Russia's tacit support. For the following thirty years, the Russo-Prussian *entente* would be the backbone of Bismarck's eastern policy.

For the time being, Bismarck was eager to take advantage of a foreign policy issue in the West.

When King Frederick VII of Denmark died in 1863, the Duchies of Schleswig and Holstein were claimed both by his Danish heir and by a German Duke. Bismarck alleged that they legally belonged to the Danes under the London Protocol signed a decade before, but that as Schleswig was mostly German speaking it should be returned to its former status. When Denmark refused this solution, Bismarck persuaded Austria to join Prussia in invading Denmark on 1st February 1864.[8] After a second war, Denmark ceded both Duchies, nominally under Prussian and Austrian control.

But Prussia did not allow this situation to last. Although, under the Treaty of Gastein, Schleswig was given to Prussia and Holstein to Austria, Prussia was given the right to build military roads through Holstein and establish a naval base at Kiel.[9] As time went on Prussia encroached more and more on Holstein's sovereignty until Austria's hostility was aroused.

The dispute with Austria over Holstein continued to smoulder until it provided a pretext for war. A hundred years earlier Frederick the Great had declared: 'If sovereigns wish to make war they are not restrained by arguments for the need for a public proclamation. They determine the course upon which they wish to embark, make war and leave to some industrious jurist the trouble of justifying their action.'[10]

Bismarck admired Frederick's logic. It matched his own sentiments exactly. Frederick also wrote, 'It is necessary to have in one's neighbour states, and especially among one's enemies, agents who report faithfully all they see and hear.' Again Bismarck agreed. He decided to employ Wilhelm Stieber, who had lately lost his job as Chief of Police and Head of Security of the Berlin police headquarters, to help him prepare the ground for a successful war against Austria.

An autobiography of Wilhelm Stieber, called *The Chancellor's Spy* was published a hundred years after his death. In an explosive article, the magazine *Der Spiegel* immediately declared it to be 'rubbish'. However, despite the inaccuracies in the book, Stieber's brilliance as a spy has been recognised by historians such as Jeffrey T Richelson (1997) in *A Century of Spies: Intelligence in the 20th Century*, Jackson and Scott (2000) in *Understanding Intelligence in the Twenty-First Century*, Terry Crowdy in *A History of Spies, Spymasters and Espionage* and also Stephen Wade in *Victoria's Spymaster: Empire and Espionage* (2011), who went as far as to call Wilhelm Stieber, one of the founding fathers of military intelligence. I have therefore inserted a few lines into this book to show the way Stieber operated to help Bismarck ascertain his foes readiness for war and to prosecute his wars successfully.

Stieber asserted that in order to assess Austria's readiness for war he would need a multitude of spies and suggested that the best way for them to operate without attracting attention was to set up a Press Bureau, like Reuters. Most of the agents would merely seem to be out to find a story and would not even need to know each other. Stieber also solved the question of payment, declaring that some brilliant forgers had been detained in Prussian prisons and that he was sure they would be able to forge undetectable bank notes.[11]

Soon Stieber had some interesting information to divulge. Firstly, he revealed that the Austrians wished to satisfy the 'longing of all Germans for unity by means of a federation of states with Austria at their head', and that this union was particularly desired by the Catholic South German states of the Confederation such as Bavaria and Hesse. Secondly, he reported that the authorities in Vienna had no idea that a war was in the offing; indeed the Austrian people were resolutely against the idea of war. Thirdly, he revealed that three-quarters of Austria's military manoeuvres were purely defensive, and fourthly, that it would take a good two weeks longer for Austria to mobilise its forces than Prussia. Finally, he announced that unlike Prussia, Austria did not have the latest Dreyse needle gun, said to be the first reliable breech-loading gun guaranteed to mow down the enemy.[12]

Bismarck declared that although it was 'repugnant' to him to take advantage of members of the same race, the Austrian Emperor, Franz Joseph, was determined to reduce Prussia to a powerless, petty state and so co-existence was impossible. He urged Stieber to stir up animosity between Austria and its neighbours and to persuade the Austrians to become dissatisfied with their government.

Soon tales of corruption swept the Austrian newspapers, also alarming reports of incidents where the police had exceeded their authority. Stieber also used eight hundred 'generously paid agitators' to incite the Hungarians, Slavs and Czechs against Austrian rule. An even more provocative plan, instigated with the help of counterfeit money, was to establish a 'Hungarian Freedom Legion', made up of deserters from the Austrian army. Finally Stieber promoted a report that Italy was about to invade Austria.[13]

Bismarck had managed to secure a defensive and offensive alliance with Italy 'in pursuit of the necessary reform of the German Confederation'. Under this treaty Italy pledged to declare war on Austria, if and only if, Prussia attacked Austria within three months. Prussia's pledge to Italy did not leave Bismarck much time to incite Austria into declaring war!

Prussia was by far the largest state in the German Confederation. The smaller German states disliked Bismarck's predatory plans for Schleswig-Holstein and sided with Austria in the Federal Diet over the issue. On 27th March 1866 Prussia partially mobilised its troops.[14] Then Bismarck, who had proclaimed, 'I am not a democrat and can never be one', stated that the Federal Diet was not legitimate, and that a new National Assembly must be elected by universal suffrage instead. The proposal was met with cynicism and horror.

On 9th May the Federal Diet voted to demand why Prussia had mobilised its troops, but Bismarck gave no explanation. On the contrary, one month later, a huge total of 330,000 soldiers assembled on Prussia's borders.[15] But Bismarck still had no pretext for war.

The Austrians asked the Federal Diet to intervene in the Schleswig-Holstein conflict and to mobilise the non-Prussian army corps. They also ordered the Governor General in Holstein to call the estates of the Duchy into session. Unfortunately, by this action, Austria 'revoked' the recently signed Gastein Convention, and according to Bismarck's press office, 'endangered the sovereign rights of the King of Prussia as co-regent of Schleswig-Holstein.' His press release concluded menacingly: 'Our Government will respond to the treaty violation with its full energy in defence of our rights.'[16]

Bismarck then presented the smaller German states with the text of a new federal constitution, which would exclude Austria and contain a Lower House based on universal suffrage. On 15th June 1866, Prussia invaded Hanover, Saxony and Hesse while simultaneously presenting them with a twelve-hour ultimatum.[17] Bismarck had managed to engineer war against Austria while proclaiming to his king and the wider world that Austria was responsible for the conflict.

A total of 120,000 soldiers from Saxony, Hanover, Bavaria, Württemberg, Baden, the Electorate of Hesse, Nassau, Frankfurt and several German principalities fought on Austria's side.[18] The Hungarians also forgot their grievances and rallied to Austria's support. Yet Austria was faced with war on two fronts. Although the Austrian army defeated Italy at Custoza, it was no match for the Prussians 'needle gun' which produced a steady stream of 'lightning-fast' salvos, routing the Austrian armies at Königgrätz and Sadowa.

In 1742, after Frederick the Great succeeded in seizing Silesia from Austria, he wrote to his Minister, Heinrich von Podewils: 'At the present moment our task consists in making the capitals of Europe accustomed to seeing Prussia occupy the great position which she had obtained by her war with Austria, and I believe that great moderation and a conciliatory attitude towards our neighbours will help us in this.'[19]

Bismarck sensibly took the same course at the Peace of Prague on 23rd August 1866. Although he demanded a hefty indemnity he did not actually grab any of Austria's territory. He was not so conciliatory to the German states. He absorbed the Duchies of Schleswig and Holstein into the Kingdom of Prussia, along with Hanover, Nassau and the free city of Frankfurt, while Bavaria and the other southern states had to pay war indemnities and agreed that their armies would fight for the Prussian King, if (and when) war came again.

As the citizens of the former 'free' city of Frankfurt were unhappy about having to pay indemnities, Bismarck decided to make an example of the city, which had been home to Germany's largest Jewish community from the fifteenth until the nineteenth century. Frankfurt was initially fined six million thalers and then another twenty-five million. When there was opposition to this impost, Bismarck threatened Frankfurt with an additional fine for every day it failed to pay, and if the money was still not forthcoming, he declared that he would bring all traffic, mail and business dealings to a halt. No wonder the mayor of Frankfurt hanged himself! The defeated Hanoverians were also targeted. They were reduced to calling their dogs 'William' and 'Bismarck' so that they could insult them in public without incurring the long arm of the law.

After uncovering a stash of guns in a Hanoverian castle cellar and finding and appropriating the famous Guelph treasure from a Hanoverian bank, Wilhelm Stieber was dispatched to Paris to scout out France's readiness for war, with Bismarck's words ringing in his ears: 'Despite all the sympathy I feel for the poor Emperor of France because of his dwindling prestige in his own country, I do not believe that we can avoid going to war with him for very long.'[20]

Bismarck's surreptitious use of the Guelph treasure meant that the costs of Stieber's undercover operations in Paris would not appear on the official Prussian defence budget and therefore the entire operation could remain secret. Stieber set up a huge network of spies across France, whilst posing as a journalist. Thousands of dossiers were scoured to find Frenchmen who might betray their homeland with the right inducements. Yet it was one of his own agents who discovered the most exciting news. While he was pretending to be an Alsatian house-painter looking for work, he found employment with the French War Ministry, painting a dilapidated wall. As soon as he was alone he scouted the area, found the right door and there on the table, marked 'Secret', lay the precious plan for the deployment of French troops in the event of a war with Germany.[21]

The Austrians had suffered in their war against Prussia from their lack of the most modern weapon, the Dreyse 'needle gun'. In 1870 the French were equipped with the breech-loading Chassepot rifle, said to be one of the most modern mass-produced firearms in the world, with a far longer range than Prussia's needle gun.[22] However, Stieber examined the Chassepot rifle and declared that it worked on the same principle as Prussia's gun and did not constitute such a leap in technology as the French claimed. He regarded France's much vaunted precursor to the machine gun, the *mitrailleuse* in the same light, stating that it was prone to jamming and ineffective against moving targets.[23] Meanwhile, Prussia had Krupp's famous 6-pounder (3kg) steel breech-loading cannons in its armoury, ready to pound the enemy in future battles.

Stieber asserted that France was ill-prepared for war as many French troops were in Rome protecting the Papal States and Emperor Napoleon III's many illnesses, which included kidney disease, bladder stones, chronic bladder and prostrate infections, were affecting his ability to run the country, yet alone to wage war.

Bismarck declared the situation in France to be an 'invitation to the German soldier's boot'. He would also have liked to have used a 'soldier's boot' to bring some of the recalcitrant German states into line but decided that might be unproductive. A glorious war against the historic enemy, France, was what was needed to persuade them to accept Prussian control. If only Bismarck could persuade the French to declare war![24]

Napoleon was already upset with Bismarck. Bismarck had reneged on his promise to Napoleon to give France the Duchy of Luxembourg as a reward for not intervening in his war against Austria. Relations between Prussia and France deteriorated until eventually the British found a compromise. The Prussian garrison was removed from Luxembourg and the Duchy was declared an independent neutral state. Yet Napoleon had been made to look a fool and it rankled.

In 1868 the Spaniards expelled their delinquent Queen Isabella and started the search for a new king. Bismarck sensed an opportunity. He gave his emissary, Theo von Bernardi, money from the booty he had secured during his war against the kingdom of Hanover, to bribe officials who could help Wilhelm I's young Hohenzollern relative, Prince Leopold, in his application to become King of Spain.[25] The Spanish duly offered their crown to the Prussian prince. King Wilhelm I, however, had obviously not been a party to Bismarck's scurrilous plan. On 20th April King Wilhelm and Leopold's father, Prince Anton, wrote to Madrid to refuse the proposal.

Bismarck was annoyed. Prussia had a great army, ready to go to war against France but King Wilhelm wouldn't help him create the opportunity. Bismarck did not give up hope. He secretly sent a letter to Spain's General Prim, through another confidant, asking Prim to write to King Wilhelm again, offering the Spanish crown to Prince Leopold, while insisting that Bismarck had nothing to do with his offer.

On 28th May Bismarck told young Prince Leopold's father, Prince Anton, that the Spanish had finally managed to change King Wilhelm's mind. General Adjutant, Alfred von Waldersee, who was at Bad Ems with the King wrote in his diary:

'the Spaniards ... knocked on the door again and now all of a sudden the father and son Hohenzollern have become passionately in favour ... They have allowed themselves to be talked into it by Bismarck, and the Prince who doubted that he had the guts to be King of Spain, is suddenly filled with the idea that he has a mission to make Spain happy'.[26]

On 19th June 1870 Prince Leopold sent his letter of acceptance of the Spanish crown. On 2nd July the provisional Spanish government welcomed its arrival. The French were horrified. They did not want France to be hemmed in by Prussian kings to the north and south. Their ambassador, Count Benedetti, protested that the Hohenzollern candidacy for the Spanish throne constituted a serious attempt to change the balance of power in Europe. Leopold's father was pressured to withdraw his son's candidacy and King Wilhelm of Prussia, who was never keen on the idea in the first place, renounced it in the name of the House of Hohenzollern. On 12th July 1870 Prince Leopold's candidature was officially withdrawn.

Bismarck did not give up. He decided upon a diplomatic offensive against France's ambassador, emphasising the restraint and moderation as shown by Wilhelm I and his Ministry in withdrawing Prince Leopold's candidature.[27] The French were incensed. Egged on by the press and the Empress Eugenie, Napoleon instructed Count Benedetti to demand that King Wilhelm never change his mind again. King Wilhelm, who was taking the waters at Bad Ems, was by now annoyed by the whole affair. He described the French request as 'impertinent', and sent a private report about it to Bismarck as follows:

'13th June 1870. Count Benedetti intercepted me while I was out walking, and in what became a very importunate manner, demanded that I authorise him to immediately telegraph the message that I promised never again, at any time in the future, to give my consent if the Hohenzollerns were to renew their candidacy. Finally I refused his demand somewhat sternly for on no account can one enter into undertakings of this kind. Naturally I told him that I had not received any information, and that, since he had been informed sooner than I about what was going on in Paris and Madrid, he could easily understand that my government had nothing to do with the matter.'[28]

Most of the King's government 'had nothing to do with the matter' but Bismarck had cooked the whole idea up in the first place and he was not going to let the opportunity slip. He quickly altered the Dispatch, which King Wilhelm had sent him so that it read:

'Ems, 13th June, 1870. Today, France's Ambassador, Benedetti, intercepted the King of Prussia when he was out for a walk and importunately demanded that he promise to forbid the Hohenzollerns to assume the throne of Spain at any time in the future. In view of this unreasonable demand, the King of Prussia refused to reply to the French ambassador and sent an adjutant on duty to inform him that he had nothing further to say to him.'[29]

The very next day Bismarck published his version of the Ems Dispatch in all the German newspapers and informed all the foreign courts that Benedetti had 'addressed the old and sickly King of Prussia, against his will and in a provocative manner'. The following day, the French voted for war.

The French were foolish. Whatever their anxieties, they should have employed a spy like Wilhelm Stieber to ascertain the Germans' battle-readiness before embarking on war.

Prussia's Chief of Staff, Helmuth von Moltke, had been devising a war plan since 1857, and had an intimate knowledge of the railway timetables so that he could get his troops to the front at lightning speed. Within a period of only fourteen days the Prussian army was mobilised and ready to attack.

Frederick the Great used to lead his men in battle. This was impossible for Bismarck as he has never been in the army, but he admired the Prussian military tradition. So throughout the campaign he wore the silver helmet and yellow coat of a cavalry division, decorated either with the sparkling Order of the Eagle, or a gleaming white service cap.

Victories at Wissembourg and Wörth on the 4th and 6th August 1870 shook the morale of the French army. Von Moltke was a brilliant tactician and he was helped by Krupp's brilliant six-pounder cannons, which were far speedier and more accurate than the muzzle-loaded bronze cannons of France. Napoleon III surrendered and the Germans marched on to Paris. After four months besieging Paris, Bismarck ordered two hundred and fifty of Krupp's cannons to bombard the city. They silenced the defences and destroyed the tunnels bringing food to the starving population.

Wilhelm Stieber had been at Bismarck's right hand during the military campaign against France. Bismarck ordered him to prepare well-guarded lodgings for the 'Revolutionary Minister', Jules Favre. Jules Favre was the Vice-President and Secretary of State for Foreign Affairs in the new Republican government, and he had come with his stepson, Martinez del Roi, to negotiate peace terms.

There could not have been a more striking contrast between well-fed Bismarck, 'beaming' with health, and the two half-starved Frenchmen, who arrived to negotiate peace. Their ravenous appearance gave Stieber an idea. He decided that he would play the part of a valet to gain some inside information. He hurried back to where the secret police had their headquarters, made all his officers put on civilian clothes, and laid on a sumptuous meal. After dinner he gave Favre his feather coverlet and led him to a bedroom he had prepared for him, where he had drilled a hole to overhear his conversations. Meanwhile Bismarck left for a Council of War with the Kaiser and army leaders.

Favre did not snuggle down under the coverlet in his bedroom but spent the whole night nervously pacing up and down, debating the peace options with his stepson. These were carefully listened to by Stieber's assistants before being passed on to Bismarck.

Favre was deceived by the solicitude of his valet, Stieber, and thanked Bismarck for providing him with such a good attendant. In return, Bismarck refused Favre's request for a month's truce and thirty-six thousand cattle for Paris's starving population, declaring: 'We will keep them on scanty rations unless they agree to the peace terms we choose to set.'[30] Meanwhile Stieber oversaw the surveillance of the town using his secret police to make brutal arrests.[31]

Eventually Paris surrendered after one hundred and thirty-two days under siege. On 28th January 1871 Count Bismarck and Jules Favre signed a ceasefire agreement and the city turned over all its arms. Stieber took hostages, who were forced to walk ahead of the soldiers until Bismarck was sure that the fortresses were not mined.

The Prussian army won the battle at the cost of over 138,000 French dead and 143,000 wounded. Although less than 30,000 of the Prussian army had died, nearly 90,000 had been injured.[32] Wilhelm I was proclaimed German Emperor in the Gallery of the Hall of Mirrors at Versailles. Yet neither Bismarck nor his new Kaiser were happy. Bismarck was in a rage about the defects of the ceremony while Wilhelm objected to being called German Emperor instead of Emperor of Germany.

It was still, however, a momentous occasion. The Holy Roman Empire was called the First (German) Reich. Bismarck and his Kaiser would name their new empire the Second Reich, even though Wilhelm Stieber's spies related that the kings and princes and governmental leaders in the states of Hanover, Bavaria, Württemberg and Saxony were all opposed to the idea of a 'German Empire' under the rule of a Prussian king. They would still far prefer Austria to regain its ascendancy in Germany and Prussia to submit to it.[33]

Under the Peace Treaty of Frankfurt, France agreed to cede the French provinces of Alsace (except the town of Belfort) and North East Lorraine, and to pay a massive reparations bill. Then the Kaiser and his Chancellor returned to administer their discontented new Reich. Not surprisingly, the new Reichstag was little more than a popular façade to hide the new empire's autocratic structure. Although elected by universal franchise, its power was confined to making suggestions, which the government could refuse, to checking the income and expenditure of the budget, to passing bills which did not affect the Emperor's right to appoint and control the military and to appoint the Chancellor and deal with foreign affairs. Yet, although more autocratic, Bismarck's new empire shared some remarkable similarities with the European Union.

It was comprised of twenty-six states, as opposed to the twenty-eight states in the European Union, and, as in the European Union, the states were of wildly differing sizes. There were four kingdoms, six grand duchies, five duchies, seven principalities and three republics, each with its own constitution, representative system and divergent economy.[34] They retained practically the whole of their internal administration but Prussia was the dominant state, just as Germany would become the dominant state in the European Union.

There was another similarity. Both Bismarck's Reich and the European Union decided to adopt a new currency. On

1st January 1999 the European Union adopted the euro, instead of the d-mark, the franc and other venerable European currencies. In 1871 Bismarck decided to adopt the gold mark instead of the currencies currently prevailing in the different states of his new Reich.

Traditionally, Prussia and many northern German states had used a silver coin called the Vereinsthaler for their currency. The Austro-Hungarian Empire also used silver for its currency although its coin was called the gulden and had a slightly lower silver content than in Prussia. Many of the southern states in Bismarck's new Reich had traditionally used the gulden too, although their gulden was slightly less valuable than Austria's.[35]

As with the arrival of the euro, the gold mark initially created no problems. The French were forced to pay the stupendous sum of five billion gold marks in reparations after the Franco-Prussian war. (If the sum is converted using RPI, it amounts to 342 billion gold francs today![36]) More than half of the money was earmarked to be spent on improving the German armies and modernising the fortifications.[37] Yet there still seemed to be plenty of cash around. A bubble of money was created and speculation ensued, just as it happened after the arrival of the euro. Even Austria joined in the fun.

After its defeat by Prussia, the Austrian Empire had devolved into the Austro-Hungarian Empire. To encourage confidence in the new regime, Austria and Hungary sponsored building works. Some of the most beautiful buildings in their capital cities were built at this time. Mortgages were easy to come by, and a construction boom took off, not only in Vienna but also in Berlin and southern Germany. As land values soared, borrowers took added risks, using unbuilt or half-built houses as collateral for loans, just as would happen between 2001 and 2008.[38]

The party spread to America where Europeans and Americans speculated on American railroad shares. Then interest rates rose, and rose again,[39] and cash became scarce everywhere. Ominously it was also announced that silver would no longer be used as currency from July 1873.

Bismarck's adoption of the gold mark, and the forthcoming abandonment of silver, created a glut of silver on world markets, debasing the value of other countries' reserves based on silver. The deflation of silver-backed currencies cascaded throughout the world[40] and the value of the Austrian gulden plummeted. On 9th May the Vienna Stock Exchange suffered a devastating crash, followed by a crash on Wall Street and eventually in Berlin.

The stock market crash came at a handy time for Bismarck. 150 years later, on 23rd March 2006, the newspaper *Der Spiegel* would declare that the real divide in Germany was not between the former East Germans and those in the West, but between the Protestant North and the Catholic South. Bismarck was no longer indulging in military warfare by 1873 but he was determined to wage war against the Catholic Church, whose adherents in southern Germany yearned for ties with Catholic Austria, rather than with the autocratic Prussians. In 1871, he initiated his so-called *Kulturkampf*, and abolished the Catholic Department of the Prussian Kultusministerium.[41] Then, in May 1873, just as the stock market was crashing, he instituted his infamous May Laws, which would eventually lead to hundreds of Catholics, and scores of priests and bishops, either being imprisoned or exiled.[42]

Bismarck's experts argued that the Austrians were to blame for the stock market catastrophe in Vienna because of their irresponsible lending. Yet basically Bismarck had been responsible both for the easy money after 1870 and for its disappearance in 1873. Huge care should be taken in introducing a large new currency. Whether by accident or design, Bismarck's over-hasty decision to tighten the purse strings and abandon silver seemed to be the primary cause of the crash, both in Vienna and in New York. Nonetheless, Bismarck accused the Austrian Emperor of allowing the Austrian State Bank to issue a larger volume of bank notes than had previously been authorised. He declared that 'the Vienna Stock Exchange had been the arena in which speculation had called forth a lot of companies ... for which the existing capital proved insufficient'. [43]

The Austrian Emperor's brother, Archduke Ludwig Viktor, was alleged to have indulged in unwise speculation. Stephen Keglevich, a relative of Hungary's Royal Treasurer, was also declared bankrupt. The Austro-Hungarian Empire received a grievous blow. Thousands of Austrian public figures were ruined. They had hoped to recover their self-esteem after Bismarck's victory against France. Instead they received a shattering blow. Naturally they didn't dare answer back. Instead they diverted all their anger against the Jews' 'unwise expansion, insolvency and dishonest manipulation' of the Vienna Stock Exchange. Their enmity against the Jews lasted until the First World War.

Banks in Munich, Stuttgart and Frankfurt, which had links to Vienna, also suffered. The Catholic southern states were horrified by the imprisonment of their bishops and they realised the unpalatable fact that in future they would have to go 'cap in hand' to Berlin if they wanted money.

After the Austrian stock market collapsed, the crash extended to New York and Berlin. Then Bismarck's Reich adopted a policy of 'austerity', producing a lengthy economic depression. This caused an alarming increase in anti-Semitism, which Bismarck was prepared to countenance in aid of his policy of 'negative integration'.

With its 'intoxicating propaganda', anti-Semitism was able to attract mass support and form a unifying force in Bismarck's Reich. It became an acceptable, and in time increasingly violent, expression of all those who were anxious about the social and economic changes that resulted from the rapid pace of Germany's industrialisation. In 1899 the programme of the United Anti-Semitic Parties would call for the solution of the 'world problem' of the Jews by having them all rounded up and destroyed in what they called their *Endlösung*.[44]

After Bismarck's victorious wars against France and Austria, the Reichstag allowed the Prussian standing army to remain at the formidable figure of 400,000 men until 1874. The Reichstag then had the right to vote on reducing its size, but the generals and Bismarck were determined to keep it permanently at 400,000.[45] A confrontation with the Reichstag loomed while Bismarck searched for an excuse to maintain it at its present level without creating a constitutional crisis.

France had paid its enormous reparations bill with astonishing haste in order to get rid of the German occupying force. Yet this did not mean that the French were rich. Far from it. The French population hardly increased in size in the next forty years because the country felt so poor. The sandy colonial empire that France acquired in North Africa was little compensation for the loss of land in resource-rich Lorraine or the fertile farms and valuable vineyards of Alsace. The German standing army of 400,000 battle-ready troops was threatening. In 1875 France decided to increase the number of her cavalry battalions from three to four.

Bismarck immediately seized on the news of France's increase in cavalry with an article in the *Berlin Post* called 'Is war in sight?' He told every capital in Europe that France was bent on revenge. Russia's ambassador in London, Count Peter Shouvaloff, commented cynically to British Foreign Secretary, Lord Derby, that it was the state of Bismarck's nerves that was a danger to Europe! The order for a German 'preventative war' was averted by British and Russian intervention[46] and Bismarck secured what he had been aiming for all along, the agreement of the Reichstag that the size of the German standing army could be fixed at 400,000 men for the next seven years.

The German philosopher, Constantin Frantz, mourned for the German Confederation of States, which Bismarck had destroyed in 1866:

'It was of paramount importance for the whole European system ... Its dissolution ... made the whole European system lose its former stability so that from that moment onward the relations of all European states became based on bayonets, and the whole continent groans under the burden of militarism'.[47]

The German people suffered from the Long Depression. However, the iron and steel industrialists of the Ruhr prospered, helped by the rich coal seams of the Ruhr, the iron ore from Lorraine, a competitive exchange rate and indirect subsidies from the state. This was fortunate for the armaments company, A G Krupp, because it had over expanded after the victorious 1870 war. The Emperor and his Chancellor said a public 'Nein' to coming to the aid of Europe's largest company. However, they were not going to let it go bankrupt! Soon a group of Prussian banks came to its rescue. Smaller companies would go to the wall in these difficult times but Krupp and the armaments concerns were subsidised by their orders for the army and used cartels, syndicates and agricultural tariffs at home to secure industrial markets abroad.

After the railways spread to the corn-belt in America, America flooded the European market with cheap wheat and in 1878 Bismarck introduced protectionist tariffs. Eventually this gave German industry an advantage, as many countries who wanted industrial goods had nothing to sell but wheat. However, the workers in the great factories were increasingly angry about the higher prices because so much of their income was spent on food. Bismarck responded to the fight. Initially, he adopted the 'Law concerning the Combating of the Criminal

Aims of Social Democracy' which dissolved over six hundred newspapers and journals and exiled leading activists, but eventually he passed progressive compulsory insurance against sickness (1883) accidents (1884) and old age (1889).

The health insurance scheme was inspired by the cooperative model in the coal mining industry, which already offered cover for employees for accidents, with medical support, health payments and even pensions for invalids. However, as there were still countless conflicts between injured workers and their bosses, the employers pressed for a national scheme, with the workers paying two-thirds of the contributions.

The Accident Insurance Law of 1884 made employers pay two-thirds of the workers' wages after the 14th week if the worker was fully disabled. Finally the Old Age Pensions Scheme offered pensions to employees over seventy, equally financed by employers and workers. It was the great industries of the Ruhr and other industrial centres which would create the German economic miracle, but the cost to the German worker in the Ruhr was hard. He would be paying contributions towards his pension but would have little chance of enjoying it because of the acrid polluted environment. Coal fires, 'used for heating, hot water and cooking' were lit an hour before the start of the morning shift every day, and 'coals were mended in grates that had smouldered overnight, sending up plumes of smoke' from thousands of chimneys, fouling the atmosphere.[48]

Although German coal miners worked 51.5 hours a week in 1895, employees in the chemical industry worked 60 hours a week and steel workers 63 hours a week.[49] However, the insurance schemes were valuable in reducing the country's high emigration rate to America, as many of the brightest and best were lured by the prospects of the New World.

Bismarck never returned to military warfare after 1870 but he did not look peaceful! His large empire and huge standing army gave him political clout. He built up a complicated system of alliances in the early 1880s, which resulted in Germany being the dominant power in a weighty Central European bloc containing Austria, Russia, Italy, Serbia and Romania.

Soon however, relationships with Russia worsened. Germany's ever-heightening agricultural tariffs were seen by Russia as deliberately unfriendly.[50] Previously over 30 per cent of Russia's agricultural exports had gone to Germany to enable her to buy German industrial goods, but Bismarck lost interest in trading with her. After Russia resigned from the Triple Alliance over a crisis in Bulgaria, Bismarck concluded a Reinsurance Treaty with her but as she refused to remain neutral in the event of a German war against France, Bismarck became deliberately unfriendly.

Bismarck's expulsion of over 30,000 Poles and Jews from German-occupied Poland prompted the Czar to issue an edict prohibiting the tenure of land in Russia by any foreigners, most of whom seemed to be German. Then, the German press, with Bismarck's blessing, attacked the value of Russian State Bonds. In November 1887 the Prussian State Bank stated officially that it would not offer any loans against the Russian State Bonds. As Russia's shaky economy could not exist without foreign loans she had to turn to France.[51]

Bismarck was determined to secure a new seven-year mandate for the expansion of the army before the 90-year-old Emperor, Wilhelm I, died. So, even though he received a report from the German ambassador in Paris, Graf Münster von Derneburg, saying that there was absolutely no sign of France preparing for war, he won a huge electoral victory in December 1887 by frightening the German electorate into believing that France was about to invade, with scary newspaper headlines like 'On the Razor's Edge'.

Then he asked the newly elected members of the Reichstag to vote on the bill proclaiming: 'Since 1870 there has been danger of war every year' but 'even if Germany were at war with France, a Russian war would not necessarily follow'. 'There is no need to fear the hatred of Russia,'[52] he declared, alarming the Reichstag and winning its backing for increasing the German army to 491,000 men.[53]

Bismarck then triumphantly published the text of a new Austro-German Treaty, declaring: 'We no longer sue for love either in France or in Russia.' He obviously believed that the German Reich was strong enough to defy both of them.

Soon afterwards, Wilhelm I died and Bismarck, aged seventy-five, was sacked by the new young Kaiser, Wilhelm II. He left a powerful country in a 'chronic crisis of overproduction', looking for ways out of the depression,[54] and he had some advice for the new Kaiser: 'The German Empire is just jogging along. You try and make Prussia strong!'[55]

CHAPTER TWO

The Coming War

On 15th June 1888, Queen Victoria's eldest grandson, Wilhelm II, became Emperor of Germany. 'Kaiser Bill', as he was popularly known in England, had a difficult birth at the hands of an English doctor and grew up with one arm paralyzed and six inches shorter than the other. He resisted his English mother's attempts to educate him in British attitudes towards democracy, blaming her and her English doctor for his deformity. Wilhelm II regarded himself as a Prussian, with a great military destiny.

After he came to the throne he was seldom out of uniform. Wildly jealous of the British and encouraged by the shipbuilding industry, he decided that the path to glory for the German Empire was to build a great navy and attack America, whose defences he believed to be weak. Wilhelm elevated a man with steely ambition and a magnificent two-pronged beard, called Alfred Tirpitz, to become State Secretary of the Imperial Navy Office and Tirpitz was soon given the coveted title 'von' to elevate him into the nobility. The plan was not to conquer the US physically: Operational Plan Three called for a deliberate attack on the international systems of trade, credit and insurance with the goal of bringing America to its knees by killing capitalism.

Tirpitz toured the US on his way back from the Far East. He reported that America was filled with societies of German origin and organisers of pro-German sentiment. By early 1898 Naval Lieutenant (and later General) Eberhard von Mantey had drawn up his first plan. It called for a great German fleet to cross the Atlantic and destroy the Norfolk Naval Shipyard and the Newport News Shipbuilding Center, with another attack aimed at the 'the most sensitive point' of American defences, Portsmouth Naval Shipyard at the junction of Maine and New Hampshire.[1] But the Kaiser found the funding for the project difficult and the Spanish-American War broke out in 1898.

Then the Kaiser had the idea of tempting Britain into forming a naval coalition with Germany and France against America during the Spanish War, but Arthur Balfour, who commanded the world's most powerful navy, defended America, saying: 'No: if the British fleet takes any part in this war, it will be to put itself between the American fleet and those of your coalition.'[2]

So the Kaiser reverted to his previous schemes. In 1899 he changed his plan to an attack on America's Eastern Seaboard by sixty warships, with 100,000 soldiers and a large artillery force, but the designer of the famous Schlieffen Plan, General von Schlieffen, poured cold water on all his projects.[3]

Von Tirpitz and his Kaiser were frustrated but another opportunity presented itself in the New World. The Venezuelans had refused to pay their debts so the Kaiser persuaded Britain and Italy to join him in blockading the Venezuelan coast until they paid them. After a while he threatened to bombard the coastal towns with a view to occupying them if he did not get satisfaction.

Ebullient extravert Theodore Roosevelt became US President in 1901. He had no illusions about what the Kaiser's threat to occupy the Venezuelan coastal towns would mean. If a German regiment managed to obtain a base within striking distance of the projected Panama Canal, Venezuela would be powerless to drive it out. So Roosevelt decided to kill the Kaiser's initiative. Having sounded out Italy and Britain, he warned the German ambassador, Dr von Holleben, that unless the Kaiser accepted arbitration over the debts within a strict timetable, the American fleet under Admiral Dewey would appear off the Venezuelan coast and defend it from German attack.

Dr von Holleben was aghast. 'Blind obedience' was not only expected of soldiers serving the German Officer Corps but also of civil servants serving their imperial master. Dr von Holleben declared that when his imperial master, the Kaiser, refused to accept arbitration that was the end of the matter. He asked Roosevelt if he realised what his words meant. President Roosevelt declared that it meant war. A week went by without any communication from Berlin. Then von Holleben called at the White House again. The President asked him if he had heard anything from Berlin. 'No,' said von Holleben. 'Of course His Majesty cannot arbitrate.'

'Very well,' replied President Roosevelt. 'You may think it worthwhile to cable to Berlin that I have changed my mind. I am sending instructions to Admiral Dewey to take our fleet to Venezuela next Monday instead of Tuesday.'

Von Holleben shot out of the door and returned less than thirty-six hours later with the news: 'His Imperial Majesty consents to arbitrate.' Von Holleben had consulted Karl Buenz, the German Consul-General in New York, who assured him that Roosevelt was not bluffing and that Admiral Dewey could blow up all the German navy in half an hour.[4] After this episode the Kaiser turned his attention to Turkey and Africa.

Hopefully the Europeans would be easier to intimidate!

German heavy industry was interested in Turkey. The Kaiser had already visited Palestine and Syria in 1898 and declared himself the protector of all the Muslims. This found favour with Abdul Hamid II of Turkey, who alarmed the British by granting Germany a concession to build a railway from Constantinople to Baghdad. German heavy industrial leaders were excited by the possibilities of the so-called Berlin-Baghdad railway. The projected route would eventually run close to the British oilfields of Persia (Iran), and beyond that lay India.

The railway concession was followed by military agreements. Most of the leaders of the Young Turks Revolt of 1908 would receive their military training from the German Reich. By December 1913, the Turkish army would be virtually under the control of the German General, Liman von Sanders[5] and in a very strategic position.

Meanwhile relationships with Britain worsened. R J Unstead, in his *A Century of Change* (1963) declared:

'The German Emperor, who had neither brains nor manners, seemed to go out of his way to give and take offence. He wrote rudely to his grandmother (Queen Victoria), openly sided with the Boers, and told Britain to mind her own business in Egypt instead of complaining about German plans to build a railway from Berlin to Baghdad.'

The German industrial magnates were also interested in Morocco. After France had lost valuable territory in the Franco-Prussian war, she acquired an empire in North Africa. Much of it consisted of desert sand but Morocco contained valuable iron ore deposits. France's ally, Russia, had suffered from revolution after a disastrous war with Japan, and France itself was identified as vulnerable by the German military establishment.

General von Schlieffen prepared a plan to invade France through Belgium. The Kaiser then spilled the beans, and angered King Leopold of the Belgians, by saying that Leopold would have to guarantee the German Reich 'the use of Belgian railways and fortified places'[6] during the conflict, and by informing Queen Wilhelmina of the Netherlands that Germany would need to occupy the entire Dutch coast to prevent the British from landing there.[7]

That might have been a more propitious moment for Germany to invade France, while Russia was still recovering from revolution, but because of the Kaiser's bellicose statements, France had managed to sign an *entente cordiale* with Britain.

The first Moroccan crisis could have been seen as a German attempt to test the strength of France's *entente* with Britain. The French 'with blissful disregard for international agreements' had set about turning Morocco into a protectorate over which they would have a trade monopoly.[8] The British were torn because they believed in free trade. The Kaiser made a state visit and declared his support for a sovereign and independent Morocco, suggesting a conference to decide the matter.

When French Foreign Minister Théophile Delcassé, opposed the idea of Moroccan independence, German Chancellor Bernhard von Bülow, threatened war and Delcassé was forced to resign. The delighted Kaiser elevated von Bülow to the rank of Prince. Yet the 1906 conference at Algeciras was not a success for the German Reich. Indeed it was a diplomatic disaster. Theodore Roosevelt had been alarmed by the threat to the Panama Canal if a German garrison was stationed in neighbouring Venezuela; the British were equally disturbed by the threat to the Strait of Gibraltar if German troops became entrenched in Tangier. The Kaiser's sudden arrival in Tangier, and his procession through the city on horseback, was treated with the greatest suspicion by the whole of Europe.[9]

Five years later Morocco became the scene of another German adventure. The great iron and steel tycoons of the Ruhr, like Hugo Stinnes, August Thyssen, Gustav Krupp, and Albert Vögler were immensely rich. Their income surged between 1895 and 1907.[10] They forged their vast combines on a 'vertical plan' which meant that they owned or controlled the iron ore fields, the ships which brought the ore back home, the coal fields that provided the power to smelt the ore and the steel factories that produced the finished products. Owing to their great wealth they exercised an enormous influence in Kaiser Bill's Germany. The growth of German steel production since 1880 had been spectacular. How much had been due to the remarkable growth in German shipbuilding and armaments production was not recorded but the German Reich's share of world steel production rose from 14.6 per cent in 1880 to 22.75 per cent in 1910 and would surge to 25.2 per cent in 1913.

In July 1911, the gunboat SMS *Panther* was sent to Agadir 'for the protection of German interests', which meant the profits of a German-owned iron ore concern. This brought France and Germany to the brink of war. A tactful but firm speech by Lloyd George saved the situation. His hint that Britain would stand by France in her hour of need made Germany recoil. Instead of the German Reich being able to bully the French into surrendering French Congo as the cornerstone of a great continuous German-African Empire, it was merely given what it considered two 'meagre' strips of French territory on the Congo and Ubangi.

A crucial factor in the German decision to retreat was the lack of support from Austria. Austro-Hungarian Foreign Minister Graf von Aehrenthal, vowed his perfect loyalty to the Triple Alliance but pointed out that Germany could count on Austria's support only when questions of European impor-tance were at stake.[11] This virtually ensured that there would be no more colonial wars to achieve the Reich's coveted 'place in the sun'. The Kaiser was blamed for Germany's colonial setbacks. He lost his influence in domestic and foreign spheres to the military/industrial hierarchy and especially the Pan-German League. The Pan-German League's most powerful but secret supporter was the head of the Krupp concern, Gustav Krupp von Bohlen und Halbach.

The Pan-German League's traditional plan had been to expand in Europe. Bismarck either defeated in battle or bullied into submission, Denmark Austria and France and all the lesser states of the German Confederation in the nineteenth century. He had got away with his wars without international censure because his actions were labelled by what could be called 'appeasing foreigners' as 'unification'.

The Pan-German League wanted to bully more states into joining the Reich in the twentieth century. So its publicist, Heinrich Class, cleverly declared that 'Germany was incomplete because Bismarck had failed to include all the people of German ethnicity'. Class asserted that the borders of Bismarck's Reich were only temporary. Soon the moment would come for the national 'redemption' of all those unsuspecting mortals who the Pan-German League considered of German blood in the Hapsburg lands of the Austrian Empire; also in Switzerland, Holland, Luxemburg, Belgium and Romania (because of its strategic position at the mouth of the Danube). Their plan was to attract these nations into their lair by means of a customs union like the Zollverein, which would prepare the way for community-wide legal and political institutions. Finally, if necessary, force might have had to be used to complete the unification process.[12]

The Pan-German League shared many of Bismarck's hatreds. Bismarck fought the Socialists. In his book, *If I were the Kaiser* (1912), Class declared that all who stood in the service of socialist propaganda should be expelled from the German Empire.

Class did realise that in a modern world the voice of the people could not be completely ignored, but he was determined to take up the 'struggle for the soul of the people'. He advocated holidays to celebrate the Fatherland and proposed that the army gave lectures drawn from German – or rather Prussian – history to entertain the masses. But the carrot was to be accompanied by the stick. Socialist strikers must be shown a firm hand. Class was no fan of the Jewish community either. Anti-Jewish sentiment had already risen since Bismarck imposed tariffs on agricultural produce in 1879. Bismarck condoned the use of the Jews as a scapegoat. Celebrated historian Heinrich von Treitschke had started the campaign against the Jews and soon it permeated the heights of the establishment. Even Wilhelm II became a disciple. Whether the Kaiser had actually met any Jews is not recorded but he often declared that he 'cannot bear the Jews'.

Class was an extremist. In *If I were the Kaiser*, Class, who would eventually become a member of Hitler's Nazi party in the Reichstag between 1933 and 1939, wrote:

'Today the borders must be totally barred to any further Jewish immigration ... foreign Jews who have not yet acquired citizenship rights must be speedily and unconditionally expelled, to the last man ... and resident Jews be placed under an Aliens Law'.

Class's definition of who was Jewish was anyone who belonged to a Jewish religious corporation as of 18th January 1871, as well as the descendants of such persons who were Jews at that date, even when only one parent was a Jew by that definition. Class declared that the Kaiser should announce that all public offices remain closed to Jews and they would not be allowed to serve in the army or navy.

Class also made clear that the Germans were a superior race, and that anyone who could claim German blood in southern Russia, Galicia, Russian Poland and North America should be welcomed home. Other nationals, however, were not welcomed in the lands his Volk had appropriated. Class declared that Germany should pursue a resolutely militant policy against the Poles through the application of expropriation and the introduction of a prohibition against the parcelization of land.[13]

In this respect Class was copying Bismarck. Bismarck's 'expulsion law' (Aussiedlungsgesetz) of 1886, forced many Poles to leave their land, even though they were living on former Polish territory that had been annexed by Prussia. About 32,000 Poles, who could not demonstrate that they had German nationality, were evicted in a campaign which combined anti-Slav with anti-Semitic hatreds, 25 per cent of the people expelled being Jewish. It seemed that expropriation of Polish land was still continuing in the years before the First World War as the Reichstag passed a motion in January 1912 stating that, 'the expropriation of Polish landowners for the purposes of the Prussian Settlement Commission is at variance with the judgment of the Reichstag'. This was the first vote of censure ever passed by the Reichstag, but it had no practical effect as the Kaiser and his ministers were not responsible to parliament.

Class was no kinder to the people of Alsace-Lorraine and Denmark, whose lands Bismarck had appropriated in his wars before 1870. He declared:

'When we consider that in Alsace-Lorraine the number of French speakers has grown constantly since 1871, we need to speak out in cold blood. We didn't take the Reichsland "for the sake of your beautiful eyes" we took it out of military necessity. The inhabitants are an extra. Every adult must declare publicly and without reservation ... that the French language will be used neither in the home nor outside it and that no newspapers, periodicals, or books will be brought in from France. The constitution will be abolished. The territory will be placed under a minister for Alsace-Lorraine ... and ruled dictatorially ... We must also consider the Danes and also place before them a new deciding choice. Whoever fails to declare himself unconditionally for the Prussian state must cross the border to Denmark.'

Class felt that his initial idea, to create a larger Germany – or Mitteleuropa – gradually, initially by means of a customs union, had largely been overtaken by events. His answer to the German Reich's setback in Morocco was for it to grab European territory in the traditional Prussian manner. He declared:

'We must pursue an active foreign policy – in a word, an aggressive one ... Obviously, any expansion in Europe is to be brought about only through victorious wars ... If we have been victorious and force cessions of territory, we will thereby get regions inhabited by Frenchmen or Russians, people who are hostile toward us. We then have to ask whether such an increase in territory improves our situation ... Since we have broached the question of evacuation (of native populations) in passing, so to speak, it is perhaps not out of order to speak of it publicly on occasion. By so doing, our enemies will recognise that such desperate measures already have their advocates in Germany ... In other words; we ought not to think of an aggressive war to take foreign territory for purposes of evacuating (inhabitants). But we ought to accustom ourselves to thinking of such a measure as an allowable response to foreign attack. A predatory war contradicts our principles. But a punishment for a ruthless attack justifies us, even to this severest measure, for there is such a thing as "iron necessity". A defensive war in this sense may legitimately be conducted in an aggressive way on the German side, for we must undertake to pre-empt the enemy.'

Class was making horrific remarks, but he had influential friends, including bearded, broad-shouldered, pebble-spectacled lawyer, Alfred Hugenberg, who co-founded the Pan-German League in 1894. French Ambassador Francois-Poncet would later observe that Hugenberg's 'round-gold-spectacles, his potbelly, his bristly white moustache lend him the reassuring aspect of a worthy country doctor, but in reality he is ... one of Germany's evil spirits'.[14]

Between 1894 and 1899 Hugenberg was employed by the Prussian Settlement Commission in the Polish province of Poznan to buy land from the Poles for ethnic German settlement. In 1899 Hugenberg openly envisioned the 'annihilation' of the Polish population.[15]

The German Reich's population had expanded rapidly since 1870. Hugenberg felt that *lebensraum* (more living space), should be found for its population, if necessary by force, and he knew influential industrialists who were sympathetic to his view. In 1910 Emil Kirdorf, founder of the German Coal Syndicate, agreed to put up substantial sums in return for a position on the Pan-German League's executive committee. Gustav Krupp, whose armaments company employed 77,000 people[16] and was alleged to have closer ties with the German government than any other comparable firm in the world,[17] was another major funder. Krupp's sole proviso being that word must never get out that he was paying the bills.[18]

Hugenberg revealed that his and Krupp's mission was 'to do practical work, and surreptitiously lay cuckoo eggs all over the place – without insisting on taking credit for it'. The German people were told that the barbaric Russian hordes were massing in the East and the nation was surrounded by a string of enemies, waiting for the moment to attack. The Pan-German League was suddenly awash with cash and it soon gained influence and attention. Class's memoirs revealed that it was instrumental in mobilising popular support in favour of the two major army bills of 1912 and 1913.

The Kaiser had appointed the former Prussian Minister for the Interior, Theobald von Bethmann Hollweg, as Chancellor in 1909. Tall, elegant Bethmann Hollweg, on whose soothing words the British would fatally come to rely, had a Swiss mother and eminent and cultured ancestors on his father's side. He was a consummate politician but he was first and foremost a Prussian. He told the Reichstag the army had to be increased because, 'Nobody could do away with the chance of war ... If there was a war it would become a world war and we would have to fight on two fronts.'[19]

Although the legislation would make him deeply unpopular, it would not deter him from his task. The first army bill in 1912 raised the numbers of the already large standing army from 595,000 to 622,000 men. The second army bill in 1913 increased the German standing army to 694,000 men, enabling it to put fully trained reserve formations into the field on the first day of war.[20] The Navy League had also been busy canvassing for funds for expansion. It planned to construct another battleship, another large cruiser, two small cruisers, a flotilla of torpedo-boats and a large number of U-boats. Ten airships and fifty aeroplanes were also to be built.

One would have thought that the Social Democrats would have fought against the armaments bills as they had just won a huge electoral victory in the Reichstag. Yet Bismarck had merely side-lined parliament when it opposed his armaments bill in the 1860s and the framework of the new German Reich's constitution. Bismarck's bitter campaign against the Social Democrats in the 1870s and 1880s, exiling their spokesmen and banning their magazines, had made them wary of taking on the establishment again. Although as a pressure group the Social Democrats had been instrumental in prodding Bismarck to introduce very progressive social legislation, they were subject to repeated threats of attack. So, after a half-hearted attempt at criticism, they accepted the new increases in the army.

The task was then to condition the peaceful German people to accept the prospect of war. In December 1912 the conservative East Prussian paper the *Ostpreussiche Zeitung* expressed itself in favour of a 'brisk, merry *(fröhlich)* war' while the *Post* announced at New Year in 1913:

'If, as a hundred years ago, a war is required, if the year of fire and flood was really to be followed by a year of blood – then the German people will demonstrate that today, as in the past, it can defy a world of enemies.'[21]

Germans liked to portray the coming war as a final settlement of accounts between the 'Teuton and the Slav' because the Social Democrats criticised Russia as a despotic regime. Yet the Austrians were not so keen on this portrayal, as about a third of their subjects could be called Slavs. The pretext for war would therefore have to constitute an affront to the 'Teutons'. The Balkan wars of 1912 and 1913 did not fit into this category.

In the first Balkan War, which lasted from October 1912 to May 1913, Serbia, Greece, Montenegro and Bulgaria fought the Ottoman Empire and captured nearly all its remaining European territories. The second Balkan War was provoked because of Bulgaria's unhappiness with its share of the spoils after the first Balkan War. When Austria-Hungary mobilised in the winter of 1912–13 to prevent Serbia from extending her frontier to the Adriatic, Chief of the German General Staff Helmuth von Moltke, warned the Austrians that Germany could not be expected to excite her people over a border dispute.

Britain was pleased that Germany did not want to become involved in the Balkans and took this as proof of the country's peaceful intent. So she sent Viscount Haldane to Germany in February 1912 to come to an agreement on halting its dreadnought warship-building programme.

Viscount Haldane was born in Edinburgh and had the distinction of being able to speak fluent German. A member of the Liberal Party, he was a supporter of women's suffrage and in 1895 helped Sidney Webb found the London School of Economics, whose aim was to 'teach political economy on more modern and more socialist lines'.

Beatrice Webb recorded in 1897 that Haldane's 'bulky awkward form and pompous ways, his absolute lack of masculine vices and manly tastes ... would have made him an unattractive figure if it were not for the beaming kindness of his nature'.

Unfortunately, Haldane was only allowed to meet the Kaiser and Tirpitz. Naturally there was no meeting of minds between them. The Kaiser would not have noticed 'the beaming kindness' of Haldane's nature and would have viewed his support for women's suffrage with the greatest suspicion. There was absolutely no chance of Haldane wringing concessions on reducing navel expenditure out of Tirpitz and the Kaiser.

Indeed, at that very moment, a book was published by a General Bernhardi called *Germany and the Next War*. In this book Bernhardi maintained that the German warlike spirit was only waiting to be awakened by an appeal to force. Bernhardi declared that Germany must claim 'not only a place in the sun but a full share in the mastery of the world'. France should be 'completely brought to the ground, so that she will never again be able to obstruct our path', and Germany should destroy the balance of power in Europe and set up a system of States with Germany at its heart. And, above all, he wrote, 'England is the enemy' which would have to be beaten at sea!

Bernhardi's book was an embarrassment to Bethmann Hollweg, who wanted to secure a promise of Britain's neutrality in the coming war. He rejected the Pan-Germans' plans for a *coup d'état* to make the constitution even more autocratic and persisted with his task of trying to prise Britain away from her *entente* with Russia and France, specifically asking the German ambassador to Britain, von Lichnowsky, to sound out British Foreign Minister Sir Edward Grey, before persuading the Reichstag to vote to provide funds to increase Germany's armaments.

Bethmann Hollweg attempted to portray his country's friendship with Britain like a business deal, most easily made between strong partners.[22] He felt that he made real progress in gaining Britain's friendship during the Balkan wars. Although the German army clung to the Schlieffen War Plan which envisaged Germany invading France through neutral Belgium, Foreign Minister Gottlieb von Jagow warned Austria-Hungary that before she went to war there must be an 'obviously hostile act by Serbia' and emphasised, 'It is very important that we should appear to have been provoked because I believe that then – probably only then – Britain can remain neutral.'[23]

In January 1912 France elected a new Prime Minister and Minister for Foreign Affairs, Raymond Poincaré. Small, neat and punctilious, Poincaré had a formidable intellect and a prodigious capacity for work. Before entering parliament he was lawyer to the French iron ore magnates in Lorraine, so he was acutely aware of how the German iron and steel bosses coveted France's iron. He was convinced that France should present a strong negotiating front, and defended his attitude by declaring: 'I have studied all the documents relating to the Morocco affair. There results from this study a conviction: it is that each time that we have desired to be conciliatory towards Germany she has abused our overtures. Each time, on the other hand, that we have shown ourselves firm, she has retreated. Germany does not understand the language of right; she understands only the use of force.'

In the face of the increases in the German army in 1912 and 1913, France introduced a 'Three Year Law' in the summer of 1913 to equalise the number of soldiers on both sides of the border. Putting the same number of soldiers into the field of battle as Germany was a tall order, as France's population was only forty million compared to Germany's sixty million. Poincaré received support for three-year conscription. However, the radical Socialists, led by former Prime Minister, Joseph Caillaux opposed his bill.

In 1913 an astonishing incident occurred in the part of Alsace that Bismarck had grabbed in the Franco-Prussian war. A young Lieutenant named Günter Freiherr von Forstner was reported to have stated to his recruits in Zaberne (Saverne), that they would each be given a present of ten marks if they stabbed a Wackes (a local expression for a native of Alsace), if the Wackes insulted them. This caused outrage in the area. That same evening some pupils from the secondary school were said to have made offensive remarks to the German officers returning from fencing school, where-upon von Forstner ordered his regiment to load their rifles and arrest all the civilians who were out of doors. Von Forstner's regiment zealously carried out his orders and arrested twenty-seven people, including the Judge and Council of the Civil Court, who were leaving for home after a long day. A further aggravation was caused by von Forstner's wounding of a lame cobbler, who he alleged had insulted him 'by contemptuous cries'. The affair caused an explosion of indignation among the mass of the German people who disagreed with his excessive high-handedness. Bethmann Hollweg tried to play down the incident by declaring that the authorities 'can make no progress in Alsace-Lorraine unless they abandon the fruitless attempt to turn the South Germans of the Reichsland into North German Prussians'.[24]

Yet Bethmann Hollweg's words were not enough to pacify the members of the Reichstag about von Forstner's conduct. A motion was proposed under the new rules of procedure, stating that the Reichstag disapproved of Bethmann Hollweg's treatment of the whole affair. It was adopted by the huge majority of 293 votes against 54. Von Forstner was sentenced by court martial to forty-three days for 'assault and wounding and the unlawful employment of weapons' in striking the lame cobbler with his sword.

However, the Officer Corps fought back. It had always been the army's creed that 'the soldier, whether ... an officer, an NCO, or a private, was never subject, even in peacetime, so long as he was serving with the colours, to the civil courts, no matter what offence he might commit'.[25] On 5th January 1914 the military court of appeal reversed von Forstner's sentence, accepting his plea that the sword was only an ordinary military sword and had not been specially ground for the occasion and moreover that he was a Prussian officer and executed the orders of his King.[26]

The battle lines were emerging between the Reichstag and the Emperor. Many in the military believed that the only way to retain their power and prestige was to wage a successful war. The Officer Corps and the soldiers under their command did not believe that they would 'die as cattle' because of the greed of the industrialists, who paid their wages and coveted France's iron ore. Their fight was for their place in society, above the civilian herd, with their great estates subsidised and their rights secure from civilian courts. Members of the civil service owed their employment to the Kaiser too. The lower ranks of the civil service (with the exception of purely clerical and technical posts), were staffed exclusively by ex-servicemen 'hammered by years of discipline into the Prussian pattern'.

The postman who delivered the officer's letters, the inspector who clipped the officer's railway ticket, and the customs officer who examined the officer's railway ticket, would all come smartly to attention whenever they met an officer. They were horrified at the modern concepts of liberty and equality emanating from revolutionary France and were prepared to die in an external war in order to preserve the status quo at home. In 1893 General Graf von Haeseler, who commanded the German troops in Lorraine, declared: 'Our civilisation must build its temple on mountains of corpses, an ocean of tears and the groans of innumerable dying men. It cannot be otherwise.' Most soldiers would not have used that language but in essence they agreed.

Kaiser Bill and his military chiefs created an immense army but had no war to use it in. Meanwhile increasing the size of the armed forces was so expensive that the country was running out of cash. By the autumn of 1913 the country's capital coverage had become extremely thin and the military/industrial leadership became increasingly worried lest the Austro-Hungarian Empire slipped over to the Entente camp. By December 1913 both Turkey and Austria-Hungary began looking at enlisting Entente capital to help their projects. In May 1914, Chairman of the Deutsche Bank, Karl Helfferich, expressed his frustration:

'Not one man can take the responsibility of going one step further with the advances for the construction of the Baghdad railway without certain prospect that a Baghdad loan will come in the very near future. If the market is upset for us by Bulgarian or Turkish armaments loans we shall have to shut up shop.'[27]

In 1870 Bismarck failed to invade enough of France to secure all her iron ore deposits. France's iron ore was now desperately needed by the iron and steel and armaments magnates. German prospectors had been active in Asia, Australia and Africa to fund their insatiable appetite for iron, but the French deposits in the Briey basin in Lorraine, were so much nearer and more convenient. August Thyssen was the first to buy an iron ore concession in France. By 1913 seventeen concessions were partly or completely owned by German companies. Finally, in

December 1913, alarmed by Germany's penetration *pacifique*, the French stopped the granting of new iron ore concessions to Germany. When it became apparent that there was no hope of continuing the peaceful penetration of France, a deputation of German industrialists spoke openly to the former Italian Minister of Commerce, Francesco Nitti, of their need to lay their hands on the iron ore basin of French Lorraine. Indeed in 1917 Albert Vögler, future director of vast conglomerate, United Steel, would declare, 'To obtain Briey we would fight for a further ten years.'[28]

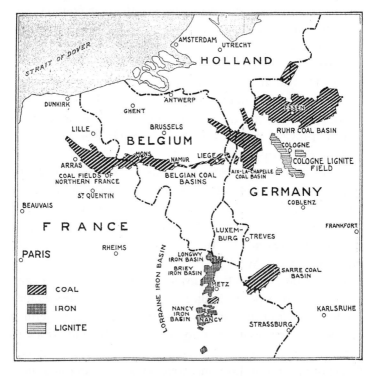

The French had been frightened of another invasion since 1870. Sooner or later they believed that the 'Prussians' would invade again. The great iron and steel factories had initially expanded in Germany rather than France because of the simple fact that it was cheaper to move iron to coal rather than coal to iron. With the threat of war, France expanded her iron production too. Yet her iron production was still less than a third of Germany's in 1914.[29] The railways had played such an important part in Germany's success in the Franco-Prussian war. Poincaré had lent Russia money to modernise its armed forces so that the two countries could present a united front against German aggression, but more was needed to complete the modernisation programme and to bring Russia's strategic railways up to date.

Russia was concerned about the construction of the Berlin-Baghdad railway. By December 1913, the Turkish army would be virtually placed under the control of the German General, Liman von Sanders.[30] When the railway was completed Germany would be able to speed troops and guns to Turkey, threatening the Russian navy's access to the Mediterranean.

The Japanese defeat of the Russian army in 1904 had led to an increase in the size of the Russian army and an eagerness to modernise it. The great programme for its enlargement to over 2 million was prepared in October 1913, but the Russians did not vote on approving it until June 1914.[31]

Only the British were not thinking of arming at this time. Lulled by Bethmann Hollweg's attempts to woo them, the British seemed to turn their backs on Europe. Although British Foreign Minister Sir Edward Grey expressly told Haldane, in 1912, to emphasise that Britain 'could under no circumstances tolerate France being crushed', there was no doubt that France's historic enemies, the British, had decided to believe in the German leadership's genuine love of peace. In contrast to the rest of Europe, the British added no soldiers to their army between 1912 and 1914. And it seemed that at this critical point they succumbed to internal distractions.

Good-looking womaniser, Herbert Henry Asquith, was called 'the sledge-hammer' by his predecessor, Sir Henry Campbell-Bannerman. He introduced valuable social legislation when he became Prime Minister. However, his coalition was fatally weakened as it was dependent on the support of the Irish nationalists.

Irish Nationalist leader, John Redmond, wanted Home Rule in return for his support for the new administration. In April 1912 the government introduced a bill offering that purely Irish questions be dealt with by an Irish Parliament, while Westminster dealt with foreign affairs and security. Protestants in the booming shipbuilding area round Belfast were unhappy with these proposals, and they prepared to fight, fearing that a Catholic administration in the poor rural South would discriminate against them.

This was exactly the sort of situation which Bismarck's spy, Wilhelm Stieber, would have enjoyed. He was innovative in stoking up divisions between Austria and Hungary before Bismarck's invasion in 1866. And he taught his successors well. The groundwork that Stieber established in the nineteenth century was responsible for his country having an excellent spy system in the lead-up to the First World War. Indeed, Charles Lucieto, one of the Allies most successful spies in the First World War, described Germany's pre-First World War espionage system as 'gigantic'.[32]

Germany offered tons of ammunition to the Irish competing parties. Ulsterman Fred Crawford smuggled 25,000 rifles and three million rounds of ammunition from Hamburg in April 1914, while the Catholic Irish volunteers were caught landing a thousand rifles in broad daylight in July.

On 24th February 1914, the conservative *Post* published a leading article, declaring that the prospects for a victorious preventative war were propitious: 'France is not yet ready to fight, England is involved in domestic and colonial difficulties.

Russia shuns war because it is afraid of revolution at home. Are we to wait until our opponents are ready or shall we seize a propitious moment to bring about a decision?'[33]

The 'Prussian' leadership had relinquished the idea of fighting a battle for a colonial empire now; it knew where its future mission lay, in Europe! While the German Conservatives advocated 'a brisk and merry war' to quell the power of the workers, the employers' federation spokesman, Walter Lambach, called for a war to achieve an 'economic unit stretching from the North Sea to the frontiers of Egypt'.[34] As usual the Pan-German League had the final word by quoting from Bismarck to advocate war. Bismarck had declared in a speech to the Reichstag on 4th November 1871:

'It is very useful to follow the example of Frederick the Great before the Seven Years War, who instead of waiting for the net in which he was to be caught to envelop him, tore it with a quick thrust ... In such situations it is the duty of the government, and the nation has the right to demand from the government, that if war is really impossible to avoid, the government shall choose to fight it at a time when it can be fought with the least sacrifice and the least danger to the nation.'[35]

The most opportune time to fight a war was now. Bismarck falsified his Emperor's telegram in order to engineer a successful war against France in 1870. His successors were equally determined and ruthless in 1914.

CHAPTER THREE

Bismarck's Responsibility for the First World War

This chapter goes through the last twenty-eight days before the First World War began, with the help of the German historian Fritz Fischer's research, and concludes that Bismarck bore a heavy responsibility for the conflict.

Bismarck was responsible for the First World War by showing his successors how easy it had been to manipulate events with a mixture of deception and strong-arm tactics; how tempting it was to invade one's neighbours if one had developed an enormous armaments industry; how quickly one could achieve victory if one was well prepared, and how the outside world seemed to applaud you rather than condemn you if you succeeded. Last but not least, he had shown his successors how to engineer war by falsifying Wilhelm I's telegram!

The opportunity for Chancellor Bethmann Hollweg and the German military to provoke a major European war came at a most convenient moment on 28th June 1914. On that fateful day a Serb extremist committed a crime which could be presented as an offence against the whole Germanic race. He assassinated the heir presumptive to the Austro-Hungarian throne, Archduke Franz Ferdinand, in the city of Sarajevo.

Franz Ferdinand's murder did not cause quite the amount of weeping and gnashing of teeth that might have been expected in Austrian court circles. Chief of the Austro-Hungarian General Staff, Baron Conrad von Hötzendorf, and his military friends actually welcomed the news because it presented them with the opportunity of securing Germany's help in bringing Serbia to heel.

The Austrian army had wanted to bring the Serbians down a peg for a long time, but it had been difficult to persuade the Germans to help. Many had a low view of the Austro-Hungarian Empire. Balding ambassador to Vienna, Heinrich von Tschirschky, who had served as German Foreign Minister between 1906 and 1907, asked wearily on 22nd May 1914 'whether it is really still worth our while to tie ourselves so closely to this decrepit construct of states and to continue the irksome task of dragging it along'.[1] Yet the Germans needed the Austrians for their 'brisk and merry war' against France. The murder of the Archduke could provide the pretext for the conflict. Indeed the timing of the Archduke's murder was so propitious that conspiracy theorists could even believe that a German spy might be behind it. *Der Post* spoke the truth in February 1914 when it declared that Britain and France were 'in disarray'. Wilhelm Stieber himself could not have done a better job of stirring up turmoil in France and Britain at this critical time.

Britain was facing near civil war in Ireland, and the French were also totally preoccupied at home after Henriette Caillaux, former mistress and now wife of leading left-winger and former Prime Minister, Joseph Caillaux, murdered France's most powerful journalist, Gaston Calmette.[2]

Joseph Caillaux had been accused of having German sympathies. He was the most prominent opponent of the three-year conscription law, which France had adopted in response to increases in Germany's army.

The French iron ore magnates of Lorraine had a very strong influence in government circles, just like Krupp and the iron and steel magnates in Germany. The President of the iron and steel association, the Comité des Forges, had been criticised by Joseph Caillaux as 'the symbol of the plutocracy'. Yet the French iron magnates knew that the Germans coveted their iron ore fields, lying as they did so temptingly close to the border, and it was precisely to avoid them marching into their country and grabbing them that they supported the three-year conscription law.

The conservative press had been out to discredit Caillaux for trying to undermine the law. After Gaston Calmette published a letter in *Le Figaro* revealing Caillaux's former marital infidelities, Henriette Caillaux followed Calmette to his office.

'Do you know why I have come?' Henriette asked.

'Not at all, Madame,' Calmette replied. But he soon found out. Henriette Caillaux took out a revolver and shot Calmette six times. Hours later, he died of his wounds.

The French public were convulsed by Calmette's murder and forgot about the death of Franz Ferdinand. Henriette Caillaux's trial would start on July 20th, three days before Austria-Hungary's Ultimatum to Serbia.

The Kaiser, who had a close relationship with the Austrian Archduke, was stunned by the news of Franz Ferdinand's death. His vision of the two Emperors ruling the continent of Europe together, after the death of Franz Joseph, was shattered by the Archduke's murder. He immediately declared: 'It's now or never!' The Austrian ambassador to Berlin was summoned forthwith to send a message to Vienna that the Kaiser 'would regret it if we let this present chance … (to go to war) go by without utilising it'.[3]

The Kaiser was very close to the Krupp family. He had been accused of being weak during the Morocco crises but now he promised Gustav Krupp (née von Bohlen und Halbach), that he would declare war at once if Russia mobilised, assuring him that this time he was not 'falling out'.

Gustav Krupp was a head shorter and sixteen years older than his wife, Bertha. Portrayed as a man with a fanatical love of order, he forbade all talk of politics, never lost his temper and rarely displayed emotion of any sort. One biographer even declared of him: 'It is … doubtful that he entertained a single original thought in his entire life.'[4]

Yet that portrayal grossly underestimates Gustav Krupp's ability, ambition and the threat he posed to peace in Europe before the First World War. His father-in-law, Fritz Krupp, was the first of the family to bankroll the Pan-German League in the 1890s, distributing display signs to shops reading, 'The World belongs to Germans'. Gustav was arguably the Pan-German League's largest funder by 1914. His firm had developed the 420 mm Big Bertha Howitzer, the most powerful cannon in the world, and his finance for the Pan-German League had borne fruit, with vast increases in the size of the German army agreed by the Reichstag in 1912 and 1913. Kaiser Bill was so nervous of Gustav Krupp in 1914 that his 'repeated protestations' that no one would be able to reproach him, ever again, for his failure to declare war at the appropriate moment, were to the Kaiser's confidant, 'almost comical to hear'.[5]

At the time of Franz Ferdinand's death, the 84-year-old Austrian Emperor, Franz Joseph, had been on the throne for over sixty years and had become nervous and brittle with age. Following his crucial defeat by Bismarck, he had been forced to share the Austrian Empire with the Hungarians. Each day he rose at 5.00 a.m. and worked long lonely hours on his Dispatch boxes. Now he wrote a letter in his own quivering hand appealing for Germany's help. After the Archduke's murder, he was eager to have a show down with Serbia in order to prevent his empire from being swallowed up in the 'Pan Slav flood'.

After initial hesitation, the Kaiser declared that Austria-Hungary could 'count on Germany's full support' even in the case of 'grave European complications', consoling himself that 'Russia is not at all ready for war, and would certainly think long before appealing to arms.'[6]

Austria's partners, the Hungarians, also had to give their consent to reprisals being taken against Serbia. Hungarian Prime Minister, Count Stephen Tisza, was alarmed that an Austrian attack on Serbia might lead to 'intervention by Russia and consequently to world war'. However, Germany's 'unconditional attitude' that 'the Monarchy had to reach an energetic conclusion' persuaded him to change his mind.[7]

Germany had already been told of the contents of the Ultimatum to be delivered to Serbia, but both countries decided that it should be delivered only after French President Raymond Poincaré had finished his trip to St Petersburg, and was on the sea journey home, cut off from communication.[8]

'What a pity!' about the lateness of the date, declared the Kaiser, who had already set off on a cruise and was trying to keep abreast of developments by telegram.

German Ambassador to Britain, small, thin aristocratic Prince Karl von Lichnowsky, had languished on his estates in Silesia for thirteen years before the Kaiser chose him to become British Ambassador. He was instructed to mobilise the British press against Serbia whilst being careful not to give the impression that Germany was 'egging Austria on to war'.[9]

In Vienna, German Ambassador Heinrich von Tschirschky, was confident that Britain 'will not at this juncture intervene in a war which breaks out over a Balkan state, even if this should lead to a conflict with Russia, possibly also France'.[10]

Gustav Krupp had industrial spies everywhere. His agents stole over a thousand documents from the German War Office files in 1912. Moreover, his firm had fomented anti-German attacks in the French press to rattle the German government into giving him more orders.[11] When he declared in 1914 that the Russian artillery was 'far from being either good or complete' while Germany's 'has never been better', people believed him.[12] Foreign Minister Gottlieb von Jagow, envisaged the coming conflict becoming a war 'between the Teuton and the Slav'.[13] He said happily, 'if the conflict cannot be localised, and Russia attacks Austria, this gives the *casus foederis*'.[14]

Jagow was a close friend of Gustav Krupp.[15] On 18th July, he suggested that 'His Majesty might spend the last days of his cruise closer to home in the Baltic … in case unpredictable developments should force us to take important decisions, such as (the army's) mobilisation'.[16]

On 19th July the text of the Austrian Ultimatum to Serbia was finalised by Germany and Austria-Hungary. Jagow promised that Germany would stand behind Austria 'unreservedly and with all her power'.[17]

On 20th July, the day that the French were transfixed by the wife of the former Prime Minister, Madame Caillaux's actual appearance in court on a charge of murder, the Directors of the Hapag and Norddeutscher Lloyd were given warning of the Austrian Emperor's impending Ultimatum, so that they could take measures for the protection of their ships in foreign waters. The Kaiser also ordered the concentration of the fleet.[18]

The 23rd July was decided as the day for the Ultimatum's delivery to Serbia, and the time of the delivery was put back an hour to make quite sure that President Poincaré and Prime Minister Viviani would have left St Petersburg and be on the high seas on their way home when it arrived.[19]

At 6.00 p.m. on 23rd July, the Ultimatum was presented. Besides the trial of those involved in the Archduke's assassination, the Ultimatum demanded that the Serbian state formally and publicly condemned its 'dangerous propaganda' against Austria-Hungary, whose ultimate aim, it alleged, was to detach 'a part of the territories of Austria-Hungary from the Monarchy'.

The Ultimatum also demanded that the Serbs 'suppress by every means this criminal and terrorist propaganda' which it alleged was propagated in subversive magazines and in 'school books'. In addition it demanded that Serbia remove all the people from public office that Austria-Hungary disliked and accepted in their stead Austro-Hungarian government officials who could seek out and suppress all the elements in Serbia they consider insurrectionary. The Ultimatum demanded a response in only two days' time, at 5.00 p.m. on Saturday evening, 25th July.

The wording of the Ultimatum caused consternation in European capitals. Britain had been completely unaware of the impending conflict on its doorstep. First Lord of the Admiralty, Winston Churchill wrote: 'Europe is trembling on the verge of a general war, the Austrian Ultimatum being the most insolent document of its kind ever devised.'

Long-serving British Foreign Minister Sir Edward Grey, was held in high esteem in Europe.[20] Although rooted in love of the countryside, and with a passion for fishing in his spare time, he had been sorting out international problems for years. In 1913, he persuaded the Germans to curb Austrian ambitions in return for Britain preaching moderation in St Petersburg,[21] and he was confident that he and his German 'friends' could sort out the present situation. He told Ambassador Lichnowsky, that Germany should impress upon Austria-Hungary the need to retract some of its 'impossible demands' while Britain worked on Russia to influence Serbia.

The Germans quickly instructed their ambassador, Prince Lichnowsky, to tell the British, 'We did not know what Austria was going to demand, but regarded the question as an internal affair of Austria-Hungary, in which we had no standing to intervene.'

Sir Edward Grey was not content with this reply. On 24th July, he suggested mediation over the Ultimatum by the four powers not directly affected – Britain, France, Germany and Italy – in the event of 'dangerous tension between Russia and Austria' but the suggestion was not sent on until after the time limit given in the Ultimatum.[22]

Meanwhile the Austrians' resolve seemed to waver. They told German Ambassador Tschirschky that Austria wanted 'no alteration in the existing power relationships in the Balkans'. Serbian Crown Prince Alexander had already visited the Russian Legation in Belgrade on the night of 23rd/24th to express his despair over the Austrian Ultimatum.[23] Subsequently the Austrians received the Russian chargé d'affaires to discuss the situation.

Russia was naturally alarmed at the thought of the obliteration of its fellow Slav and Eastern Orthodox friend, Serbia. The maintenance of the balance of power in the Balkans was vital to Russia. The Berlin-Baghdad railway, on which so many German ambitions were pinned, was alleged by alarmists to threaten Russia's very existence because Russia's only access from the Black Sea to the Mediterranean at that time was through the narrow channel of the Bosphorus, the so-called boundary between Europe and Asia. When the Bosphorus Straits were briefly closed in 1911–12 'the economy of southern Russia nearly shut down as well'.[24]

In 1913 a German General, Liman von Sanders, was appointed to command an Ottoman army corps at Constantinople. This caused uproar in the Russian press. Although Sanders was eventually appointed to the less provocative role of Inspector-General of the Turkish Army, Russian anxieties remained. Yet Russia only received the first tranche of a large French loan to improve its strategic railways and enlarge the army on 9th February 1914.[25] So it confined itself to declaring in an official communiqué that it could not remain 'uninterested' if Austria actually annexed Serbian territory.[26]

On 25th July Serbia's answer to the Ultimatum was received. Serbia accepted all the onerous terms of Austria's Ultimatum except for the demand that Austro-Hungarian police should be allowed a free hand in Serbia.

Grey said that Berlin should intervene in Vienna to say that it found Serbia's answer satisfactory. He differentiated sharply between the Austria-Serbia dispute and an Austria-Russian conflict. Lichnowsky sent three increasingly urgent messages asking Germany to give Austria 'the hint'.

Late in the evening of 25th July, Jagow agreed to Grey's proposal to 'localise' the conflict, but Chancellor Bethmann Hollweg destroyed his happy moment by threatening that Germany would mobilise if reports of an alleged call-up of Russian reservists were confirmed.[27]

On 25th July Austrian Emperor Franz Joseph, decided that Serbia's response to the Ultimatum had been inadequate. He signed the order mobilising eight army corps. Hungarian Prime Minister Tisza revealed that Germany had influenced Franz Joseph's decision by declaring that hesitation would 'greatly impair belief in the Monarchy's energy and capacity for action, in the eyes of both friend and foe'.[28]

Sunday 26th July came and went. President Poincaré and French Prime Minister Viviani were on the high seas at this crucial time. Poincaré would later write: 'In our floating home there reached us only the deadened echoes of the outside world. We received nothing precise, either from St Petersburg or from Paris. We were more and more anxious in our solitude and in our remoteness and the Sunday passed away without bringing us, lost between the sky and the waves, positive news from land.'[29]

That same Sunday, 26th July, while Poincaré was stuck on the sea, Chief of the German General Staff, General von

Moltke, was plotting his French invasion, busily drafting a demand to Belgium to allow the passage of German troops in the event of 'the imminent war against France and Russia'.[30]

Moltke had little respect for the French armed forces. When asked how long the Austro-Hungarian armies would have to hold out against the Russian armies unaided, he confidently declared: 'We hope to be finished with France in six weeks after the commencement of operations, or at least to have got so far that we can transfer our main forces to the East.'[31]

At last, late in the evening on 26th July, the Kaiser arrived back from his cruise at Potsdam station.[32] He was met by Bethmann Hollweg, whose apprehension stemmed 'not from the dangers of the looming war, but rather from his fear of the Kaiser's wrath when the extent of his deceptions are revealed'.

'How did it all happen?' asked the Kaiser brusquely. Bethmann Hollweg quickly offered his resignation. Unfortunately the Kaiser refused to accept it. So Bethmann Hollweg continued to deceive his Kaiser, but he realised that he must act quickly to get Russia to mobilise because the Kaiser would almost certainly try and quell the coming storm when he actually saw Serbia's answer to Austria-Hungary's Ultimatum.

Franz Joseph had already mobilised eight army corps. On 27th July, Grey's trusted aide in the Foreign Office, Sir Eyre Crowe, warned that Austria's mobilisation could have serious consequences:

'I am afraid that the real difficulty to be overcome will be found in the question of mobilisation. Austria is already mobilising. This, if the war does come, is a serious menace to Russia, who cannot be expected to delay her own mobilisation which, as it is, can only become effective in something like double the time required by Austria and Germany. If

Russia mobilises, we have been warned that Germany will do the same, and as German mobilisation is directed almost entirely against France, the latter cannot possibly delay her own mobilisation for the fraction of a day. This however means that within 24 hours His Majesty's Government will be faced with the question whether ... Great Britain will stand idly by, or take sides.'[33]

Sir Edward Grey was growing frustrated. He alleged that if Germany really wanted peace, it could prevent Austria from pursuing a 'foolhardy policy'.[34]

But the German leadership had other ideas, and it was in a hurry. On the 27th, Austria's actual 'declaration of war' was laid before the old Emperor for his signature. German Ambassador to Austria, Tschirschky, promised Berlin that it would 'go off on the 28th or 29th at latest 'in order to eliminate any possibility of intervention'.[35]

Meanwhile, Germany's Ambassador in Britain, Lichnowsky, warned his master that Germany could not continually reject Britain's peace proposals:

'If we rejected every attempt at mediation the whole world would hold us responsible for the conflagration and represent us as the real warmongers. *That would also make our position impossible here in Germany, where we have got to appear as though the war had been forced upon us.* Our position is the more difficult because Serbia seems to have given way extensively. We cannot therefore reject the role of mediator; we have to pass on the British proposal to Vienna for consideration, especially since London and Paris are continuously using their influence on Petersburg.'[36]

Bethmann Hollweg and Foreign Minister Jagow did belatedly pass on Grey's peace initiative to Austria, but left out the all-important last line of the latest British telegram, which read: 'Also, the whole world here is convinced ... that the key to the situation lies in Berlin, and that if Berlin seriously wants peace, it will prevent Vienna from following a fool-hardy path.'[37]

Meanwhile Grey was sent a soothing message which read: 'We have immediately initiated mediation in Vienna in the sense desired by Sir Edward Grey.'[38]

The Kaiser had arrived home from his cruise, late in the evening of 26th July. Yet it was only on the morning of 28th July, over a day after Serbia's reply to the Ultimatum arrived, that he actually had sight of it.[39]

The Kaiser had been full of spite against the Serbs. Even just before he landed at Kiel, he declared: 'These fellows (the Serbs) have been intriguing and murdering, and they must be taken down a peg'.[40] Yet when at last he saw Serbia's response he immediately declared that it represented Serb 'capitulation of the most humiliating kind' and stated 'because of it there no longer exists any reason for war'. In his opinion, 'The few reservations which Serbia has made with respect to certain points can surely be cleared up by negotiation ...' [41]

This was the moment that the military, the armaments manufacturers and their friends in government had been dreading, the moment that their Emperor's nerve would give way before the certainty of war, like it allegedly had in 1905 and 1911. But Chancellor Bethmann Hollweg had a solution, and it had, to him, the merit of historical precedent.

In 1870 Bismarck decided to change the Kaiser Wilhelm I's Ems telegram in order to goad France into war. In 1914 Bethmann Hollweg decided to change the text of Kaiser Wilhelm II's so-called 'Halt in Belgrade' to ensure that war began.

The only condition that the Kaiser had insisted upon in his 'Halt in Belgrade' was that Austria had 'to have a guar-antee that the promises are carried out by a "temporary" occupation of parts of Serbia'.

Bethmann Hollweg changed the wording to stress that the Austro-Hungarian occupation must be the means of compelling 'complete fulfilment by the Serbian government of the Austrian demands', emphasising to his ambassador in Vienna, Heinrich von Tschirschky (in the telegram 174) 'You must most carefully avoid giving any impression that we want to hold Austria back. We are concerned only to find a modus to enable the realisation of Austria-Hungary's aim without at the same time unleashing a world war, and should this after all prove unavoidable, to improve as far as possible the conditions under which it is to be waged.'[42]

At 11.00 a.m. on 28th July 1914, with Bethmann Hollweg's words ringing in her ears, Austria presented her declaration of war on Serbia. Von Tschirschky did not even bother to show Bethmann Hollweg's amended version of the Kaiser's 'Halt in Belgrade' to the Austrians until the afternoon.

On the same day, Bethmann Hollweg offered Turkey an alliance guaranteeing Turkey's territorial integrity vis-à-vis Russia if Turkey would bind herself to Germany and would place her army under German control during the war.[43]

Russia was alarmed by events in the Balkans. She had already stated that she could not remain 'uninterested' if Austria annexed Serbia. She ordered a partial mobilisation of her troops as a warning.

Although the Russian army was 300,000 larger than the combined German and Austrian armies in 1914, the Prussian military was not frightened by its size. The Russian army had been humiliated by the little respected Japanese in 1904. Then the country had suffered from a revolution. The modernisation of the army and its strategic railways would not be completed until 1917. Bethmann Hollweg declared 'Russia alone must bear the responsibility if a European war breaks out.'[44] He only needed to nudge Russia into a general mobilisation in order to be able to provide the *casus foederis* to attack Russia's ally, France.

After Austria-Hungary actually presented her declaration of war against Serbia, Bethmann Hollweg realised with horror that Austria was physically unable to begin hostilities until 12th August. He complained:

'The Imperial government is thus put into the extraordinarily difficult position of being exposed during the intervening period to the other Powers' proposals for mediation and conferences ... It is imperative that the responsibility for any extension of the conflict to Powers not directly concerned should under all circumstances fall on Russia alone.'[45]

Bethmann Hollweg believed that he could count on the Social Democrats' support and Britain's neutrality in the coming war against France, provided that Russia appeared as the warmonger. So he refused Generals von Moltke and von Falkenhayn permission to use Russia's partial mobilisation as an excuse to proclaim a state of emergency.

Meanwhile, he continued to emphasise Germany's wish for peace to British Ambassador Sir Edward Goschen. However, the army's pressure was mounting. In the evening of the 29th, von Moltke and von Falkenhayn queued up again. Their troops were ready; they wanted to go to war and had already, that day, sent a demand to the German Minister in Brussels to allow the passage of the German armies through Belgium.[46]

Once again Bethmann Hollweg told them that Russia's partial mobilisation did not create a *casus foederis* for them to go to war against France; they must wait until Russia's general mobilisation to ensure German and British public support.[47] But he couldn't put the army off for ever. Under Bismarck's Prussian structure for the German Reich, the leaders of the armed forces carried equal weight to the Chancellor.

Austria had already declared war on Serbia on 28th July. On the 29th Austria bombed Belgrade. The Tsar of Russia and his advisors were racked with anxiety that if Russia mobilised partially and there was a war with Austria-Hungary, Russia would be completely unprepared for a war against Germany.[48]

At last, on the 29th, the boat bringing French President Poincaré and Prime Minister Viviani from Russia, arrived at Dunkirk. The two men took the train to Paris. All the members of the government were waiting for them at the Gare du Nord and people crammed the windows and pavements to see their four-wheeled carriage as it went past. Their attention had abruptly shifted from the murder trial of Madame Caillaux, whose husband did not see the point of France adopting three-year conscription, to the horror of an imminent war. The three-year conscription had been adopted to deter the Germans from marching into France, but it had not worked.[49]

At 11.05 at night on 29th July, Bethmann Hollweg summoned Russia in almost ultimatum terms, not to provoke any warlike conflict with Austria. An hour and a half later, he informed Vienna of Russia's partial mobilisation and added:

'To avert a general catastrophe, or in any case to put Russia in the wrong, we must urgently wish to begin and to continue conversations (with Russia) in accordance with telegram 174.'[50] Telegram 174 was the one where Bethmann Hollweg wrote: 'You must most carefully avoid giving any impression that we want to hold Austria back. We are concerned only to find a modus to enable the realisation of Austria-Hungary's aim without at the same time unleashing a world war, and should this after all prove unavoidable, to improve as far as possible the conditions under which it is to be waged.'

Then late in the night of 29th and into the early hours of 30th, encouraged by hearing that George V wanted Britain to remain neutral, Bethmann Hollweg met the British ambassador, Sir Edward Goschen, to explain to him the naked truth of the

70

matter. Previously Bethmann Hollweg had dissuaded the British from joining the arms race by stressing his country's peaceful intent and encouraging Britain to join Germany in solving the Balkan disputes. Now that Germany had the ascendancy, with an immense army about to fall upon its neighbours, he decided that the time had come to show his hand, to ensure deluded Britain's neutrality in the coming war.

Bethmann Hollweg spilled the beans to Goschen – who was of German descent, and therefore hopefully would understand the German Empire's needs – to tell Sir Edward Grey that Germany would soon be going to war against France. He asserted that the French colonies, which Germany had so long coveted, would be forfeited but that Germany would not grab any French territory unless Britain entered the war, in which case Germany would claim a free hand. The offer also applied to Belgium.[51]

Tall, slim Sir Edward Grey came from a long line of Whig politicians. He had been Foreign Minister since 1905 and carried immense prestige in England. In October 1908 the Kaiser had caused disquiet in Britain when he published an article in the *Daily Telegraph*, in which he declared:

'Germany is a young and growing empire. She has a world-wide commerce which is rapidly expanding and to which the legitimate ambition of patriotic Germans refuses to assign any bounds. Germany must have a powerful fleet to protect that commerce and her manifold interests in even the most distant seas.'

Grey realised that the Kaiser was reflecting a view shared by a wide section of the Prussian establishment at the time, so he stated in his response:

'He (the Kaiser) has the strongest army in the world and the Germans ... are looking for somebody on whom to vent their anger and use their strength ... It is 38 years since Germany had her last war, and she is very strong and very restless ... I

71

don't think there will be war at present, but it will be difficult to keep the peace of Europe for another five years'.[52]

Grey's assessment of the situation in 1908 was correct. Six years later the Germans were looking to upset the peace of Europe. They understood only too well that it was Britain's backing for France which had thwarted their colonial ambitions in 1905 and 1911. So they had concentrated their efforts on lulling Grey and his country into a false sense of security and friendship in 1913. The British had responded enthusiastically. Their artistic and cultural links with Germany went back a long way. It was the French, after all, who had been Britain's historic enemies not the Germans.

Yet the British government did not realise that the country which had been chatting them up in 1912 and 1913 was not Germany but the Prussian Empire writ large. In 1912 between 75 per cent and 85 per cent of the whole net revenue of the German Empire was spent on the army, skewing its economy, unless justified in war.[53] In 1913 Germany voted for further army increases, leaving it critically short of funds.[54]

Britain had a great navy but if she wanted to keep the peace in Europe she needed a land force. Although the British Expeditionary Force was 'the best trained, best organised and best equipped British Army' ever, its size was insufficient to command German respect, while Britain's projected expenditure on the army in 1914 was less in real terms than it was in the year 1907–8.[55]

Grey realised that he had been fooled when he turned a blind eye to Germany's armaments drive in 1913. He did not believe that warfare was the way to conduct negotiations in the twentieth century but he realised that Prussia/Germany took a different view. However, even with the knowledge of Bismarck's wars against the Austrian Empire and France, a man as intelligent and civilised as Grey would have found it difficult to accept that Germany was prepared to go to war against both France and Russia in 1914. Finally, on the night of 29/30th, he did. So he sent a telegram to the German ambassador, von Tschirschky, via Ambassador Lichnowsky, stating that Britain as a neutral power was prepared, with German help, to mediate between Austria-Hungary on the one side and Serbia and Russia on the other, but that the moment that France was drawn into the war, Britain would not be able to stand aside.[56]

Bethmann Hollweg was momentarily shattered by Grey's telegram, after all his efforts to secure British neutrality. At 3.00 a.m. on the 30th he sent his Ambassador von Tschirschky a message, telling him that circumstances had changed and he no longer supported Austria's fight against Serbia:

'If therefore, Austria should reject all mediation, we are faced with a conflagration in which Britain would be against us, Italy and Romania in all probability not with us. We should be two Great Powers against four. With Britain an enemy, the weight of the operations would fall on Germany … Under these circumstances we must urgently and emphatically suggest to the Vienna cabinet acceptance of mediation under the present honourable conditions. The responsibility falling on us and Austria for the consequences, which would ensue in case of refusal, would be uncommonly heavy.'

And at 3.05 a.m. Bethmann Hollweg sent another telegram ordering Austria-Hungary to stop 'refusing any exchange of views with Russia'. He declared to the no doubt astonished Austrians: 'We are prepared to fulfil our duty as allies, but must refuse to allow Vienna to draw us into a world conflagration frivolously and without regard to our advice.'[57]

If Bethmann Hollweg had continued in this vein, a European war might have been averted but the generals were already clamouring for a declaration of war. Bethmann Hollweg had set the ball rolling. Encouraged by a night's sleep, he continued with his task.

The Kaiser had great nominal power but he had been side-lined. When he saw the news that Russia had partially mobilised at 7.00 a.m. on the 30th July (two days after the event occurred),[58] he commented in his marginal notes on the information 'Then I must mobilise too ... He (Tsar Nicholas II) is taking on himself the guilt ... I regard my attempted mediation as having failed'.[59]

The Foreign Ministry passed the Kaiser's marginal notes on to the General Staff. Neither Austria-Hungary nor Serbia, let alone Russia, had seen the Kaiser's 'Halt in Belgrade' before Bethmann Hollweg doctored it, but that was neither here nor there. When von Moltke saw that the Kaiser had said 'Then I must mobilise', he felt justified in pressing Austria-Hungary to adopt general mobilisation (without actually declaring war on Russia), and also to mobilise against Russia rather than Serbia.[60]

The Kaiser was a loud-mouthed fool, but it was not his fault that his 'Halt in Belgrade' had failed to stop the war. He had been deceived big time. He was distraught at the thought of war and at midday on 30th July he received more unsubstantiated news from his naval attaché in London, to the effect that the 'British fleet would launch an instant and immediate attack on us at sea if it comes to war between Britain and France'. This drove the Kaiser crazy. After venting his anger against 'that filthy cur, Grey', he declared that 'England alone is responsible for the war and peace, not we anymore!'[61]

Although Bethmann Hollweg was still reluctant to proclaim an 'imminent threat of war', General Moltke then took independent action. He sent an urgent warning to the Chief of the Austro-Hungarian General Staff, Conrad, to mobilise immediately against Russia (letting the dispositions against Serbia take second place) and to announce as his reason the Russian proclamation of partial mobilisation (so as to make Russia appear the aggressor).[62]

Russian Foreign Minister Sergei Sazonov declared that it was clear to everybody that Germany had decided to bring about a collision, as otherwise it would not have rejected all the peace proposals that had been made and could easily have brought her ally to reason.[63] He therefore urged Russia to adopt general mobilisation. Germany resumed talks with Turkey with the aim of making Turkey the base for revolution against Britain. Preparations were also made to stir up revolution against Russia in Poland.

The French were acutely aware of the threat to their nation. The covering troops of the German army were already massed all along the frontier between Luxemburg and Alsace.[64] They had adopted three-year conscription to deter the German troops from attacking France. As this had proved ineffectual they felt that their only hope was to withdraw the French troops well behind their frontier in order to avoid giving the Germans the slightest pretext to invade. In an unprecedented move, Prime Minister René Viviani (who had only been appointed by Poincaré a couple of weeks earlier), ordered the French troops to leave a zone of ten kilometres (six miles), between the French army outposts and the border.[65]

This did not worry the 'Prussian' leadership, but before attacking France it was imperative for Bethmann Hollweg to identify Russia as the aggressor in order to secure the support of the peace-loving German people. At 9.00 p.m. on 30th July, Bethmann Hollweg and Foreign Minister Jagow yielded to Generals Moltke and Falkenhayn's insistence that the 'state of imminent war' had to be proclaimed the next day.[66] The report of Russia's general mobilisation was confirmed on the 31st.[67] On 1st August the Press Office of the German Foreign Ministry declared: 'Russia alone forces a war on Europe which nobody has wanted except Russia; the full force of responsibility falls on Russia alone.'[68]

Now that Russia had been identified as the warmonger, the Social Democrats who had demonstrated in favour of peace were reported to be 'keeping quite quiet'. Persuading the German socialists that Russia was the enemy was of primary importance, not only to ensure their support but also to persuade British socialists to campaign for Britain to remain neutral. To make absolutely certain of German and British backing, Bethmann Hollweg postponed the date for Germany's general mobilisation to 1st August.[69]

British socialists did not realise that Germany, whose culture they admired so much, had been hijacked by the Prussian military and industrial hierarchy. The left in Britain were united with their German socialist brethren in their loathing for the repressive Tsarist regime in Russia, which had denied liberal ambitions ever since the revolution of 1905. In contrast they admired German states like Saxony, who had been in the forefront of introducing garden cities and clearing slums, and promoting elementary and adult education. In Württemberg and Baden, art, theatre, music and literature were generously supported.[70] A large portrait of the Kaiser hung in the Oxford Examination Schools and a host of distinguished German figures such as Lichnowsky, and the composer Richard Strauss had just received honorary degrees.[71] On 1st August when a number of British academics realised that Britain was on the brink of war on Russia's side, they expressed their opposition in a letter to *The Times*:

'We regard Germany as a nation leading the way in the Arts and Sciences, and have all learnt and are learning from German scholars. War upon her in the interest of Serbia and Russia will be a sin against civilisation.'

The influential journalist, Norman Angell, also wrote:

'The object and effect of our entering this war would be to ensure the victory of Russia and her Slavonic allies. Will a dominant Slavonic federation of say 200,000,000 autocratically governed people with very rudimentary civilisation but heavily equipped for military aggression, be a less dangerous factor in Europe than a dominant Germany of 65,000,000 highly civilised people, mainly given to the arts of trade and commerce?'[72]

On 1st August, after the German order for mobilisation had been signed, the British King, George V, sent a direct personal telegram to the Tsar.[73] An offer also arrived in Germany to guarantee France's neutrality. The Kaiser accepted the offer and ordered Moltke 'to hold up the advance westward'.[74] However, Moltke protested that he could not; the patrols had already penetrated Luxembourg. When the Emperor persisted with his demand, Moltke remarked bitterly, 'Now it only remains for Russia to back out too.'

Unfortunately however, after sharp arguments, Bethmann Hollweg and Moltke agreed that the military advance would have to go on 'for technical reasons'. Britain's offer had come too late.

On 2nd August Germany managed to conclude a most useful military agreement with Turkey, under which the Turkish army was placed under German military command. The German cruisers, SMS *Goeben* and *Breslau* were dispatched to Constantinople.[75]

Meanwhile, Britain had been having a two-day debate about entering the war. The Conservative Party supported it but four Ministers in Grey's own Liberal Party opposed it, as did the Labour Party.

Almost all the information in this chapter leading up to the First World War came from Fritz Fischer's *Griff nach der Weltmacht*, published in English as *Germany's Aims in the First World War* except this one curious incident, reproduced by the website 'Spartacus Educational' (a website used by history teachers and their students). It is reproduced here as it gives an inkling to the character and outlook of Bethmann Hollweg and Sir Edward Grey at this critical time.

An American journalist working for the *Chicago Daily News* (Raymond Gram Swing) met Chancellor Bethmann Hollweg. He asked Swing to approach Sir Edward Grey, in confidence, with a new peace offer.

Late at night, on the 29th/30th July, Bethmann Hollweg had told Britain's ambassador, Sir Edward Goschen, that Germany would respect the integrity of France and Belgium if Britain agreed to stay neutral, saying that Germany only intended to grab France and Belgium's colonies. In Bethmann Hollweg's new peace offer there was no mention of respecting the integrity of France. However, Bethmann Hollweg promised not to actually annex any Belgian territory and to guarantee Belgium's independence after the war, in return for Britain paying Germany an indemnity. Belgium's powerful steel industry had helped to make Belgium one of the most industrialised small nations in the world. Bethmann Hollweg wanted compensation for forgoing the 'spoils of war'.

Raymond Gram Swing described Sir Edward Grey at this time as 'having the personal appearance of a shaggy ascetic' with crumpled clothes and 'thin but untidy hair'. Yet the former real tennis player was under greater pressure than the immaculately turned out Bethmann Hollweg, as he was leading a divided party while Bethmann Hollweg had the Prussian military solidly behind him.

In the month since Franz Ferdinand's murder, Grey had received numerous messages from Bethmann Hollweg stating that he was striving to stop war between Austria and Serbia, only to find out that he was actually using Franz Ferdinand's murder as a pretext to invade France. Now Bethmann Hollweg was asking Grey to believe him when he said that if Britain stayed out of the war he would not annex any Belgian territory during the conflict and would guarantee Belgium's independence afterwards. Talking of Britain paying Germany an indemnity to stop Germany annexing parts of Belgium was the final straw.

An irate Sir Edward Grey told Raymond Gram Swing, 'Does not Herr von Bethmann Hollweg know what must come from the war? It must be a world of international law where treaties are observed, where men welcome conferences and do not scheme for war ... Great Britain is fighting for a new basis for foreign relations, a new international morality.' France agreed.

Despite France's unprecedented move in withdrawing her troops ten kilometres (six miles) behind her frontier, Germany alleged that the French had violated its territory and that French aeroplanes had dropped bombs on the railway near Karlsruhe and Nuremberg.[76] At 6.00 p.m. on 3rd August, the German ambassador in Paris was instructed to inform the French government that Germany considered that a state of war existed between the two countries.

On 4th August Germany invaded neutral Belgium, and Britain declared war against Germany. Chancellor Bethmann Hollweg was reputedly upset over this turn of events, repeatedly asking the departing ambassador how Britain could possibly go to war over 'a mere scrap of paper'! Yet the German army was not worried about the British Expeditionary Force fighting on France's side. General Moltke remarked to Foreign Minister Jagow, 'We shall manage the 150,000 British.'[77]

English journalist Norman Angell had stated that Germany would not make money from going to war against France. Yet the Pan-German League did not agree. Despite the fact that the French had introduced three-year conscription, it envisaged the German army fighting a lightning six-week military campaign to demolish the French army. And it would soon be publishing its war aims.

CHAPTER FOUR

Who Won the War?

Chancellor Bethmann Hollweg of Germany and Sir Edward Grey of Britain represented two rival philosophies in August 1914. Prussia/Germany believed that 'might is right'. It deserved to be able to march into its neighbours and grab their coal, iron and territory because it was a stronger, more capable race and able to use its neighbours' land and raw materials more efficiently. It had always expanded by going to war. Even if there was a mountain of corpses in the short-term, the future was bright. A short, sharp war against France and Russia, like Bismarck waged against Denmark, the Austrian Empire and France, would achieve its objectives.

Grey, on the other hand, believed that in the modern, civilised world there should be international law, so that one country would not march into others, grabbing their land and stealing their wealth. Britain may have had to use minimum force for the security of her Empire, but in cultured northern Europe she believed that war was totally inappropriate and she had the support of her dominions in her wish for law and order.

So the Prussian army set off to defeat its neighbours, and Britain and her Empire decided to go to war over Germany's invasion of neutral Belgium. Neither side remembered that 750,000 people died in the American Civil War.[1] In the twentieth century, war was liable to cause infinitely more carnage.

The German leadership had terrified its citizens with tales of it being encircled by a ring of threatening enemies, and yet its army waged war against France with a light heart. It hoped to defeat the French in six weeks before demolishing Russia. It raped Belgium and swept on towards Paris. Yet all did not go quite to plan. General Gallieni, Paris's Military Governor, redeployed troops so that they could attack General von Kluck's First Army on its exposed flank, bringing in extra troops in a fleet of taxis to avert catastrophe. Paris was saved. The larger German army was repelled by thirty-nine French divisions and six British divisions, at the cost of thousands of deaths on both sides. The first Battle of the Marne, 5–12th September 1914, was an immense strategic victory for the Allies, wrecking the German army's bid for a swift victory. In spite of this setback, German morale remained high. On 22nd August 1914, Generals Paul von Hindenburg and Erich Ludendorff won a major victory against Russia at Tannenberg, and in France the army occupied the area German industry had most coveted in France in the years before the war, the Longwy-Briey iron ore field.

On 28th August the Pan-Germans produced their war aims, although not a word was allowed to be relayed by the press. They were endorsed by armaments maker Gustav Krupp, steel magnates like August Thyssen and a ruthless coal and steel magnate called Hugo Stinnes.

Thyssen's ambitions encompassed not only France and Belgium, but also central Europe, Russia and beyond. He shared the Pan-Germans' ambition to create a huge German-dominated European region called 'Mitteleuropa', which would include all the regions of weakening Austria-Hungary, the Crimea and the manganese ore-rich Caucasus. His ultimate

81

ambition was to acquire a land-bridge across South Russia, Asia Minor and Persia (Iran) from where it could deal a decisive blow against the British Empire – by now the real enemy in the war – in Egypt and India.[2]

But first things first. Bethmann Hollweg had to deal with realities on the ground. On 9th September he produced 'provisional notes' on what he would demand from Belgium and France, when France was defeated.[3]

Bethmann Hollweg declared that 'France must be so weakened that she never again recovers as a great power.'[4] A commercial treaty would make France economically dependent on Germany and exclude British commerce from the country. France would also lose her colonies, Belfort and the western slopes of the Vosges and the coast from Dunkirk to Boulogne. He resisted Pan-German pressure to annex Toulon as a fortified port but rejoiced in the capture of Germany's primary objective in France, the Longwy-Briey iron ore field.

Other nations may have coveted Notre Dame and the Arc de Triomphe, but Prussia/Germany's military-industrial complex coveted iron. The loss of Longwy-Briey's ore would ensure that France lost 80 per cent of its blast furnaces and 85 per cent of its iron ore production, destroying it as an industrial power.[5]

The Germans lost no time in exploiting the mines. They were put under a special 'Imperial Protective Administration' before being placed directly under the Supreme Army Command. The total reserves of Longwy-Briey were put at 2,775 million tons of ore. August Thyssen remarked that it would be 'only a question of a little time before Germany caught up with and passed America, which would ensure Germany's world domination on the iron market'.[6]

On the question of Belgium, Bethmann Hollweg believed that Liège and Verviers should become part of Germany and that little Belgium, the third most industrialised small state in the world, must be reduced to a vassal state. He envisaged adding French Flanders, Dunkirk, Calais and Boulogne to Belgium to salve the wounds of defeat. Industrial magnate Hugo Stinnes, who would fight a venomous and ultimately successful campaign against the eight-hour day in German mines in 1923,[7] would be called upon to organise Belgium's coal and industrial production.

The acquisition of Longwy-Briey and Belgium's industrial riches so close to the Ruhr made it infinitely cheaper for Germany to wage war than Britain, as Britain would become increasingly dependent on expensive imports,[8] perilously transported across the ocean from America.

Naturally Germany rejected American President Wilson's tentative peace initiative at this time. Prince Hohenlohe, Austro-Hungarian Ambassador to Berlin, believed that Germany was resolved 'to thrash France and England as soundly as possible', and 'Russia as soundly as the enemies in the West, or even more so'.[9]

It is easy to march into a country, less easy to hang on to it. German General Erich von Falkenhayn was determined to win on the Western Front where General von Moltke had failed. After the Battle of the Marne, there was the so-called 'race to the sea'. The British wanted at all costs to protect the French Channel ports from falling into German hands. In the battles fought in Picardy, Artois and Flanders, neither side could gain the military advantage while the Belgian army, later reinforced by the British Royal Naval Division, held out in Antwerp. In October and November, Falkenhayn tried a break-through at the strategic town of Ypres in western Belgium. Although the 150,000 British Expeditionary Force was almost wiped out by the end of the battle, the Allies temporarily won the fight.

On 2nd December 1914, Bethmann Hollweg dressed himself up in the grey service uniform of a German General and told the Reichstag that Britain and Russia were responsible for the war. 'Belgian neutrality', he declared, 'was nothing but a disguise'.[10]

This was the start of the German hierarchy's long and successful propaganda campaign to persuade the German people, the Left in Britain and the Americans that Germany was no more responsible than any other country for starting the First World War. It was the German army, however, which was occupying its neighbours' territories, and it was determined to win the military as well as the propaganda battle.

In the spring of 1915 Falkenhayn fought a second battle for control of Ypres, using poison gas to be sure of victory. After the battle of Frezenberg between 8th and 13th May, Sir John French declared:

'The effect of the gas was so overwhelming that the whole of the positions occupied by the French divisions were rendered incapable of movement ... Fumes and smoke were thrown into a stupor and after an hour the whole position had to be abandoned.'

After this the Allies used poison gas too. Bethmann Hollweg had banned all public discussion of war aims. However, in the spring of 1915, the Pan-German League wanted to reassure the weary German people that war paid. It won the legal battle to publish its 1914 war aims. Besides despoiling France and Belgium, 'shattering the Russian colossus', eliminating weak 'allegedly neutral states' on Germany's frontiers, and creating an African Empire, the Pan-Germans waxed lyrical about the creation of a German-dominated bloc in Europe called 'Mitteleuropa'. Their spokesman, Heinrich Class, declared:

'It is an absolutely imperative demand, and widely accepted as such, that Mitteleuropa, inclusive of those areas to be acquired by the German Reich and Austria-Hungary as prizes of victory, must form one great economic unit. The Netherlands and Switzerland, the three Scandinavian States and Finland, Italy, Romania and Bulgaria will attach themselves to this nucleus gradually and of compulsive necessity, without need of the least pressure from the nucleus States, the result will be a vast economic unit capable of asserting and maintaining its economic-political independence against any other in the world'.

To a cynic, the Pan-Germans' vision looked very much like a take-over bid for the Austro-Hungarian Empire. The Austrians were weakening daily and it looked as though their empire would soon fall into the Prussians' lair. Indeed, by 1917 General Ludendorff would be declaring, 'The alliance with Austria must remain but the conflict with Austria is bound to come.'[11]

Meanwhile the industrialists were crystallising their ambitions for the future of Belgium and France. Alfred Hugenberg, former director of Krupps and foundation member of the Pan-German League, invited the leading members of Germany's trade associations to a meeting in Berlin, where bellicose Pan-German spokesman Heinrich Class, who had declared in 1912, 'We didn't take the Reichsland (Alsace-Lorraine) for the sake of your beautiful eyes ... The inhabitants are an extra', was asked to give a speech outlining the Pan German's ideas on Germany's war aims in the West.

The outcome of this meeting was a memorandum signed on 20th May 1915 by the Six Associations, representing Germany's principle trade bodies, which declared that Germany needed a substantial colonial empire, 'security' in the fields of tariff and commercial policy, 'an adequately guaranteed war indemnity, and territorial acquisitions in the East and the West'.

In the West they insisted upon the military and economic dominance of Belgium, the Belgian and French Channel coasts, the strategic towns of Belfort and Verdun, the annexation of the Longwy-Brie iron-ore field and the coalfields of the department of the Nord and the Pas de Calais. The local populations in these regions were to be deprived of all political rights and all the large and medium businesses were to be transferred to German ownership.[12]

In early 1916, Falkenhayn decided on a massive battle of attrition against the French at Verdun. He reasoned that if France, which had a third less inhabitants than Germany, bled to death, Britain would be left fighting alone on the Western Front and could be starved into submission by a submarine blockade. The Battle of Verdun lasted from 21st February until 18th December 1916. The Russian General Brusilov's brilliant offensive, in June, was designed to force Germany to halt its attack. A primary reason for the British starting the Battle of the Somme in July, where they were estimated to have suffered 420,000 casualties, was also to take the pressure off France.

Falkenhayn did not win the Battle of Verdun, but from a German viewpoint, his effort was not fruitless. France suffered more casualties than Germany. Its total casualties at the Somme and Verdun amounted to over 700,000. The war costs for Britain and France also kept mounting and not only in horrific human terms. They were finding it more and more expensive to buy their raw materials from overseas. Meanwhile France's Pas de Calais was producing coal for Germany's furnaces, Longwy-Briey was producing iron to make Krupp's Big Bertha guns and Belgium's factories were turning French iron into German steel. In October 1916 the new Hindenberg-Ludendorff administration ordered 400,000 workers from occupied Belgium to be pumped into German industry. Kind America sent ships across the sea to feed the starving Belgians, paradoxically relieving Germany of the necessity.[13]

The Battle of the Somme, which lasted from 1st July until 18th November 1916 was a scene of carnage, with immense losses on both sides.[14] General Falkenhayn lost his job. On 29th August 1916, 70-year-old General Hindenburg, who was raised to a peak of adulation after his victories at

Tannenburg and the Masurian Lakes, and General Ludendorff (the brains of the combination), took military control of Germany and the German army withdrew to the more easily defendable Hindenburg Line on the Western Front, adopting a scorched earth policy on its retreat.

Ludendorff and Hindenburg had been promoted as they had made progress in the East. Since 1915 the German army had occupied the entire Russian part of Poland, including Warsaw, and the area of Courland and Lithuania. The German government decided that it would soon resume unrestricted submarine warfare in a systematic way to starve Britain into submission. The third weapon in its armoury was subversion. With the help of his spy chief, Wilhelm Stieber, Bismarck had been successful at subverting Austria and France in the nineteenth century. Since then the spy organisation that Stieber had put in place grew to become the most powerful in the world.

At the beginning of the war, the Kaiser declared: 'Our ... agents ... must inflame the whole Mohammedan world to wild revolt ... if we are to be bled to death, at least England shall lose India.'

In August 1914 the Khedive of Egypt was given a bribe of four million gold francs to liquidate the British officers in the Egyptian army and block the Suez Canal. The Turks were given £100,000 to help. However, the British thwarted the plot.[15]

On 5th September 1914, Irish nationalists decided to stage a wartime rising and accept whatever help Germany might offer. In November 1914, the German government had ex-British consular official Sir Roger Casement brought from New York to Germany, where he raised the hopes of the political and military authorities. Casement returned to Ireland on a German U-boat. However, another German boat carrying a shipment of arms for him and the rebels was scuttled by the Royal Navy and Casement was captured. The subsequent 1916 Easter Rising failed, but the heavy-handed British military occupation of Dublin afterwards helped the Irish nationalists' cause. So the money spent on arms and encouragement for the Irish nationalists had been cost-effective.

In the autumn of 1916 the big economic associations threatened to withdraw war finance unless Germany returned to unrestricted submarine warfare. Tall, stooped, and by now silver-haired, Bethmann Hollweg was given the task of reneging on his promise not to return to unrestricted submarine warfare. Bethmann Hollweg told Hindenburg and Ludendorff his plan:

'Count Bernstorff has been instructed on the personal orders of His Majesty to induce President Wilson to issue an appeal for peace. If Wilson can be got to do this, the probable rejection of the appeal by England and her Allies, while we accept it, would give us a moral justification in the eyes of the world, and in particular of the European neutrals, for withdrawing our promise to America.'[16]

Luckily for Bethmann Hollweg, early returns suggesting that American President, Woodrow Wilson, would lose his re-election campaign on 7th November 1916 proved false. The Midwest with its large German-American population bolstered Wilson's vote. However, Bismarck may have forced many of the roughly ten million Americans of German extraction to leave their former homeland, but that did not mean to say that they were eager to fight their kith and kin.

After Presbyterian Wilson's re-election he lost his former affection for Britain. As a Professor of Jurisprudence, he was incensed by what he saw as British malpractice in searching, seizing and censoring American transatlantic mail, and issuing a 'blacklist' of American firms suspected of trading with the Central Powers. He warned that the US would not tolerate the continuation of 'repeated violations of international law'.[17]

His attitude to Germany was more cordial. On 16th November 1916, German Ambassador Count Bernstorff relayed the good news that Wilson would be receptive to a peace initiative from Germany, the most important proviso being that there should be as little talk as possible about it in Germany so that the Entente powers would believe that it originated in America.[18]

Wilson had by now come to the conclusion that all the Europeans were guilty of war lust in 1914. His aim was 'peace without victory'. He knew that Britain was becoming more and more dependent on America to finance the war. To make quite sure that Britain responded to the offer of peace he was awaiting from the Germans, he put Britain under such financial pressure that its reserves were almost exhausted.[19]

On 4th December, Bernstorff reported that everything was 'ready for a peace action in Washington' and on 12th December, Bethmann Hollweg submitted his offer. He was a model for all negotiators to copy. He knew that America could not put economic pressure on Germany like it had on England. So, having launched his peace initiative, and with the Americans sworn to secrecy, he behaved as though he was making a concession even thinking about peace. Although the Austrians were desperate for the war to end, Bethmann Hollweg's peace proposal was characterised by its strong confidence in victory and its absence of any commitments. He merely declared that the Central Powers were ready to enter negotiations 'calculated to assure the existence, honour and freedom of their people'.

Even Wilson was disappointed. On 18th December 1916 he asked all the belligerents to make public the conditions on which they would make peace. After Germany refused this initiative, the Entente refused to comply too. Yet Wilson clung to his trust in Germany, fruitlessly begging the German government to communicate its war aims to him in confidence.[20]

Republican ex-President Theodore Roosevelt declared, 'I don't believe that Wilson will go to war unless Germany literally kicks him into it.'[21]

The German hierarchy was certain that Wilson would eventually be pushed into declaring war by American public opinion, when Germany explicitly refused to allow American shipping to pass freely to Britain. However, they were confident that their use of unrestricted submarine warfare would quickly win the war and believed that Bethmann's 'peace offer' had secured a propaganda victory among the neutral nations.

Large, red-blond haired and red-blooded Arthur Zimmermann, who had recently replaced the puny 'rodent' Jagow, as Foreign Minister, had an insurance policy in case America entered the war. He did not think it would take long for German submarines to sink Great Britain, telling a Danish journalist bluntly: 'If only the United States will keep its hands off and leave us alone, two or three months will be enough.'[22] Yet to make sure that American troops lingered in the US, rather than pouring over to Europe to help the Allies in the summer of 1917, he decided to persuade the Americans that Mexico was just about to invade.

In 1916 the revolutionary General Pancho Villa raided Columbus, New Mexico, killing twenty Americans. Twelve thousand troops were sent in vain to chase him while four-fifths of the regular army was tied up along the Mexican borders. So in 1917 Zimmermann sent a coded telegram to Mexico by three different routes to make sure that it arrived:

'We intend to begin unrestricted submarine warfare on the first of February. We shall endeavour in spite of this to keep the United States neutral. In the event of this not succeeding, we make Mexico a proposal of alliance on the following basis; make war together, make peace together, generous financial support, and an understanding on our part that

Mexico is to reconquer the lost territory in Texas, New Mexico, and Arizona. The settlement in detail is left to you.'[23]

Zimmermann's telegram created a huge stir in America. However, the Mexicans denied ever having received it and the cream of intellectual society in New York declared it to be a forgery. At Zimmermann's press conference he was asked straight out to deny 'this story'. 'I cannot deny it,' Zimmermann replied. 'It is true.'[24]

Zimmermann dared to admit that he sent the telegram because he believed that American anxieties that Mexico would invade their southern states, would delay their troops' arrival in Europe until Germany had won the war. The British exchequer was in a parlous state,[25] and the German naval staff promised that unrestricted submarine warfare would sink an average of 600,000 tons of enemy and neutral shipping monthly and force Britain to accept terms within five months.[26] France was also fragile. The French army had been battered by Falkenhayn's policy of attrition in 1916 and a major mutiny would occur after General Nivelle's failed offensive in April.

Yet all the Americans, including German-Americans, were horrified by Zimmermann's admission that Germany had been inciting Mexico to go to war against America. The *Omaha World Herald* declared, 'The issue shifts ... from Germany against Great Britain to Germany against the United States.' Overnight the Midwest isolationist press changed tack.[27] American sentiment became pro-British and war fever set in. The US number one popular song 'I Didn't Raise My Boy to Be a Soldier' was swiftly replaced with the jingoistic tune 'Over There'. Zimmerman's telegram helped to unite American opinion in favour of war.

Wilson declared war on Germany on 2nd April 1917 as an 'associate power'. And even though fears of Mexican attacks on Texas, New Mexico and Arizona may have contributed to his caution in sending large numbers of GIs over to Europe in 1917, Zimmermann's calculations about unrestricted submarine warfare forcing Britain into submission were proved false.

German submarines achieved extraordinary initial successes up to May and June, but defensive weapons and the convoy system gradually stemmed British shipping losses. Wilson's declaration of war against Germany also gave the Entente a tremendous boost to its morale, and on 14th June, Britain's General Plumer took the Messines Ridge just south-east of Ypres, which had been held by the German army since December 1914. Yet Britain was spending ever more of its national treasure to replace ships and to finance Russia's crumbling war effort. Meanwhile, although unrestricted submarine warfare had not defeated the British, Zimmerman's efforts on the Eastern Front were meeting with success.

In 1915 the Foreign Office discovered a Russian revolutionary in Turkey called Alexander Helphand, more commonly known as 'Parvus', who declared:

'Russian democracy can only achieve its goals through the complete destruction of Tsarism and the dismemberment of Russia into smaller states. Germany, for her part, will not achieve full success unless she succeeds in starting a major revolution in Russia.'

Parvus was brought to Germany and promised that thousands of émigrés would return to Russia to create mayhem provided that they were given finance. The German government gave him two million marks.

Parvus recommended a conference of all Russian Socialists in Switzerland, including Lenin, the radical leader, who had unexpectedly offered to come. Few in Zurich public library remarked on the bald little Russian with a red moustache and a neat short beard, who worked from morning to night demonising less extreme revolutionaries. For Lenin the war had only one purpose – the destruction of the capitalist system and the

92

substitution of the 'dictatorship of the proletariat'.[28] An Estonian called Aleksander Kesküla assured the German Foreign Office that it could bank on Lenin to achieve its ambitions.

In September 1915 Lenin stated his conditions, including Germany renouncing annexations and a war indemnity. The German negotiators were happy to say 'Yes' to anything; the serious negotiations could proceed once Lenin was in place.

In the winter of 1915–16 Parvus was given another twenty million roubles to create revolution in Russia but he found the Mensheviks, like their Social Democrat counterparts in Germany, unwilling to renounce their government in the middle of a war.[29]

At last, in mid-March 1917, the German hierarchy heard that the Russian Tsar had been toppled. Russia split into two factions: those who wanted to carry on the war and implement moderate reforms and those who were ready to conclude peace with Germany on the basis of 'no big annexations' only 'frontier rectifications'. Germany's Russian expert, Count Brockdorff-Rantzau, advised Berlin to 'create the greatest possible chaos in Russia', and on 31st March Lenin and fellow Bolsheviks received permission to travel home in a sealed train, accompanied by a larger group of pro-Entente Mensheviks so that they were not compromised as German agents.[30]

After reaching Russia, Lenin at once pressed for peace with the Central Powers. Yet he took months to achieve power. He had to flee after Bolshevik putsches failed in May and June, but the German Foreign Office continued to help 'inflame the anti-English feeling of the masses' and to strengthen the Russians' longing for peace.[31]

Despite the brilliant Russian, General Brusilov's final offensive in June there were increasing reports that the country was descending into chaos. Both Ludendorff and Bethmann Hollweg believed that 'time has become our latest ally'.[32] Yet censorship was total in Germany. The mass of the German people knew nothing about Russia. Meanwhile the submarine war was failing to defeat Britain, and Germany was facing another winter of war when Hindenburg had promised victory by August.[33] The Social Democrats believed that peace with Russia could only be achieved by a renunciation of annexations and indemnities. Their squat authoritative leader, Friedrich Ebert, warned that the Reichstag must not underestimate America as it had underestimated England, and he called for the unequal voting franchise in Germany's largest state, Prussia, to be removed.[34]

On 6th July, former arch-annexationist Matthias Erzberger called for the Reichstag to vote for a 'compromise' peace. This astounded and horrified the military, already envisaging grabbing great swathes of the Russian Empire's territory. Bethmann Hollweg finessed the situation by declaring that Germany had always favoured a defensive standpoint but had to include 'safeguards for Germany's future'.[35]

However, the pressure was tangible. It was in these circumstances that Bethmann Hollweg agreed to consider the idea of equal franchise for Prussian voters.[36] Prussia was by far the largest state in Germany. It was governed by an oral three-class franchise method, under which the richest got the lion's share of the votes. The socialists had long wanted to change the system. It seemed at last that their wishes had been granted. The Emperor supported the idea but the very next day Chancellor Bethmann Hollweg was overthrown by General Ludendorff.

New Chancellor, Michaelis, realised that he must give the socialists one concession, so allowed the Reichstag to vote on a so-called 'Peace of Understanding'. The Reichstag proclaimed, just as it did on 4th August 1914, that Germany was waging war solely in order to retain 'the integrity of its own territory'. It would never aim at any other end than a 'peace of understanding'. However, the Reichstag had never been in control of Germany and the new Chancellor confided to the Crown Prince: 'I have deprived it (The Peace of Understanding) of its most dangerous features by my interpretation of it. One can make any peace one likes with this interpretation.'[37]

Also former Navy Minister Tirpitz and friends quickly formed a new political movement called The Fatherland Party to discredit the socialists and to campaign for red-blooded war aims. Although Bismarck's Reich had been notably poor at looking after minorities such as the Danes, the Poles and the inhabitants of Alsace before the First World War, Tirpitz believed that modern Germany had a mission to grow and to rule.

The Allies did not realise the importance of their new offensive at Passchendaele, to break the German army's morale on the Western Front before the German High Command could get Lenin into power. Unfortunately the heavens opened the day that they commenced their offensive at Passchendaele, the rain soaked the ground below and they were soon floundering in the mud, waiting numbly in water-logged holes 'with the mud gusts tugging the wire, like the twitching agonies of men among its (barbed-wire) brambles'.[38] The rain, the bloodshed and the misery on the Western Front continued for the British Soldiers but Germany's efforts to put Lenin in place were in sight of victory. Tirpitz expressed his loathing for Britain and America and his confidence in the future:

'The question today is whether we can hold our own against Anglo-Americanism or whether we must sink down and become mere manure for others ... what is really at issue is the liberty of the continent of Europe and its peoples against the all-devouring tyranny of Anglo-Americanism. Germany is fighting for a great deal, and therefore I would cry out to every corner of our Fatherland: Germany awake! Thine hour of destiny has arrived.'[39]

At last, on 7th November 1917, Lenin achieved power. Zimmermann's successor at the Foreign Office, Richard von Kühlmann, patted himself and his spy department on the back, boasting, 'It was only the resources which the Bolsheviks received regularly from our side ... that enabled them ... greatly to expand the originally narrow basis of their party.'

Kühlmann responded immediately to Lenin's call for peace because he was alarmed that the Bolshevik government would collapse. To the world's astonishment he agreed to negotiate with the Bolsheviks on the basis of a peace without 'annexations or reparations'. Meanwhile Lenin's right-hand man, Leon Trotsky, revealed some shady agreements that Britain and France had made with Russia and Italy to keep them fighting on their side in the war. The publication of these agreements caused uproar in Europe and the US. The Americans felt that they had to come out with a statement of their altruistic war aims to compete with Germany's philanthropy.[40]

Woodrow Wilson was eager to show how altruistic the New World was. On 8th January 1918, he produced his, later to become famous, Fourteen Points for Peace:

1. open covenants of peace, openly arrived at,
2. absolute freedom of navigation upon the seas, alike in peace and in war,
3. the removal, so far as possible, of all economic barriers,
4. national armaments to be reduced to the lowest level consistent with domestic safety,
5. a free, open-minded and absolutely impartial adjustment of all colonial claims,
6. the evacuation of all Russian territory,
7. Belgium to be evacuated and restored,
8. all French territory to be freed and the former portions taken by Bismarck to be restored,

9. the frontiers of Italy to be readjusted along clearly recognizable lines of nationality,
10. the nations of Austria-Hungary should be accorded the freest opportunity for autonomous development,
11. Romania, Serbia and Montenegro should be evacuated,
12. the Turkish portion of the Ottoman Empire should be restored but the rest of the nationalities should be allowed an absolutely unmolested opportunity of autonomous development,
13. an independent Polish state should be created, with access to the sea,
14. a general association of nations must be formed (to police these many new territories).

Hundreds of thousands of copies of Wilson's speech were distributed in Russia, but the German leadership completely ignored it at the time and the Russians were in no position to take advantage of it.

Kühlmann was happy to agree to Lenin's request for 'no annexations' and 'no indemnities' because he was a warrior and lies and deceit were part of his armoury. Many years later he described his approach to the negotiations:

'My plan was to entangle Trotsky in a purely academic discussion on the right of self-determination ... to get for ourselves ... whatever territorial concessions we absolutely needed,'[41]

Soon Germany found that it 'absolutely needed' a lot of territory and the spoils of war too. The treaty with Ukraine was signed on 22nd January 1918. The advantage of making a separate treaty with Ukraine was that its government had absolutely no authority. Its rule, according to Lenin's irate negotiator, Trotsky, did not even extend beyond its own living rooms in Brest-Litovsk.[42] Yet Ukraine was full of natural resources, waiting for plunder. Heavy industry coveted Ukrainian manganese and its high-grade iron ore. It also wanted the 70 per cent of Russia's coal and one-third of Russia's agricultural production which currently came from Ukraine but would in future be travelling towards Germany.[43]

The negotiations with Russia dragged on. Germany wanted complete freedom to acquire and work the mines formerly owned by the Russian state. It also wanted Russia's rubber, cotton, asbestos, copper, nickel and tin and insisted that Russia became a supplier of raw materials, dependent on Germany.[44]

On 9th February General Hoffmann demanded both Russia's Black Sea and its Baltic coast. To avoid this diktat, Trotsky declared: 'No war, no peace!' Yet this merely gave the German army the chance to use 'the soldier's boot' in the name of 'chasing out the bandits'.

The *Allgemeine Evangelisch-Lutherische Kirchenzeitung* commented:

'Germany's armies pressed on, took city after city ... Russia, who wanted to give no indemnity, was forced at the last minute to yield up uncountable booty; 800 locomotives, 8,000 railway trucks with every kind of treasure and supply. God knew that we needed it. And we also needed guns and munitions for the last blow against the enemy in the west. God knew that too. So he freely gave us, since God is rich, 2,600 guns, 5,000 machine guns, two million shells for the artillery rifles, aircraft, lorries and innumerable other things.'[45]

On 3rd March 1918, in the charred and blackened ruins of the town of Brest-Litovsk, Russia ceded Poland, Lithuania and Courland and consented to the separate peace with the Ukraine. Livonia and Estonia remained Russian, but were to be occupied by German 'police forces'.[46]

Germany's use of subversion in Russia had been a huge success from the military/industrialists' viewpoint. Its final ambition was to win on the Western Front. It transferred 'some' forty divisions from the Eastern Front to knock France and Britain out of the war before the trickle of American troops became a flood.[47] On 21st March 1918, sixty-two German divisions launched the offensive. Yet, despite its superior numbers the German army failed to gain the great victory it was expecting. Meanwhile during the final seven months of the war many of the ten million Americans liable for military service were sent over to Europe. Only 32,842 Americans were killed in battle, 17,015 died of disease and 13,554 were lost at sea, but their arrival was a huge morale booster for the Allies. They played a key role in helping to stop the German thrust towards Paris during the Second Battle of the Marne and would achieve their first solo victory at Saint Mihiel in September.

In the middle of July the German army suffered a reverse on the Western Front. Soon the Allies were pushing the German army on the Western Front back to its homeland, but the German army in the East was still making progress. Under supplementary treaties Romania became a satellite state in May,[48] agreeing to give up 80 per cent of its oil and all surplus food. Marching eastwards it captured the strategic city of Rostov-on-Don,[49] cutting the main line of communication between Russia and the resource-rich Caucasus.

In order to persuade the invaders to evacuate Rostov and cease their advance, the Bolsheviks agreed to painful new demands on 27th August: half of Russia's raw materials production was to be delivered to Germany; a joint commission would decide what industrial goods would be sent in return. Russia also surrendered Estonia and Livonia and agreed to the independence of Georgia and the payment of an indemnity of 6,000 million roubles, in fine gold, currency and kind, delivery to start straight away![50] Russia also promised to deliver one-third of the Baku oil in return for its surrender by the Turks.

The German leadership reflected: 'The Bolsheviks are very evil and antipathetic people ... (Nevertheless) Politics have always been utilitarian, and will be so for a long time to come ... What ... do we want in the East? The military paralysis of Russia. The Bolsheviks are producing this better and more thoroughly than any other Russian could do, without our giving a man or a mark for it.'

Yet the German/military industrialists' greed in the East meant that the Western Front was short of troops. It has been estimated that Germany had nearly a million troops on the Eastern Front, when they were desperately needed in the West.[51] On 8th August the British army delivered a telling defeat on the Germans in the West. Ludendorff called it the 'black day'.

Finally Britain's General Haig secured his war cabinet's grudging permission to pierce the Hindenburg line and capture the Passchendaele Salient by making it clear to them 'The discipline of the German army, is quickly going, and the German officer is not what he was.'

On 28th September, the Allies won a great victory over the muddy crater-strewn ground at Passchendaele. This was the moment when America and the Allies should have consulted the memoirs of Frederick the Great, who declared that he had only avoided defeat in 1762 through his opponents' lack of unity.

Unfortunately, with military victory seemingly 'in the bag', Ray Stannard Baker's *Woodrow Wilson, Life and Letters volume 8* (published just before the Second World War) revealed that President Wilson was no longer concerned about German militarism. His prejudice was against Britain and France. He sent a coded note to his emissary, Colonel House:

'My deliberate judgement is that our whole weight should be thrown for an Armistice ... which will be as moderate as possible ... because it is certain that too much success or security on the part of the Allies will make a genuine peace settlement exceedingly difficult if not impossible.'[52]

Europeans had been horrified by the endless bloodshed of the war. Wilson's ideals, expressed in his Fourteen Points, seemed to promise a new world order where war would have no place. Writing in 1933, former British diplomat and Member of Parliament, Harold Nicolson, reflected people's belief in Wilson's altruism when he wrote:

'I believed, with him (Wilson) that the standard of political and international conduct should be as high, as sensitive, as the standard of personal conduct ... I believed, and I still believe, that the only true patriotism is an active desire that one's tribe or country should in every particular minister to that ideal.'

Wilson had great principles, which inspired a war-weary world. However, he allowed his prejudice against the British and French, and his realisation that he controlled their purse strings at this critical time, to cloud his better judgement. On 27th September he offered Germany peace on the basis of the Fourteen Points it had flatly rejected in January 1918, with an added sweetener to persuade it to come to the negotiating table, 'impartial justice'! 'The impartial justice' President Wilson declared 'must involve no discrimination between those to whom we wish to be just and those to whom we do not wish to be just'.[53]

By 1st October the combined Allied and American armies were nearing the French and Belgian frontiers. Panic-stricken Ludendorff asked the Kaiser to seek peace:

'The army cannot wait forty-eight hours longer ... Today the troops are holding their own; what may happen tomorrow cannot be foreseen ... I have ... begged H M now to draw into the government those circles whom we have chiefly to thank for being in this position ... Let them conclude the peace that must now be concluded. Let them cope with the mess! It is their mess after all.'

On 1st October General Haig commented that the German army was 'completely breaking'. Four days later, on 5th October, Prince Max, head of the new 'democratic' government which had hastily been installed, grasped at the life-line Wilson had offered, the Fourteen Points and impartial justice.

President Wilson was a man of principle, but he had also showed himself to be naïvely prejudiced and dangerously misguided when he made his peace offer. Worse, as a Democrat he could be labelled criminal because so many of his countrymen felt that he was making a terrible mistake. On 7th October, Republican contender and ex-President, Theodore Roosevelt voiced the anxiety, which was increasingly shared by the American public:

'At this point, if we make an Armistice we have lost the war and we shall leave Germany about where she started. I am sure that the American people want a complete victory and an unconditional surrender.'

Meanwhile the battle went on. On 10th October Haig declared: 'We have got the enemy down; in fact he is a beaten army and my plan is to go on hitting him as hard as we possibly can, till he begs for mercy.'

But the German army did not need to beg for mercy because President Wilson saved it from destruction. He continued to discuss peace terms with the German government without consulting the Republican opposition or the Allies. In the meantime, while many American troops waited to go to war, others who had a hard struggle fighting in the dense Argonne forest had a period of rest while Pershing handed control to General Hunter Liggett.[54] Frustrated French Premier, Georges Clemenceau, declared: 'Nobody can maintain that these fine American troops are unusable. They are merely unused.'

Wilson's peace negotiations started to weaken the Allies' will to fight and to give the German army renewed hope. By

19th October Haig observed that the enemy was 'not ready for unconditional surrender'.

On 24th October an irate Theodore Roosevelt declared that he believed that it was unconstitutional for Wilson to give Germany peace on the basis of his Fourteen Points without the support of the Senate and he pleaded, 'Let us dictate peace by the hammering of guns and not chat about peace to the accompaniment of the clicking of typewriters.'

The German army, meanwhile, started to implement its plans to turn its military defeat on the Western Front into economic victory. In 1916 the German High Command examined 4,000 industrial firms in occupied northern France, to see how Germany could benefit from destroying France's industry in the event of defeat. The research showed that the destruction would bring Germany benefits:

'iron and smelting works, will not be able to resume work before one or two years ... as a result of this long interruption of activity, production and therefore receipts will fall off heavily, and industries will be so prejudiced ... that it will be difficult for them to resume operation or to restore it to its former level'.

'Textiles: the French textile industry will during the War have lost its markets. To reconquer them, and to derive some use of the terrible blow suffered by the textile industry in occupied regions, it is particularly important for Germany to start its intact industries working as quickly as possible after the War ...'

'Coal mines: the districts will be unproductive for years to come, owing to the removal of machinery and the flooding of shafts ... France will have to buy her machinery from Germany.'[55]

This policy was put into action in October 1918. A reporter from *The New York Times* was also shocked by evidence of destruction he found in Belgium:

'This morning I visited the great Cockerill plant at Seraing near Liège. It is the largest engineering concern in Belgium and was founded 100 years ago. In normal times it employs 10,000 hands. The area covered by the works is immense and the multitude of buildings present the appearance of a town ... Now not an ingot of steel can be made at Cockerill's for the Germans with devilish ingenuity have dismantled the essential machinery and either smashed it up or taken it off to Germany ... A favourite method is to drop heavy weights on the machinery from a rolling crane. As one of the directors explained to me, the Germans deliberately aimed at crippling Belgian industry for several years so as to enable their own mills and factories to capture markets.'[56]

Ex-President Theodore Roosevelt knew of the Kaiser's audacious plan to invade the US in 1902. He had no doubt that Germany was responsible for war in 1914. An isolated figure at one stage during the conflict, he now represented majority American opinion. He was alarmed that Wilson was not going to let Americans have a vote on the vital question of war and peace in the forthcoming mid-term elections. A flood of American newspapers echoed his anxiety.

The New York Times commented bitterly: 'They (the Germans) have manoeuvred for an armistice which would save their precious Fatherland ... and omits to mention moral punishment or reparations.'

The *Boston Herald* asserted: 'Unconditional surrender is not only the sole course for us, but it is the best for our enemies ... The hour of reckoning has come, and the reckoning cannot be a matter of bargain and sale.'

The *Chicago Tribune* stated bluntly: 'There is but one mind in America on this war – that it shall go on to victory, to the utter destruction of Prussian militarism.'

President Wilson was acutely aware that the mid-term elections were coming up in two weeks' time. If he did not make a gesture to public opinion he would face a crushing defeat. So he made a final condition to his peace offer, the

Kaiser would have to abdicate. Then, happy in the belief that he had secured democracy in Germany, he turned to the Allies to force them to accept his peace terms.

Although the United States had a large sphere of influence in Central and South America, President Wilson objected very strongly to Europe's old-fashioned structured colonial empires, confiding to his assistant, Colonel House, 'There are many things in it (the peace offer) which will displease the imperialists of Great Britain, France and Italy.'

Rich, small, and soft-speaking Colonel House reassured Wilson that he was confident of bullying the Allies into accepting Wilson's terms when he met them on 29th October, stating:

'It is my intention to tell Prime Ministers today that if their conditions of peace are essentially different from the points you have laid down ... that you will probably feel obliged to go before Congress and state the new conditions and ask their advice as to whether the United States shall continue to fight for the aims of Great Britain, France and Italy. I told the British privately you anticipate that their policy would lead to the establishment of the greatest naval programme by the United States that the world had ever seen ... I would suggest that you quietly diminish the transport of troops giving as an excuse the prevalence of influenza or any other reason but the real one[57] ...'

In hindsight it is easy to say that Britain should not have submitted to blackmail and should have rejected accepting anything less than the 'Prussian' army's 'unconditional surrender'. However, the nearly bankrupt country was in a difficult position to negotiate. In 1916 Britain practically ran out of money after Wilson put a financial squeeze on the country to respond to Germany's spurious 'peace offer'. In 1918 the British economy was even weaker as it had to supply 80 per cent of the aircraft and virtually all the tanks and artillery for the American army.[58] Before the war Britain was the world's largest creditor but after the war she became its largest debtor.[59]

Whatever the state of Britain's finances, Prime Minister Lloyd George has to take the major blame for submitting to Wilson's blackmail. He could not believe that the Americans were not Britain's best friend. The British workers had been told that Wilson would listen to their pleas to introduce humane working conditions on the shop floor throughout the world and had gone on strike in support of Wilson's Fourteen Points and a new world order where the ordinary working man would be respected. The British government believed in so many of Wilson's principles and was also alarmed at the spectre of Bolshevism spreading to Britain. Unrest had swept the country and the army had to be diverted from winning the war, to ensure supplies of arms and ammunition and to operate the ambulance trains.[60]

However, the most important consideration in deciding whether to continue the war was the view of the generals. The leader of the most victorious army on the field of battle, General Haig, was asked for his opinion on accepting the Armistice. He spoke for many, if not for the majority of people in Britain, when he declared:

'The British army has done much of the fighting latterly, and everyone wants to have done with the war, *provided* that we get what we want. I therefore advise that we only ask in the Armistice for what we intend to hold and that we set our faces against the French entering Germany to pay off old scores.'[61]

Many British people would have agreed with Haig's sentiment. Once the prospect of peace arrived the British returned to their historic suspicion of the French. Haig was also upset with American General Pershing. At the end of August, Pershing removed five American divisions (150,000 men)

SOLDIER AND CIVILIAN.

Marshal Foch (*to Messrs.* Clemenceau, Wilson *and* Lloyd George).
"IF YOU'RE GOING UP THAT ROAD, GENTLEMEN, LOOK
OUT FOR BOOBY-TRAPS."

from Haig's victorious army, which Haig had trained to help him deal the decisive blow. By October 1918 the American army was larger than Britain's, but the supply lines had broken down during Pershing's offensive on Meuse-Argonne and divisions had to be relieved, according to a frustrated General Haig, because they were literally 'starving'.[62] This led Haig to lose confidence in the ability of the American army to help him defeat the German army.

Yet the reason that Frederick the Great escaped defeat in 1759 was because the Austrians and the Russians did not unite to ensure that the Prussian army was crushed when they had it at their mercy. By October 1918 the rifle strength was 2:1 in favour of America and the Allies. As the most successful general on the field of battle, Haig should have known that it was vital that he joined with French supremo Marshall Foch (who would later be bitterly criticised by the French for his decision to accept the Armistice), and America's General Pershing in advising against giving Germany an Armistice on such ill-defined terms.

The leader of the fresh young American army, John 'Black-Jack' Pershing, may have hit trouble at Meuse-Argonne at a critical time, but he still believed that the Prussian army must be defeated on the battlefield. He sent an urgent message to the Supreme War Council at Versailles, stating that the Allies were in a favourable position to secure an overwhelming victory over Germany. He believed that any cessation of hostilities short of capitulation would postpone or render impossible the imposition of satisfactory peace terms. In his view an Armistice would also lead the Allies to believe that fighting was at an end. After that it would be difficult – if not impossible – to persuade them to fight again if Germany refused to accept the peace terms, maintaining that by accepting a negotiated peace the Allies would jeopardise the moral high ground which they then held and possibly lose the chance to secure world peace on terms that would ensure its permanence.[63]

Pershing was correct on every point he made. Britain needed a clear cut victory for her very survival. In 1947, after the Second World War, the German industrial base would be 11 per cent higher than in 1936. In 1919 the German industrial base should have enlarged by a similar amount, compared to 1912. Meanwhile Britain's wealth had disappeared fighting the Huns. When Germany cried 'Pax!' Britain could be in trouble.

Unfortunately in 1918 Britain also had a dwindling number of friends in the US. The Irish and the German communities, through sheer numbers of immigrants, were the coming powers. Ex-President and future Presidential contender, Theodore Roosevelt, had been a consistent champion of the Allied cause, even when it was unpopular during the war. The Allies' acceptance of President Wilson's peace offer to Germany, instead of insisting on 'unconditional surrender', was not merely a kick in the teeth for Theodore Roosevelt, it was a mortal blow for him, for the Allies, and for the long-term peace of Europe.

Woodrow Wilson lost the mid-term elections on 5th November but not by such a huge margin as would have happened had he not insisted on the Kaiser's departure. The Americans were suspicious of his nebulous ideas on peace. Nevertheless he maintained his faith in Germany and in December 1918 declared that he would be asking for 'no indemnities'.

In January 1919 Theodore Roosevelt died. The Republicans, bereft of their leader and unconsulted about the terms of the Treaty of Versailles, would later refuse to ratify the Versailles Treaty and would turn their backs on Europe. In the 1920s they would also eventually become Germany's staunch supporters.

Following 11th November 1918, the Allied governments' PR machines went into overdrive to celebrate the end of the war and justify the stunning loss of human life, but the reality that the Allies were left with was far from victorious. A combination of factors ensured that Germany undeniably won the First World War on an economic footing and while the Allies rejoiced in 'victory', the German leadership had already started its post-war economic offensive. The unpalatable truth was that in an economic sense Germany was barely dented by the First World War while Britain was in a parlous state.

CHAPTER FIVE

Peace without Victory

In 1759, after the Battle of Kunersdorf, Frederick the Great wrote:

Prussia would have been lost if her enemies, who knew how to defeat her, had known equally well how to take advantage of their victories.[1]

Frederick the Great's words about Prussia were equally applicable to Germany in 1918. America and the Allies were in sight of victory but they did not press home their advantage because of President Wilson's peace offer.

The German army on the Western Front hastily destroyed northern France and Belgium's mines and industry on its retreat while the victorious troops from the Eastern Front hastened back from Russia, eager to do battle with the 'enemies within', who had, so they had been told, 'stabbed the victorious German army in the back' by parlaying with President Wilson.

Germany's civilians were confused because their tightly censored press had given them nothing but tales of victory. Suddenly their newly elected Chancellor, Prince Max of

Baden, astonished them by telling them that the fledgling democratic government was responding to Wilson's offer of an Armistice.

The Berlin stock market collapsed, while former Pan-German League publicist, Heinrich Class, who knew that his organisation was in danger of being accused of responsibility for the deaths of millions of German soldiers, called for 'the resolute struggle of a spirited nationalist party against Jewry, against whom the legitimate anger of the people must be diverted'.[2] Former Pan-German co-founder and ex-Chairman of the Krupp's industrial empire, Alfred Hugenberg, hastily started a newspaper war against President Wilson, the Socialists and the Jews for denying Germany a great military victory.[3]

President Wilson knew nothing of the Prussian mentality and could not envisage, in his wildest dreams, the propaganda campaign which the Pan-Germans would wage against him. He had convinced himself that Germany was no guiltier of war lust in 1914 than the Allies, telling Colonel House that 'freedom of the seas' should be included in the peace terms dictated to the Allies because of his pledge 'not only to do away with Prussian militarism but with militarism everywhere'.[4]

Subsequently Wilson's aim was to administer what he considered to be a fair peace to all, especially to defeated Germany. However, he was playing a foolish and dangerous game. Although he had the power to create his own foreign policy, any subsequent treaty would have to be ratified by the American Senate.

In October 1918, pressure had mounted for Wilson to demand 'unconditional surrender' from the Prussian army. His negotiations with the hastily assembled German government had continued to cause great disquiet. America's *Everybody's Magazine* even carried the uncannily predictive headlines:

THE GREAT WAR OF 1938
IF ONLY WE HAD SEEN IT THROUGH IN 1918

Wilson had realised that he must make another gesture if he wanted to rally American support for giving Germany a compassionate peace – he must force the Kaiser, Wilhelm II, to abdicate. On October 23rd he told the new German government:

'If it (the government of the United States) must deal with the military masters and the monarchical autocrats of Germany … it must demand not peace negotiations but surrender.'

The German military/industrial junta knew that they had to obey Wilson's order. In the words of the historian Erich Eyck: 'Wilhelm was now little more than ballast that might well have to be tossed overboard in this time of distress.' But how?

It was the Admirals of the fleet who provided the solution. They decided to steam out and fight a decisive engagement with the British navy without any authorisation from the German government. In 1917 discontent in the German fleet was severely dealt with, but there had been no indication of trouble since. However, on 30th October 1918, the very day that Wilson's envoy, Colonel House, was dictating peace terms to the Allies, the German Naval High Command secretly ordered its sailors to put to sea to confront the British.

The crews of several ships agreed to put to sea but others decided to mutiny when they received the order. Then there were tense moments, during which the ships that had mutinied and those that had not, aimed their great guns at each other at point-blank range, after which the mutineers surrendered. One thousand men were flung into prison, where they faced court martial and the execution squad. Protest meetings were held and the revolt spread. The way was open for Germany's excellent secret service to spread the virus of disorder, just as

Wilhelm Stieber had taught them to do in Bismarck's day. Even the soldiers flung open their barracks.

By 8th November all major German cities seemed to be in the grip of revolution but still the Kaiser refused to depart, declaring that he would place himself at the head of the Army immediately after the Armistice was signed. General Gröner told him bluntly: 'The Army will march back to the homeland in closed ranks and good order under its leaders and commanding generals, but not under the leadership of Your Majesty.'[5] Yet the unhappy Kaiser hung on. Finally, caretaker President, Prince Max, lost his patience and a proclamation was read out: 'The Emperor and King has decided to renounce the throne.'[6] The Kaiser had to go.

The legend that the sailors 'stabbed' the victorious German army 'in the back' survives to this day. The British people took lasting comfort from the popular tale that it was the sailors' mutiny in 1918 that brought the First World War to an end. Meanwhile former Pan-Germans like Hugenberg and his protégé, Hitler, would soon present the democratic government, which had saved Germany from defeat, as the villains who prevented the glorious German army from achieving military victory in 1918.

The 'stab in the back' story would feed extreme right-wing opinion in the future and lead to Hitler's rise to power. However, it was not correct. The revolution had been clearly engineered by the military/industrial establishment to obey Wilson's dictate to get rid of the Kaiser. The American people still voted against Wilson's peace proposals on 5th November 1918, but not by the huge margin which would otherwise have forced Wilson to take public opinion into account.

On 11th November 1918, after a long wait in the fog, the German Reichstag delegation was authorised to sign the Armistice. General Foch accepted the Allies' first concession:

THE ILLUSTRATED LONDON NEWS.

No. 4161.– VOL. CLIV.   SATURDAY, JANUARY 18, 1919.   ONE SHILLING.

The Copyright of all the Editorial Matter, both Engravings and Letterpress, is Strictly Reserved in Great Britain, the Colonies, Europe, and the United States of America.

GERMANY DECEIVING HERSELF? SOLDIERS OF THE ENEMY ARMIES RETURN TO BERLIN AS "UNDEFEATED."

The soldiers are seen with Colours of regiments of the ex-Kaiser's Guards. It is characteristic of the enemy's lack of sense of humour and, possibly, of information that the German soldiery marched into Berlin after the Armistice as bedraggled and flower-decked undefeated troops ! Thus, after decisive fighting about which Sir Douglas Haig wrote : "The military situation on the British Front on the morning of the 11th November (1918) can be stated very shortly. In the fighting since November 1st our troops had broken the enemy's resistance beyond possibility of recovery, and had forced on him a disorderly retreat along the whole front of the British Armies. Thereafter, the enemy was capable neither of accepting nor refusing battle. . . . The strategic plan of the Allies had been realised with a completeness rarely seen in war. When the Armistice was signed by the enemy, his defensive powers had already been definitely destroyed. A continuance of hostilities could only have meant disaster."

the German army was allowed to retain 5,000 of its 30,000 machine guns, as well as its small arms, in order to preserve order.[7]

Naturally, once revolution was started, it was difficult to quell. New Chancellor, Friedrich Ebert, the small, unprepossessing but authoritative son of a tailor, was given the task of saving the country from anarchy. From his lonely desk in the Chancellor's Palace he could hear the extreme Left advancing from their stronghold in the Imperial Palace. To whom could he turn to prevent a Bolshevik revolution in Germany? It was General Gröner on the telephone: 'The High Command expects the Government to cooperate with the Officer Corps in the suppression of Bolshevism, and in the maintenance of discipline.'

Chancellor Ebert agreed. On 11th December 1918, exactly one month after the Armistice, the German legions marched up the Unter den Linden with their arms and their standards, while Ebert declared: 'I salute you, who return unvanquished from the field of battle.'[8]

Although President Woodrow Wilson was loathed by the returning German soldiers from the Eastern Front because they had been misled into believing that he had denied Germany victory, he was actually Germany's champion at the peace conference. When France pleaded for its border to be moved to the Rhine to protect it from the marauding German army, Wilson, despite suffering from a high temperature, stubbornly declared: 'We agreed with Germany upon certain general principles. The whole of the Conference has been made up of a series of attempts, especially by France, to break down this agreement.'[9]

American Republicans had campaigned for the German army's 'unconditional surrender' and then to allow some regions like Bavaria, to regain their freedom. However, Wilson decided that 'self-determination' on the basis of language was how he would determine the future of Europe. He was particularly keen to reconstitute the country of Poland, which was grabbed by the vast empires surrounding it in the eighteenth century. Nevertheless, post-war Germany was allowed to retain the heart of Bismarck's Reich intact, including the Catholic southern states like Bavaria, because they spoke (roughly) the same language as Prussia. It was also allowed to keep its industrial powerhouse, the Ruhr.

Woodrow Wilson, Clemenceau, Lloyd George and Orlando
at the Peace Conference

The German military/industrial establishment lost no time in starting a propaganda offensive. The government revealed that its gold reserves had swelled from 1.25 billion gold marks in 1914 to 2.56 billion on Armistice Day in 1918.[10] It wanted to buy corn from America to feed its starving population but the Allies refused to lift their blockade until the terms of the peace had been agreed.

The American agricultural community was overjoyed to find one country in Europe actually able to pay for their corn, but France declared that Germany's gold must be used to pay for the devastation that Germany had caused in France, devastation so horrific that the German delegation en route to Paris could scarcely bear to look at it.[11]

The British decided to side with the Germans over the issue because Germany had promised that it would surrender its merchant fleet to Britain if Britain agreed to the deal. Nevertheless, it was a scurrilous agreement and Britain's Prime Minister, Lloyd George, added insult to injury by publicly accusing France's short, plump, heavily-moustached Jewish Finance Minister of putting personal greed over compassion for the starving German women and children.[12]

All Europe was short of food in the aftermath of the war but dark, handsome British occupation Brigadier General, Harry Lewin, said that he had seen worse hunger in France and Belgium than in Germany: 'The Belgians were yellow with hunger and as for the French ... the women were gaunt spectres and the children listless little skeletons with skins like parchment'.[13] Statistics support his observation[14] but a precedent had been created. Business ties with America were cemented and in the future, whenever there was a conflict between Germany's needs and the payment of reparations, Germany would cry 'starvation'.

Wilson had a bias against Great Britain. On the eve of the Armistice he revealed his prejudice when he told his confidant, Colonel House: 'Nelson Page will tell you how busy the English propagandists are destroying our prestige.' He was even angrier when Lloyd George told his audience on the campaign trail before the 14th December British elections that the Allies would be asking for the 'fullest indemnities' from Germany, mentioning the astronomical sum of £24 billion. Wilson quickly quashed Lloyd George's illusions and caused consternation to the Allies by declaring that his country would be asking for 'no indemnities'.

Indemnities were usually charged to a defeated foe to pay for all the damage and to make sure that the offending country was too weak to invade again. Germany had emerged completely unscathed from the First World War, while causing carnage to its neighbours. It had charged France a huge indemnity after the Franco-Prussian War forty years earlier and was expecting the return treatment now. Nevertheless, as Wilson had won the war, and he was to be the arbiter of the peace, he allowed no indemnities to be charged. However, the Allies had to be recompensed in some way, and so the term 'reparations' was eventually coined, and the War Guilt Clause inserted into the Treaty of Versailles, because all the nations were agreed that Germany started the war and had to make restitution for it.

Our children's history books give a long list of the indignities that Germany had to suffer as a consequence of the Treaty of Versailles. If you take the view that Germany was no guiltier than Britain or France for causing the First World War, they sounded severe. Germany lost its colonies. Tanganyika was to be given to Britain, and the Cameroons to France as 'Mandates', the idea of the mandates being that the nations should be under the eagle eye of the League of Nations, as a precursor to them achieving self-government. Alsace-Lorraine was returned to France. Children's history books declared that Germany lost three-quarters of her iron deposits (but surely the Lorraine iron ore was not hers in the first place).

The Saar coal fields were to be ruled by the League for fifteen years, with France controlling the mines because her own mines had been destroyed. The German port of Danzig, with 300,000 Germans, was to be ruled by the League as a 'Free City'. Memel, another German port with 141,000 German inhabitants, was 'seized' by the new state of Lithuania. Malmédy and Eupen went to Belgium and the Rhineland was to have an army of occupation for fifteen years before becoming a demilitarised zone.

In Eastern Europe, Germany had to recognise the independence of Czechoslovakia and to cede parts of the province of Upper Silesia. Poland was reconstituted as a state with access to the sea. An area of 51,800 square miles of land was given to Poland, a massive blow to Prussian pride.

Not many people know that the Versailles Treaty stated that the Kaiser Chancellor Bethmann Hollweg, Generals Ludendorff and Hindenburg and other war criminals should be put on trial. However, they all know that the Allies charged Germany £6,600 million in war reparations, a colossal figure for a country, which people would later declare to be no guiltier of causing the First World War than the Allies. Yet Germany was not immediately charged that amount.

After a long haggle over the figures to be charged in reparations, it was agreed that Germany, which was supposed to have been more powerful than Britain before the First World War and had suffered far less materially, would pay £1,000 million in the years up until 1921, the amount to 'be made in such instalments and in such a manner (whether in gold, commodities, ships or otherwise) as the Reparations Commission may fix'.[15]

The American army had been ordered to return to the US four months after the Peace Treaty was signed, and Britain's army was also due to disband, although Germany still had over 400,000 soldiers under arms, and gun factories pumping out weapons.

General Haig declared: 'If the existing orders are continued … there will be no organised army of occupation left. How then can our Government hope to dictate peace terms to the enemy?'[16] So the conference decided that the German army should be reduced to 100,000 men. However, it made no recommendations as to how the decision was to be enforced.

The Prussian officer had always had a special place in Germany, regarding himself as being above the common herd. In view of the 'revolution' accompanying the Kaiser's departure, the German government insisted that the Prussian officers belonging to the Sicherheitspolizei (security police), were not be treated as part of the army and could be armed, not only with machine guns and trench mortars, but also with field guns and planes.[17] Controlling the Communist 'enemies within' Germany, therefore, should not have been as difficult as outsiders imagined. Indeed at this point 7,000 munitions plants had their factories intact, and Krupp was still manufacturing weapons.[18]

Wilson's most treasured ambition was to create a League of Nations to keep the unruly European nations in order. Britain supported him. She was tired of trying to do it herself. Yet the Republicans were surly. They had little faith in the League of Nations being able to control a resurgent Germany.

Nevertheless, Wilson was happy with the peace he had negotiated until the day he met the German representative, Count Brockdorff-Rantzau, at Versailles. To begin with, the haughty, hostile Count refused to have the courtesy to rise when he addressed the Chamber, secondly he poured vitriol upon Wilson's treaty, when Wilson had tirelessly campaigned to secure what he had believed to be Germany's rights. Wilson had become increasingly aware of France's desperation during the conference, now he realised the terrible mistake he had made. France and Britain were dreadfully weak in 1919, and he had let the malicious warmonger, Germany, off the hook.

The German press started a tremendous propaganda campaign against the Treaty. The British were afraid that Germany would totally reject it. Future President and present member of the Supreme Economic Council, Herbert Hoover, asked if 'the argument of expediency ought to govern'.[19]

Wilson may have been prejudiced but he was also a man of principle. Expediency was not in his vocabulary. Up until his meeting with the German negotiators at Versailles he genuinely believed all participants in the war were warmongers. However, he was brave enough to admit that he had made a terrible mistake. The 'Prussians' had been the marauding villains all along. He was determined not to alter the terms of the Treaty of Versailles in case the whole Treaty unravelled.

The German government asked General Hindenburg whether the army could return to war. Hindenburg answered that it could in the East but not in the West. Nevertheless, Hindenburg said that he preferred honourable annihilation to a disgraceful peace[20] thus passing the odium for signing the Treaty onto the unhappy politicians.

Wilson then campaigned for America to join the League of Nations as the only way to prevent another war, telling the American people: 'For nearly fifty years the French had expected a war ... The terror had been there all the time and the war was its flame and consummation.'[21]

Unfortunately, the American people had been on one abortive military trip to Europe to save France and didn't want to contemplate another. They refused to ratify the Versailles Treaty and ousted Wilson from office in the next Presidential election. Small, brave General Ferdinand Foch, who had campaigned for the French border to be moved to the Rhine as the only way to prevent the Germans invading France again, declared prophetically: 'This is not a peace. It is an Armistice for twenty years.'

The Allies were on their own in Europe, confronted by a Germany revitalised by the victorious troops from the East. On 1st January 1920, *The Times* gave chilling evidence of its military strength: 400,000 Reichswehr (the army, still called Imperial Defence even though the Emperor had departed), 150,000 Zeitfreiwillingen (emergency volunteers), 40,000 to 50,000 Sicherheitspolizei (many of whom later joined the Gestapo) and 300,000 Einwohnenwehren (home defence) from which, later, tens of thousands of Hitler's storm troopers would emerge.

The weak and abandoned Allies were faced with enforcing the Treaty of Versailles without America, although it had been President Woodrow Wilson of America's decision to 'save' the German army and give it the Treaty of Versailles in the first place.

In this situation the Allies felt that it was impossible to implement Article 227 of the Treaty of Versailles, which called for the trial of the Kaiser, after Holland, aware of the proximity of Germany's enormous army, and reaping rich rewards from Germany's transfer of trade from Antwerp to Rotterdam, refused to hand the Kaiser over for trial. Holland hinted that if, and hopefully when, the Associate power (USA) eventually ratified the treaty and was willing to take a full part in the League of Nations, the situation might be different.[22]

The Allies also abandoned Article 228 of the Treaty of Versailles, which authorised them to try Generals Ludendorff and Hindenburg, Chancellor Bethmann Hollweg, Admiral Tirpitz and 890 other persons or groups.[23] They just didn't feel strong enough to enforce the Treaty's terms. America's troops had gone home four months after the Treaty was signed and renegade elements of the military were about to try and get rid of the Weimar Republic.

As soon as America decided against ratifying the Treaty, ex-soldiers from the victorious Eastern Front, egged on by a member of Tirpitz's wartime Fatherland Party, called Wolfgang Kapp, staged a military coup. Small, squat, Social Democrat, Friedrich Ebert, with his snub nose and shabby overcoat, was faced with another desperate situation, only this time it came from the Fascists rather than the Bolsheviks. 'Cease work,' he cried. 'Stifle the opportunity of this military dictatorship! Fight with all the means at your command to retain the Republic. Strike along the whole line.'[24]

The effect of his words was miraculous. The workers downed tools. There was a general strike and after five days of stalemate, the renegade soldiers retreated, firing at onlookers as they went. This was a great victory for the ordinary working man. The Republic won this time. Illegal military organisations were ordered to disband but the Republic was already under attack and the great industrialists would soon have their revenge. Meanwhile the ubiquitous reporter from *The New York Times* had already commented on Germany's economic warfare against its former military foes:

'It is true that in some respects Germany is ready for a trade war. They have undoubtedly a considerable stock of glassware, cutlery, electrical appliances, photographic materials and iron and steel goods stored up for exportation if the Allies will allow it ... I visited a big iron works, admirably equipped and using electrical power throughout, whose manager said proudly that he had enough mine pumps built during the intervals of big guns orders, by which he admitted that he had made enormous profits, to supply all the flooded mines of France and Belgium.'[25]

The Pan-Germans decided to change the name of their organisation. Alfred Hugenberg started a newspaper empire with three other Ruhr magnates and created a 'national opposition' to the Weimar Republic.[26] Britain's Brigadier General Morgan soon found that 'official obstruction' and 'newspaper vituperation' against the Allied Military Control Commission went hand in hand. His depressing verdict was that while the Republicans were 'in office' in the Weimar Republic, the Nationalists (i.e. the former Pan-Germans) were in actual control.[27]

The 'Nationalists' discovered Hitler and were impressed by his oratory. Ex-Pan German publicist, Heinrich Class, blamed the Jews for the loss of the war, saying, 'Kill them, the world court is not asking for your reasons!'[28] Hitler was captivated by Class's ideas and was enlisted to become a 'drummer' for the Nationalist cause.

Then the industrial magnates started to flex their muscles. Germany had been allowed to defy Articles 227 and 228 of the Treaty of Versailles, which ordered them to surrender the major war offenders for trial because the Allies were too weak to be able to enforce them. So the German coal barons decided to defy the Allies' request for reparations too. At the Versailles Peace Conference, Monsieur Gruener, President of the Civil Engineers of France, described how the German army had ruined 220 French coal mines on its retreat in 1918. The country was therefore required to send coal in reparations to France – and to sell her the mine pumps to restore her mines. Yet, in 1920, while Berlin's lights blazed and Germany exported coal to Denmark, Holland and Switzerland, Paris still lay in icy darkness and cold.[29] When unrepentant coal magnate Hugo Stinnes was asked to explain the difficulties which had held up delivery of France's coal, he merely referred to the Allies as 'our insane conquerors'.[30]

Hugo Stinnes was an antisocial man with an Assyrian beard and ill-fitting clothes, but he was reputed to own some 4,500 businesses abroad after the First World War – in Russia, Romania, Italy, Scandinavia, Spain, Luxembourg, France, Britain, Holland, Belgium, North America, China, Japan and elsewhere.[31] He and his friends had put millions abroad while encouraging the government to run down the value of the mark. Germany was murdering its neighbours' industries.

While the Danes were being flooded with 'iron and steel goods' 'stored up for exportation at rock bottom prices', Britain's vital coal, steel and shipbuilding industries were in desperate trouble from German dumping too.

Prime Minister Lloyd George declared darkly that 'there is undoubtedly in existence what is in effect a substantial bounty on export from certain countries whose exchanges are in a very abnormal state' and stated at the dinner given by the Federation of British Industries on November 30th 1920:

'We are pledged to do everything we can to shield the industries which were discovered during the war to be essential industries for the defence of the country. We are pledged to deal with the problem of dumping, and we are pledged to do something, in so far as the government can, to deal with the exchange situation, so that the exchange situation in Europe may not be utilised as a means for destroying our industries. These things we are pledged to do.'[32]

But the Treaty of Versailles had not given the British or French the power to enter Germany and exert control over its finances and without America they hesitated to use force. Lloyd George slapped on a 33 per cent tariff on German imports in the hope that it would stem the tide.

Looking at the map of the world after the First World War it seemed that Britain had become the most powerful nation on earth, enlarged by the inclusion of the 'mandated' colonies from the former German and Ottoman Empires. Yet Bismarck had believed that colonies, for the most part, were a burden on the public purse. Moreover, Britain was impoverished after 1918 and the costs of administering its empire kept mounting; President Wilson's heady doctrine of 'self-determination' had opened up a hornets' nest of discontent.

America itself was not feeling rich any more. America's farming industry was in trouble and German industry was causing damage to America's industrial base.[33] On 11th

February 1921 America asked the Germans to furnish them with all the data on German production to see if they were indulging in unfair practices. In 1922, the newly elected Republican President, Warren Harding, slapped on the Fordney-McCumber Tariff to protect American industry from German competition, but as he dared not tell his countrymen that a defeated Germany was the culprit, Britain and France's exports would also be discriminated against.

The British people were alarmed and angry after the huge sacrifices of war. They were beginning to ask why they had fought at all. Britain had spent nearly all her financial reserves on the conflict and, unknown to her citizens, Germany's coal and steel magnates were doing their best to ensure that her great industrial heart died too.

France was also suffering. She had received no money to restore her shattered provinces. Even obtaining coal reparations from the Ruhr magnates was fruitless until the offer of a bribe from Lloyd George.[34] Lloyd George's appeasing gesture facilitated coal deliveries to France, but it would encourage the German coal owners in the future to take greater liberties with the international community, to the detriment of the world economy.

Regrettably, in 1919 a young, idealistic British economist, John Maynard Keynes, heavily influenced by the militant pacifism of his friend, Lytton Strachey, had published a polemic called *The Economic Consequences of the Peace*. The book asserted that the Treaty of Versailles reparations clauses were far too harsh on Germany. Indeed, Keynes had a field day describing his bile against the Treaty, calling the reparations clauses 'dishonourable', 'abhorrent and detestable' and declaring that they would 'sow the decay of the whole of the civilised life of Europe'. In conclusion he asserted the Treaty to be 'one of the most outrageous acts of a cruel victor in civilised history'.[35]

It would have been better if the book had never been published but unfortunately it gained massive sales in the run up to the American Presidential elections by claiming that President Wilson had been slow-witted and incompetent at Versailles, indeed a 'blind and deaf Don Quixote' who let the avenging French Premier Clemenceau lead him by the nose.[36] The book also gained massive sales in Germany and gave its leaders new ammunition to defy the Treaty of Versailles.

In fact, in 1921, the Reparations Commission recorded that 'no' money had so far been received in war reparations. Trains, ships, war material, etc., had been surrendered and credited as reparations after the war, but not a single penny had been received in cash towards the £1,000,000,000 due by 1921.[37] As Niall Ferguson states in his book *The Pity of War*: 'The real problem with the peace was not that it was too harsh, but that the Allies failed to enforce it; not so much "won't pay" as "can't collect".'[38]

Eventually the Allies decided to get tough with Germany. They occupied the German towns of Düsseldorf, Duisburg and Ruhrort and gave Germany seven days to fulfil its disarmament provisions, try some of its lesser war criminals like the 'brutal' camp guards, and to pay its war reparations. To reassure the public a high headline figure of £6.6 billion was set as the total due from Germany, although the small print revealed that the Allies were only expecting to receive £2.5 billion. The first £50 million was eventually paid with the help of short-term loans from abroad. After paying another £25 million Germany put in its first official request for a moratorium.[39] Extracting cash reparations from Germany was going to be like getting blood out of a stone.

CHAPTER SIX

Germany's Great Inflation

By the early 1920s Germany had already succeeded in defying the edicts of the Treaty of Versailles to bring the Kaiser, Chancellor Bethmann Hollweg and Generals Hindenburg and Ludendorff to trial. It was also in an excellent position to compete in the post-war world. Having destroyed France and Belgium's mines and industry with its scorched earth policy on its retreat, it was now maiming British industry with the low value of the mark.

The popular picture of Germany in the early 1920s was of law and order breaking down and the country on the verge of revolution. There was a belief abroad that this social disorder was a popular revolt. It was nothing of the sort. Germany had been made to sign the Treaty of Versailles by the Western Allies, but Germany's fledgling democracy was in for no easy ride. The industrialists were in a perfect position to reduce the power of the workers before the currency was stabilised, and they had a perfect propaganda issue to blame for the workers impoverishment – the reparations!

In 1922 the French threw their socialist Prime Minister, Aristide Briand, out of office, and replaced him with their hard-line ex-President, Raymond Poincaré, who looked at the destruction of France's coal mines and industry, crater-pocked farmland and burned out towns and was determined to make Germany pay for the destruction its army had caused.

There was no meeting of minds between Poincaré and Lloyd George. Poincaré believed that Lloyd George had forgotten 'the 438,000' Frenchmen 'martyred in German prisons' while Lloyd George, safely across the Channel, wanted bygones to be bygones and for Britain to renew its ties with Germany. Indeed, that had already happened. Over a hundred British companies had taken advantage of Germany's low exchange rate to set up operations in Cologne. The British and the Hanoverians had fought side by side with Frederick the Great in the eighteenth century and the English began to believe Germany's post-First World War tale that it was a bulwark against Bolshevism.

Indeed, Lloyd George himself had begun to trust Germany. In 1922, his ambition was to encourage the country not to trade with the Bolsheviks until they had paid their war debts, but his plan misfired. Under the Treaty of Rapallo, Germany and the Soviet Union forged a new friendship, under which 'impoverished' Germany waived all governmental – and private – IOUs against the Bolsheviks, provided that the Russians treated other (Allied) claimants in the same fashion. Britain was left with a multitude of Russian IOUs from the First World War, which would never be repaid, while the German army was permitted to establish officer training courses in Russia and given tracts of land for testing rockets and heavy artillery.[1]

Lenin had only just had a bullet removed from his neck by a German surgeon. He was desperately short of hard currency to pay for new trains and military hardware, so former Pan-German Gustav Krupp, had an idea. In April 1922 Krupp took a lease on 50,000 hectares of land in the North Caucasus so that Russia could export wheat to pay for his trains and military hardware.[2]

On 12th July 1922, *The New York Times* wrote an article called *'Prosperity Seen In German Journey'* remarking on the abundance of 'pretty luxurious things, including watches and jewellery' in the shops, and the absence of 'maimed men' in the streets.

Life was good for the families of the rich industrialists and even for some of the workers who could go on strike to maintain the buying power of their pay, but people on fixed incomes, the old, and the poor, lived in abject poverty.

Jewish Foreign Minister, Walther Rathenau, was accused of the 'pulverisation of our middle classes' by advocating the payment of the reparations,[3] and on 24th July 1922 he was murdered. The value of the mark collapsed and Germany asked the alarmed Allies for a moratorium on paying war reparations not only for 1922, but also for 1923 and 1924.

The strength or weakness of a currency was usually an indicator of the strength of a country's economy, but not in this case. Having managed to evade surrendering for trial, amongst others, Generals Falkenhayn, who tried to bleed the French 'white' at Verdun, and Ludendorff who would become the godfather of Hitler's Nazi party, the leadership were never going to pay any monetary war reparations except under duress. The reparations were just a scapegoat for propagandists to use to soften the blow to the millions of German savers who had patriotically bought war bonds during the war and must now see them wiped out, and live in penury for the rest of their lives, so that German industry could reduce Britain to penury.

By 1922 the German national debt had been reduced to the same as it had been at the onset of war in 1914, compared to the huge national debt which remained in Britain and America.[4] Britain's industries were being critically wounded too. On 7th July Winston Churchill wrote to Lloyd George to tell him that the 33 per cent tariff Lloyd George had slapped on German imports was insufficient:

'Suppose we were confronted by tremendous importations from Germany at prices out of all relations to anything we could produce, and this was due to the extraordinary fall in the mark, surely the remedy would be to proceed by embargo and licence until conditions become more normal. Embargo and licence are undoubtedly effective, whereas a trumpery 33% duty bears no relation to the present fluctuations of the exchange. We should, therefore, wait until the danger comes – if it ever did come – and then apply a remedy which would certainly save us.'[5]

The 'danger' Winston Churchill referred to in his letter seems to have related to fears of Germany resorting to military action again by launching a poisonous gas attack on Britain. However, the Inter-Allied Military Commission of Control's President, General Nollet, stated that the work of destruction in the German chemical factories was, with few exceptions, well advanced[6] and Sir Maurice Hankey came to the conclusion that a poison gas attack would be impossible for Germany to carry out.[7]

Indeed, German heavy industry had other preoccupations on its mind. The wealth of the salaried classes had vanished, but the workers had retained the value of their pay through strike action. Ruining the currency so that the workers became completely bankrupt was an attractive option for men like the coal magnate Hugo Stinnes. The eight-hour day had been one of the workers' principle ambitions, secured after the war. Trashing the value of the mark would bankrupt them and halt their defiance to their employers (and to the idea of Germany's return to dictatorship).

It was easy to incite Poincaré into occupying the Ruhr, just cut off the coal supply. In January 1923 Poincaré embarked on a low-key intervention to collect coal and monetary reparations for the repair of his devastated provinces. The German coal syndicate, including Kirdorf, Krupp, von Bohlen, Klöckner, Hugo Stinnes and Fritz Thyssen, decided to whip up public opinion against the French.[8] Dr Grimm, who appeared as attorney for the coal barons, and Fritz Thyssen, who came to the car window in every town, led the crowd in the singing of 'Deutschland über Alles'.[9] The companies in the Ruhr decided on a policy of 'passive resistance' against delivering the coal and the workers were encouraged to go on a general strike to save their beloved country from invasion by the 'rapacious French'.

The Americans realised that their war loans were at risk and came hot-foot over to Europe to secure watertight agreements. Poincaré declared doggedly that he could pay no war debts until he received reparations from Germany, maintaining stoutly that Germany's 'present state of ruin is not consequent upon the occupation of the Ruhr but is the work of Germany herself'.[10]

The Americans were not going to allow the British to shilly-shally over paying their war debts, however. The Democrats had become increasingly anti-British during the war and since 1918 the British had lost the respect of the Republicans too. It is not known whether America had ever repaid Britain for the tanks, ships and artillery that its troops used during the conflict. General Pershing himself admitted: 'We were literally beggars as to every important weapon, except the rifle.'[11] However, the repayment of war debts was required and Britain's Chancellor of the Exchequer, Stanley Baldwin, did not want to lose the few friends Britain had left in America; so he agreed to repay the £938 million that Britain owed in war debts, despite Britain's lack of reparations from Germany.[12]

Wilson's advisor, Bernard Beruch, declared that Britain's sincere offer to pay its war debts to America at this time was made 'at a cost almost impossible for others to realise'. Britain's industries were being crucified by German competition. Her foremost business was shipbuilding but by 1923 even Germany's ship production was almost overtaking Britain's.[13] In 1920 Germany had produced 204,000 tons of shipping, in 1921 it had produced 632,000 tons of shipping, and by 1922 it had become the second-largest shipbuilder in the world.[14]

At first the British press was sympathetic to France's efforts to secure reparations from Germany but soon there was an incident at Krupp's factory in Essen, which caused the British public alarm. Six employees were killed and thirteen wounded in the fracas. France was criticised for the carnage, and for its decision to increase the number of its troops in Germany too. Historic British suspicions of France returned as they witnessed the increasing suffering of the German people. With paper money daily lessening in value, even food was vanishing from the shops. Bismarck's Reich was in danger of disintegrating into individual states too. The Rhineland was getting restive but it was the secessionist movement in Bavaria that gave the greatest concern to the German Nationalists.

Catholic Bavaria had a long and illustrious history before being sucked into Bismarck's empire. Then it made careful plans to seek independence again. On 26th September 1923 the Bavarian government proclaimed a state of martial law and appointed Gustav von Kahr as head of state. Von Kahr declared that everything he did was for Bavaria's traditional monarch, Prince Utrecht, who would soon be in a position to take responsibility.

Yet the Nationalists (whose leaders formerly called themselves Pan-Germans), had already taken steps to counter this threat. On 2nd September Hitler was invited to make a rousing speech in front of 100,000 Nationalists at the anniversary of the French defeat at Sedan in 1870. On 25th September the leaders of the newly formed Deutscher Kampbund assembled in Munich and elected Hitler as their leader.

Hitler told the Bavarian leader, von Kahr, that he wanted to march on Berlin and overthrow the Weimar Republic. Von Kahr said that he would forbid any *coup d'état* except the one he was making. Hitler and his accomplices then disturbed von Kahr while he was addressing a meeting in an eastern suburb of Munich. They led von Kahr and his associates to an anteroom to meet a hastily summoned General Ludendorff. After a brief discussion, Ludendorff and von Kahr and his associates walked back into the hall, swore loyalty to Hitler and shook hands. But the next day von Kahr reneged on the deal, and when Hitler and Ludendorff marched through Munich with about two thousand men they were met with police fire.

Although Hitler and Ludendorff's Putsch failed, it had the effect of splitting the reactionary forces in Bavaria. Bavaria did not cede from Germany and although Hitler was put in prison, he was rewarded by being treated as an officer, and encouraged to write his memoirs, in which many of the Pan-Germans' themes would reappear, such as their anti-Semitism and their idea of Germany gaining Lebensraum in the East.[15] His book would be called *Mein Kampf*.

On 23rd September 1923, the German government declared that it had abandoned 'passive resistance', but Hugo Stinnes and his friends in heavy industry refused to agree terms over renewing reparations payments unless the government gave them, amongst other things, compensation for all coal 'confiscated by the French during their occupation', and a free hand to lengthen the working day in the mines 'to eight and half hours under-ground and ten hours above ground'.[16]

The French and Belgian engineers at the head of the Control Commission argued that the delivery price of coal in Düsseldorf was already so far below the delivery price of English coal that even after delivering 20 per cent of their output, (as reparations), the German mine owners could far undercut the

THE COAST OF VICTORY.

GERMANY, "I give in!"

M. POINCARÉ. "Good! Now pay up."

GERMANY. "Pay up? You don't suppose I'd have stopped passive
resistance if I'd got any money left?"

British coal owners, without lengthening the miners' working hours. However, the spokesman for the German coal magnates, Hugo Stinnes, did not agree, declaring:

'I do not hesitate to say that I am convinced that the German people will have to work two extra hours per day for the next ten to fifteen years.' As the value of the German currency was reduced to waste paper he was in a strong position to negotiate with his workers.

In the autumn, conditions grew desperate in Germany. On 2nd November *The New York Times* reported on the food riots in Berlin and how, in their desperation, the rioters had been turning against the Jews:

'Mass food riots and plunderings ... occurred today in Berlin and they continue tonight in all sections of the city. A mass mob attack on the Bourse was one feature of the outbreak, and for the first time a pogrom spirit manifested itself in brutal treatment of Jews and others who looked like Jews ...'

On 8th November under the heading: RUHR WORK HANGS ON THE TEN-HOUR DAY, *The New York Times* described how the negotiations had proceeded:

'The German industrialists told their workforce that they could only afford to make reparations deliveries to the French and what they called "the resumption of economic life" provided that the workforce worked a ten hour day above ground and eight and a half below'.

It commented, 'Already grim starvation is staring several hundred thousand workmen in the face with the cold dark winter nights creeping in ... If all the industrial plants close as threatened the total unemployed will reach from 700,000 to 800,000'.[17]

Beaten, with the value of their wages reduced to waste paper, and their savings exhausted, the German workers finally agreed to work the longer hours for wages between

14 per cent and 18 per cent lower than they had been in 1913.[18] In return, the employees gained an arbitration system for industrial disputes which seemed, on the face of it, to be highly advantageous to them.[19] However, as all the workers were by now penniless, it would be extremely hazardous for them to summon up the courage to complain.

In 1919, John Maynard Keynes protested in *The Economic Consequences of the Peace* that the Treaty of Versailles' onerous reparations would keep 'Germany ... impoverished and her children starved and crippled'.[20] It appeared that his prophecy was coming true in 1923.

However, ailing ex-President Woodrow Wilson, who had realised his dreadful mistake in letting Germany off the hook at the end of the war, took a different view. He asked his financial adviser, Bernard Beruch, to try and persuade the British Imperial Conference to ensure that Germany paid an adequate war reparations bill, stating:

'There seems to be little realisation in England and America of what it would mean to them if Germany should escape too lightly. In the United States of America the increased borrowing of the Federal Government continues; industries and dues to the war have piled up and added tax burdens; our Federal budget has risen from one billion to four billion dollars annually. While the amount of money we have to raise in taxes because of these increased expenses and borrowings has risen so greatly, the taxes of the German government and the fixed charge on German industries have been practically wiped out owing to the use of the printing press. This means that there must be taken from the efforts of our people in taxes for the Federal Government four billion dollars a year and nothing from the Germans unless they are compelled to pay some fixed tax in the way of reparations. Unless this is done Germany will conquer the world industrially.'[21]

The New York Times agreed with Woodrow Wilson and Baruch's assessment. Its reporters were astonished that despite the German people's suffering, Germany was still the best customer for America's valuable cotton crop, importing 'approximately double' the amount of cotton going to either France or England in the first eight months of 1923. It also noted that Germany's copper imports were 'larger than those of any other country'.

It concluded: 'It may be true that Germany today is not able to pay appreciable sums on her reparations' account, except for 'deliveries in kind' but what she may be able to pay in five or six years' time is significantly indicated by what she is doing now through putting her hand upon great supplies of the raw materials ... ready for an immense economic expansion in the near future'.[22]

New President of the Reichsbank, Hjalmar Schacht, was acclaimed as an 'economic wizard' for ending Germany's Great Inflation. The lowly mark disappeared in a flurry of waste paper and the Reichsmark arrived instead to parade Germany's new quality status (as a nascent Reich!).

Then Schacht, who was raised in New York and spoke perfect English, had a bright idea. He contacted Britain's Governor of the Bank of England, Montagu Norman, and asked him if he could visit him in London. Wispy-bearded Norman, who had spent much time in the past in Dresden, was delighted. Yet when Schacht arrived on a foggy winter's day, he alarmed Norman with a tale of a group of Rhineland and French bankers intending to set up their own Central Bank in the Rhineland, with the blessing of the German government.

This was an unlikely story. The Right was on the ascendant in Germany. It wouldn't countenance French banks controlling Germany's richest area. Social Democrat President Friedrich Ebert would even be tried for treason in December

1924. Yet Montagu Norman was perturbed by what he saw as a threat to the City in London and attracted by Schacht's idea of stabilising the mark on gold.

The son of a salesman, Schacht had studied medicine in Kiel, philology in Munich and political science in Berlin before graduating in economics and working his way through the German banking system. So he was reassuringly well qualified for his position as head of the Reichsbank.

Schacht promised Norman that if Norman lent him the money to start his new Gold Discount Bank, he would raise one hundred million gold marks in foreign currency in Germany and issue its notes entirely in sterling.[23] The proposal sounded like a wonderful opportunity to Norman – but there was a catch. Because of Britain's impotence, Britain had publicly accepted the lie that Germany was weak in 1923, although Germany's Great Inflation had been a confidence trick designed to impoverish the German workers and evade paying debt at home and abroad. If Montagu Norman agreed to back Schacht's new Gold Discount Bank he would immediately be pressurised to return Britain to the Gold Standard at the same rate as Germany before the war, and that would crucify British industry.

Montagu Norman had been at the helm of the Bank of England since 1920. If the Bank of England's selection process had been made on the basis of pedigree he would have been an obvious choice because his grandfather on his mother's side had been Governor and his grandfather on his father's side, a director. Yet Norman was a sickly, neurotic youth and viewed as a misfit during his years with the merchant bank, Brown Shipley. Nevertheless, he had many useful traits for a central banker: a formidable memory for places, names and facts; restless, abundant energy and, when he chose to use it, persuasive charm. So eventually he became the Bank of England's most famous and 'infamous' Governor.

It may be that Norman did not know that the German industrialists had slashed wages and reintroduced the ten-hour day in those last dark days of autumn before Schacht contacted him. At any event Schacht left him spellbound with talk of the Reichsbank's 'supreme power within the German Reich'. Norman would soon become completely under the thumb of the brilliantly able and deceitful financier, Hjalmar Schacht.

On 3rd February 1924 ex-President Woodrow Wilson died. Republican Americans now ruled the roost. They were oblivious to the significance of the fact that the German embassy in Washington initially refused to fly its flag at half-mast because it was becoming dogma in Germany that President Woodrow Wilson had denied the German army victory in 1918.

The American Republican party now regarded Germany as its friend. It could not actually believe that Germany was as poor as it made out because *The New York Times* estimated that Germany had $500 million abroad. However, it was thrilled that Germany now believed in stable currencies and wanted to return to the Gold Standard.[24]

The Gold Standard was important to America because Germany was refusing to sign the new Dawes Plan reparations agreement without loans from America, in addition to the initially promised £40 million Dawes Plan Loan. The anti-Republican German Nationalists (or DNVP) Party, stuffed with members like the former Pan-German Alfred Hugenberg, refused to sign the agreement unless America accepted German loans, which they temptingly promised would be endorsed by Schacht's Gold Discount Bank.[25]

Many Americans wanted to invest in Germany. The main drawback was the size of the reparations bill. The American government speedily sent a delegation over to Europe in 1924 to judge if Germany had been overcharged. The German negotiators had a field day exaggerating the cost of the ships they had surrendered, the railway carriages and the value of the German factories and schools in the territories they occupied before the war, in order to be able to assert that they had already paid most of the reparations bill. They even tried to claim for the fleet that they scuppered at Scapa Flow!

Luckily France's Raymond Poincaré looked at payments in a more grounded fashion. The Germans had only paid £80 million in cash since 1919.[26] Poincaré insisted that the new Dawes Plan must only look at Germany's present capacity to pay, not to fix the final amount due in reparations. He also put French inspectors into the German Treasury to ensure that France was not short-changed. However, the German negotiators secured a huge success by forcing the Allies to agree to 'Transfer Protection'. This promised that if Germany was ever threatened with an economic depression, it could suspend reparations payments.

The American economic historian, Stephen A Schuker, in his book *The End of French Predominance in Europe*, declared: 'When the Germans accepted the Dawes Plan, they fully intended to ask for another reduction in reparations within three or four years .... Meanwhile, the French troops were unconditionally bound to leave the Ruhr – as they did on schedule in August 1925 .... In the following years German businessmen would often demonstrate greater willingness to work toward the creation of ... a 'West European Zollverein' than their protectionist-minded French counterparts. But this very fact bore eloquent witness to the Germans' confidence that the formidable economic organisation of the Reich would enable them to dominate any such precursor of the Common Market.'[27]

In 1925, in accordance with an agreement the German government had made with Hugo Stinnes, the German government paid the Ruhr industrialists 706 million gold marks in compensation for their loss of trade during the Ruhr conflict in 1923, even though cash reparations to the Allies for the year only amounted to 65 million gold marks (roughly £3 million.) In the opinion of historian C Bresciani-Turroni, this represented the most scandalous chapter in the whole history of Germany's Great Inflation.[28]

The story still circulates today in the American heartlands, that America paid Germany's war reparations between 1924 and 1929. 'Wall Street' so the fable goes, 'made the loans to Germany so that Germany could pay reparations to France, which could then pay war debts to Britain and the US'.

This story has no basis in fact. Although America poured money into Germany, in the mid-1920s it continued to be almost impossible to persuade Germany to pay cash in reparations to the Allies. So the French had to accept an unsatisfactory system through which the Ruhr magnates delivered coal to France in reparations and were then reimbursed by their government through a tax on the railways, sugar, etc. Once France's coal mines were repaired, the German industrialists were happy to export other more exciting goods to France in reparations but not the cash, which France so desperately needed to start paying its war debts to America.

Meanwhile Britain agreed to accept her reparations through a 30 per cent tariff on German imports.[29] Montagu Norman knew that the pound was too high and that wages would have to be lowered, but he felt that Britain could compete with Germany with the 30 per cent tariff in place.

In order to make quite sure that the Germans did not devalue again, the Americans also wanted Britain to return to the Gold Standard to set a good example, and they were prepared to offer a bribe.

Governor of the Federal Reserve Bank of New York, Benjamin Strong, was a close friend of Montagu Norman's. He promised $200 million from the Fed and another $300 from J P Morgan, if Britain returned to the Gold Standard and Norman remained in office. Norman was overcome with gratitude for Benjamin Strong's vote of confidence. He wrote to Strong:

'As you know, Ben, I am grateful for all your welcome and hospitality; and for all you do for me and are for me. God bless you.'[30]

Benjamin Strong came from a banking family with a strong Presbyterian social conscience. Tall, slim and 'good-looking but for a prematurely receding hairline and a large nose that spoke of ruthlessness', he was always going to succeed in his chosen profession. His personal life was less happy, however. His first wife Margaret committed suicide after the birth of their fourth child and he developed TB in 1916, struggling with the effects for the rest of his life.

Strong chose to accept the immensely prestigious job of becoming Governor of the newly created Federal Reserve Bank but it only offered a salary, which was a fraction of what he would have received as President of a large New York bank. In 1920 he was divorced by his second wife, Katherine, whose father had always been against him taking the job. By the mid-1920s, he was living in a small two-bedroom apartment and was using morphine to control the pain of his TB.

Strong was an ardent advocate of Britain returning to the Gold Standard. It was true that the Bank of England would have to raise interest rates if there was a run on its gold reserves[31] but Strong looked upon himself as Norman's guardian angel. He retained both his authority in the banking world and his friendship with Norman until his death in 1928.

Norman did not understand that Germany had ruthlessly reorganised its finances and industry to destroy British competition before it returned to the Gold Standard. He was concerned about restoring peace and financial stability not only at home but also in Britain's great empire and the wider world. England was not only the repository of Great Britain and its empire's savings; the US, Russia, Japan and Argentina also kept a portion of their cash reserves in London.[32] A measure of devaluation would be prudent but it would cause an international upset. Norman advised the Chancellor of the Exchequer, Winston Churchill, to take Britain back on the Gold Standard at the same rate as Germany before the war.

Winston Churchill was a flamboyant figure and a great administrator but economics was not his forte. Keynes fought against Britain's return to the Gold Standard, saying that it would condemn the British people to unemployment and political unrest, but Keynes was a maverick who had made ridiculous statements about Woodrow Wilson like, 'There can seldom have been a statesman of the first rank more incompetent' after the war. Churchill reluctantly accepted Norman's advice and Norman promised him, 'I will make you the golden Chancellor.'[33]

Norman knew that it was going to be hard for the British people to live with a high exchange rate, but deluded himself that Germany was in the same boat, telling his friend Hjalmar Schacht in 1925, 'You and we are indeed suffering – and are likely to suffer on the commercial and industrial side.'

France's unloved French Bank Governor, Émile Moreau, described Norman at this time: 'He does not like the French … On the other hand he seems to feel the deepest sympathy for the Germans. He is very close to Dr Schacht. They see each other often and hatch secret plans,'

As soon as the Great War was over, France had embarked upon plans to restore her ruined cities, her crater-pocked land and her systemically ruined coal mines, the source of her light and power. But the reparations to pay for their restoration were never forthcoming. After Germany engineered its Great Inflation, the only way forward, France believed, was to embark on a Great Inflation of its own to use its own citizens' savings to pay for the war. France wanted to leave its savers with a modicum of money, however, so the franc was finally stabilised at 20 per cent of its former value. Nevertheless, the French middle classes became very anti-Semitic as there was no propaganda issue like the reparations to blame for their misfortunes. This would have dreadful repercussions in the Second World War.

Montagu Norman shared the British people's historic distrust of the French. He believed that Britain was a world power, while Germany was only a regional European power, which had lost some of its land (and a little of its coal), under the terms of the Versailles Treaty.[34] He did not realise that, besides lengthening the hours of work in the mines to ten hours above ground and eight and half hours below, the industrialists had been able to lower wages in the mines to between 14 per cent and 18 per cent below what they had received in 1913,[35] making it almost impossible for the British coal mining industry to compete.

The shop floor in Britain had campaigned for peace on the basis of Woodrow Wilson's Fourteen Points in 1918 and a committee was set up at the peace conference in 1919 to coordinate social legislation with a view to banning child labour and introducing the eight-hour working day throughout the world. In view of some countries' reservations it was not legally binding, but it was intended to provide a goal for nations to aim for.[36] So, Lloyd George allowed the British miners a shorter working day. The Sankey Commission Report even proposed a seven-hour day for Britain's 800,000 miners, being shortened to six in 1921, if circumstances allowed.

In 1926, the British coal owners' desperate attempt to cut wages and lengthen coal mining hours in order to compete with German industry provoked a lengthy strike. Unfortunately the coal owners could not explain that ruthless German competition was destroying their employees' livelihoods because Britain had just accepted the little white lie that Germany was poor.

'We never forgot 1926. The wicked Thirties came after,' a miner from Sheffield would later recall. The British coal industry was not able to achieve anything like the cost reductions required to compete with the Ruhr.[37] By 1931, 432,000 miners, representing 41.6 per cent of the workforce, would be unemployed.[38]

In 1927 General Wauchope, Chief of the British Section Military Inter-Allied Commission of Control in Berlin, asserted that output per man in Germany (because of mechanisation and long working hours) was now 40 per cent above output per man in Britain, stating in his chilling memorandum to London: 'The greatest loss which Germany suffered (in its Great Inflation) was the ruin of her middle classes. If her "natural leaders" are now to be found in the present party of the Right, Germany may again become a danger. It is common knowledge that great numbers of factories could be rapidly reorganised, as in 1914–15, for the production of war material if the government wished. Many are so overbuilt at present that they could produce a large military as well as a large commercial output.'[39]

Norman soon became alarmed at Britain's penurious state. He complained to Schacht about Germany's high interest rates[40] which were causing 'the continuous drain of gold from this market to Berlin'. He even dared to assert, 'Your German concerns borrow money in America (of which I do not think they have need)'.[41] His suspicions were correct.

Short, fat and genial, German Foreign Minister Gustav Stresemann, had come to the conclusion that, 'The granting of a loan would give us an army of 300,000 people in America who would make propaganda for Germany because they would be interested in her welfare.'[42]

His plan was a wild success. Investing in Germany was an attractive option. In 1920 the Americans had complained that the German chemical industry was charging 'extortionate prices' for the dyes that America could not produce, and undercutting American prices on the dyes it could. By the mid-1920s Germany made its chemical industry even more competitive with the development of a huge industrial cartel.

I G Farben was founded in 1925 with the merger of six chemical companies, BASF (27.4 per cent), Bayer (27.4 per cent), Hoechst and Chemische Fabrik Kalle (27.4 per cent), Agfa (9.0 per cent), Chemische Fabrik Griesheim-Elektron (6.9 per cent), and from Chemische Fabrik vorm. It had a market capitalisation of 1.4 billion Reichsmarks and a workforce of 100,000 people. Germany had other huge industrial concerns.

The Vereinigte Stahlwerke of Düsseldorf – United Steel – was founded in 1926 from a group of coal and steel companies. It included 151 coal mines, 71 coking plants, 63 blast furnaces, 32 Bessemer converters, 116 large open-hearth furnaces, rolling mills, railways and port facilities. Enriched by selling coal to England during the miners' strike, it managed to attract funds for investment amounting to double the original total of the British Steel Corporation between 1927 and 1929.[43]

A G Krupp was a private concern which had been the largest company in Europe in 1900 and had made a fortune out of the First World War. Although it reputedly made a loss in the war's aftermath, it was rich enough to secretly buy the Swedish arms company Bofors, in 1921, and to continue clandestinely designing ships, submarines and artillery in the Netherlands, Russia and elsewhere.

In 1924 the Raw Steel Association was established in Luxembourg as a quota-fixing cartel. Germany chose to violate the quotas and pay fines in order to try and corner the market. A G Krupp was an innovative steel company. In 1926 it developed the production of cobalt-tungsten carbide, which was twice as tough as ordinary steel (and ideal for cladding tanks). In 1929 it produced a special stainless steel to clad the new prestigious art deco Chrysler Building in New York, which would retain the title of the highest building in the world for eleven months until the Empire State Building took the crown.

American financial advisors didn't like cartels. However, they had a duty to look after their customers. They felt that their clients were safe investing in huge companies like these, especially after Germany signed the Treaty of Locarno in December 1925 and became a member of the League of Nations in 1926. The Bolsheviks in Russia paraded the fact that Germany had also signed a treaty with them, demonstrating the eternal friendship between the two formerly pariah states.[44] However, the Americans chose to ignore the Treaty. They regarded Germany as their close friend. Indeed, they were in danger of lending so much money to Germany that if, in more straitened economic times, a stark choice arrived between Germany repaying American loans or paying reparations to the Allies, they would insist that the repayment of their loans came first.

The Americans were already beginning to believe German propaganda that it had been wrongly charged with responsibility for the First World War in the first place. The German Nationalists published telegrams such as the one Bethmann Hollweg's sent at 3.05 a.m. on 30th July 1914, in which he stated:

'We are prepared to fulfil our duty as allies, but must refuse to allow Vienna to draw us into a world conflagration frivolously and without regard to our advice.'[45]

But they did not give the context in which this telegram was sent, when Bethmann Hollweg momentarily lost his nerve, after he asked Britain to remain neutral when he invaded France, and Sir Edward Grey refused.[46]

Nor did the German Nationalist publicists mention General Moltke's telegram sent a little later that same morning, pressing Austria-Hungary to adopt general mobilisation (without actually declaring war on Russia), and also saying that Austria-Hungary should mobilise against Russia rather than Serbia[47] (which would hopefully push the Russians into general mobilisation and provide the pretext for war).

Unfortunately these incriminating telegrams would not be made public until long after the Second World War. Meanwhile Hitler declared in *Mein Kampf* that Germany should keep protesting its complete innocence of starting the First World War, asserting: '… The vast mass of a nation consists of men who are disposed to doubt and uncertainty. If the propaganda admits the least shadow of right on the enemy's side, the way has been paved for doubting its own right. And this is particularly true of a nation so inclined to an unhealthy impartiality as is the German.'

Ominously, Hitler also ranted against the immorality of 'American' capitalism declaring: 'We are enemies of today's capitalistic economic system for the exploitation of the economically weak … and we are determined to destroy this system under all conditions.'

Hitler's words were addressed to the embittered German middle classes who had been robbed of their savings in 1923 and were alienated by the ostentatious spending of visiting Americans. They had no idea of the wealth of their own heavy industrialists, who were not frittering away their cash on personal consumption but were busy rationalising their industries at home and constructing armaments factories abroad. Besides Krupp's many armaments plants, Fokker had a factory in Holland; Dornier, one in Russia, at Kronstadt, and another at Manzell on the German shores of Lake Constance, a third on the opposite shore at Altenhein and another in Holland. Junkers had established itself in Turkey, at Eski-Shehire, with the firm of Rohrhach, which specialised in mounting machine gun turrets, light cannon, and bomb racks on bombers. Heinkel was based in Sweden where it produced bombers and fighters, and U-boats were built by German engineers at Vigo.[48]

Cooperation between the German and Russian armed forces also flourished. An agreement had been concluded to build an aviation school in Lipetsk, to complement the existing military school, and to set up a tank school at Kazan. In the spring of 1927 the German chemical expert, Auer, led a delegation to view the joint Soviet and German mustard gas trials at Orenburg.[49]

It was no wonder that the French government still feared another German invasion. In 1927, on the tenth anniversary of America's intervention in the First World War, French Foreign Minister Aristide Briand, asked America for a bilateral security pact but he was merely offered the Kellogg-Briand Pact – which solemnly voted to 'Outlaw War'. Faced with this nebulous offer, the French decided that they had no option but to build what would become the Maginot Line of fortifications 'armed with cannons, mortars and machine guns' to protect their country in a concrete fashion from the threat of another German invasion. Unfortunately, however, for political and economic reasons, it did not include the area opposite the Ardennes forest in Belgium.

Due to the controls that Poincaré had put upon the German economy, the Allies had received the handsome total of nearly £400 million in reparations in the five years between 1924 and 1929.[50] But most of this sizeable sum was due to the German 'deliveries in kind' to France which should more accurately be called unpaid-for German exports of coal and other goods (with the German exporters being reimbursed by their government through levies on the railways, sugar, etc.) and to the 30 per cent tariff on German exports to

Britain.[51] Only £47 million net (937 million gold marks) was received in cash in reparations.[52] Meanwhile Germany's deluge of exports was weakening France and Britain's economies, and France desperately needed 'cash' to start paying her war debts to America.

CHAPTER SEVEN

The 1929 Wall Street Crash

It has been claimed that the Wall Street Crash was caused by the failures of the capitalist system. However, there was another more sinister reason which has never been properly investigated, that it could have been engineered by powerful forces in Germany to renege on the reparations, and start Hitler on the road to power.

When the German people went to the polls in 1928 they recoiled from the avowed enemy of the Weimar Republic, the DNVP, which still hankered after more 'living space in Eastern Europe' and planned to build a 'pocket battleship'. The DNVP suffered a severe defeat while the Social Democrats achieved power in coalition with the Centre Party.

The iron ore magnates of the Ruhr locked out their 225,000 workers for four weeks rather than allow the new socialist administration to shorten the working week and allow an increase in wages, while their spare cash fled the Fatherland before the threat of heavier taxation. Although the German local authorities had been much more frugal than their British counterparts, borrowing 80 per cent less than the British state and local authorities put together,[1] Dr Schacht told the young American reparations agent, Parker

Gilbert, that the socialists had been squandering America's precious loans on swimming pools and lavish parks. Nevertheless, Schacht, who seemingly had performed such miracles in stabilising the mark after Germany's Great Inflation, assured Parker Gilbert that he would force the Socialists to behave responsibly if America would give Germany a new, less onerous deal over the reparations.

Meanwhile sinister former Pan-German Alfred Hugenberg, became leader of the anti-democratic Nationalist Party, the DNVP. Known as the 'Randolph Hearst of Germany' because of his vast publishing empire, Hugenberg was determined not to let Socialism take root in his country. The German people had turned to extremist parties, like Hitler's and the DNVP, in the last dark days of the Great Inflation of 1923 and Hugenberg was confident that he could also persuade them to reject democracy altogether if dark times came again, and the aspiring dictator was a man of the people, like Mussolini in Italy.[2]

There were only two problems for Hugenberg; first he had to find a likely candidate to become dictator, and second, he had to create the sort of dire economic conditions which would persuade the German people to vote for him.

Adolf Hitler had not been completely out of the public eye since his attempted Putsch in 1923. On 21st March 1927, a band of six hundred Nazi Brown Shirts beat up a group of Communists in eastern Berlin; then they marched into the centre of the city, attacking anyone who looked Jewish. The authorities responded by banning Nazi activity in Berlin for a year.[3] Yet, although Hitler was treated as a freak by most of the German population, 800,000 people still voted for him in the 1928 elections.

Hitler had many attributes which appealed to Hugenberg: he was a natural orator, had been a corporal in the German army, was an Austrian – which would come in handy if Germany

Hitler was promoted by newspaper magnate Alfred Hugenberg in 1929

invaded Austria – and had similar sentiments to the Pan-Germans, even if his policy of sterilisation, euthanasia and eventually extermination against the Bolsheviks and Jews, was a little extreme. He had been a 'drummer' for the Nationalist cause since the early 1920s, which presumably meant that Hugenberg and other anti-republic figures had already been bank-noting him. Hitler's 800,000 votes also provided him with a power base. Hugenberg decided to promote him.

By the end of the 1920s the Americans become worried that the 1924 Dawes Plan had given an immense artificial stimulus to Germany's exports,[4] while producing very little 'actual cash' reparations to help France pay its war debts to them.[5] They knew that Germany could pay a sizeable sum as its national income in 1929 amounted to the handsome total of 75,900,000,000 gold marks or £3,800,000,000. So they decided to negotiate a new reparations agreement with Germany called the Young Plan, with the object of removing the political overtones from the reparations demands and transforming them into an ordinary bond. President of the Reichsbank, Dr Schacht, and head of United Steel, Dr Vögler, were the German negotiators, the Allied representatives being two Americans, Dr Owen Young and Mr J P Morgan.

The comparison between the period before the 1929 crash and the period before the 1873 crash is startling. By returning to the Gold Standard in the 1920s, Europe and America had in effect adopted a large new currency, just like Bismarck had in 1870. The huge amount of German money arriving in America to escape the socialist menace would create a 'bubble' of money, just like the 'bubble' of money that appeared after Bismarck extorted a huge indemnity from France in 1871. As there was no good place to invest such a large amount of cash, foolish speculation would be indulged in. Then interest rates would rise and tight money ensue, followed by a panic and a stock market collapse as happened in 1873.

Dr Schacht was very excited. He had long prepared the ground to take Germany's former foes for a ride. No doubt encouraged by Alfred Hugenberg, he wrote to a more hesitant and sceptical Stresemann on 28th September 1928:

'The psychological moment has now come to strike for everything. Almost more important than the sums at stake is the opportunity to regain our absolute international freedom. Every remnant of obligations, controls (i.e. the French controls on the German economy to ensure German compliance with the Dawes Plan) unresolved questions must disappear.'[6]

Ultimately, in a single currency, a powerful nation can affect all the other nations in its orbit. It is interesting to note that the rises and falls of the American stock market in 1929 (see below) almost exactly mirrored Germany's brinkmanship over the Young Plan negotiations.

In May 1928 the German Social Democrats had won a big victory at the polls and became the majority party in the subsequent coalition government. Their victory precipitated an exodus of cash by nervous right-wing investors.

Some German money had probably remained on Wall Street since 1923. A flood more arrived on Wall Street in the autumn of 1928 to influence the negotiations. Cash from other countries soon followed, excited by the rising stock market. Germany's gold holdings on 7th January 1929 stood at the magnificent total of 2,729,345,000 marks, the highest in the Reichsbank's history.[7]

Preliminaries for the new agreement on the reparations started on 11th February and finished on 18th February. Wall Street soared, giving confidence to the American negotiators that they could soon wrap up the deal. The American press, however, soon became uncomfortable with the way that the stock market was behaving.

NEW YORK STOCK EXCHANGE BULLETIN

STOCK PRICE INDEX AND MONTHLY AVERAGES OF ALL
LISTED SHARES JAN 1928 TILL DEC 1930

On 2nd March 1929 *The New York Times* commented:
'There were times yesterday when even Wall Street began to
think that the stock market was running absolutely wild.'
On 4th March 1929 the same newspaper sympathised with
the new President Hoover on the eve of his inauguration:
'He is hardly likely to have watched with pleasure the tight-
ening of credit under the strain of the speculative market's
requisitions, until money rates now prevailing are such as
have never been equalled in any new administration.'

Handsome new President, Herbert Hoover, had been a
mining engineer by training. He had come to fame because
of his efficiency in distributing American food to Europe after
the First World War. He had always had the greatest sympathy
for Germany.

158

In January 1919, 'Hoover commandeered the railroad system of central Europe, sent battleships hither and yon, took control of coal mines ... dictated policy to municipal and other authorities, and actively intervened in all sorts of areas of life and politics.' Insistent that his food programme should be an American one, independent of the Allies, his aides also distributed food to the Germans and Austrians in order 'to combat the menace of communism', even the blockade was lifted.

Hoover had been upset with the terms of the Treaty of Versailles. At daybreak on 7th May 1919 he got dressed and went out to pace the empty streets after reading his copy of the Treaty. He met up with Keynes and Smuts. 'It all flashed into our minds,' according to Hoover, 'why each was walking about at that time of the morning, because of their distress over the Treaty's terms.' Keynes wrote to his mother: 'The Peace is outrageous and impossible and can bring nothing but misfortune.'[8] Hoover was similarly upset. But Keynes and Hoover were wrong in 1919 in believing that the economic strictures of the Treaty of Versailles would cripple the German economy. In 1929 they would have been astonished to find out that bellicose Hugenberg's DNVP had just passed a resolution which stated simply:

'We hate the present form of the German state with all our hearts because it denies to us the hope ... of gaining necessary living-space in Eastern Europe.'[9]

Respected international banker Paul Warburg, who had also been at the peace conference at Versailles in 1919, asserted that control of the cumbersome US Federal Reserve Board had passed into the hands of stock exchange operators 'who have now for many months governed the flow of money, not only in the United States but in the principal parts of the world'. He declared: 'The banking system of the United States today is tossing about without its helm being under the control of its pilots. Its aftermath is likely to be a depression involving the whole country.'[10]

By the end of March the concept of a Bank for International Settlements was agreed. On 25th March the second stage of the negotiations began. There was a lot of discussion about the problems of transferring the reparations across the ocean to America but in view of the amount of German money that *The New York Times* had already claimed was in America during Germany's Great Inflation in 1923, the problem seemed to be a bit of a red herring.

Alfred Hugenberg intervened at the start of the monetary negotiations by sending a much publicised letter to prominent right-wing American businessmen and politicians, informing them that the ocean of money that they had lent to Germany since 1924 had benefited only Socialism, not business. He declared that Germany needed a generous settlement to prevent it from falling into 'Bolshevism'.[11]

In April the stock market sagged after Dr Schacht offered only a paltry sum in reparations and claimed that even that amount was dependent on the return of the Saar and Upper Silesia to Germany. *The New York Times* reporter declared Schacht's offer to be 'outrageous'.

The Reichsbank had held a record amount of gold before the start of the reparations negotiations.[12] Then it started to ebb away in a worrying manner. When faced with a similar inexplicable exit of gold in the autumn of 1928, the British had put up interest rates from 4.5 per cent to 5.5 per cent, but the Germans did nothing to stop the exodus of gold. In the spring of 1929 Germany's loss of gold was not attributed to the country's poor economy but to a negotiating ploy of Dr Schacht.

The New York Times reporter declared accusingly:

'No-one could doubt, when the Reichsbank was drawing gold in quantity from the Bank of England and elsewhere between last June and the end of 1928, that its aspirations were certain to drive down German money rates; yet every observant financier knew also that Germany's position made high rates a prime necessity, in order to retain command of the foreign exchanges with a view ... to transferring reparations money. Instead of this, the Reichsbank turned its foreign credits into cash, nearly exhausted its own holdings of foreign exchange (which were very large in the middle of 1928), and forced down the Berlin market's rate for money at the moment when Wall Street was bidding nine and ten per cent for European credits ... There will doubtless be talk of the Reichsbank's past or present action being part of a concerted program to influence the reparations controversy'.[13]

At the end of April the mark slipped to its lowest level since 1924. Germany at last decided to raise its interest rates but by a full one per cent, which triggered immediate rises in Vienna, Warsaw and Hungary, and subsequent rises in Bucharest in May, Brussels in June and Belgrade.

Over the very last weekend of April details were agreed on the Young Plan between the German and American negotiators alone. Britain was upset with the agreement because Dr Schacht had won the right to pay less in reparations – £103 million a year –[14] than the Allies owed in war debts to America. Wall Street was relieved, however, and started climbing again.

On 24th May, Wall Street suffered a mini-collapse after Dr Vögler resigned from the Young Plan negotiations. His resignation was directly related to the banquet given in his and Dr Schacht's honour by the coal and steel barons at Gustav Krupp's palace in Essen. Herr Georg Bernhard, editor in chief of the *Vossiche Zeitung* wrote disgustedly:

'These circles know quite well that, hard as the Paris agreements would be for the German nation to bear, the relief that they would involve for the German budget would be used for the restitution of ordered economic conditions in Germany ...

that is also the deeper reason for the fresh attempts by working on Dr Vögler to blow the plan to pieces at the last moment.' Money in German bank deposits had contracted by 5 per cent since the end of March, supposedly fleeing to Switzerland.[15]

The Allied negotiators then reluctantly agreed to remove all the untrusting controls over German finances, which France had successfully imposed to ensure the payment of the reparations in 1924. There was only one outstanding issue. *The New York Times* explained the history of the matter:

'When they occupied Belgium (in 1914) the Germans removed all the Belgian gold and money and "planted" marks in the banks in place of Belgian currency. Neither the facts nor the justice of the Belgian claim for restitution has ever been denied by Berlin ... Yet for one reason or another a settlement has always been postponed ... Émile Francqui, chief Belgian delegate ... has gone so far as to accuse Dr Schacht of having been party to the wholesale pillage of the Belgian banks when he was on von Bissing's staff during the occupation, and such an accusation has envenomed the already delicate question.' But in the end the delegates decided that they would have to sign the Young Plan without agreement on Belgium's claim.

It was a different Raymond Poincaré, weary and sick, who pleaded for the ratification of the Young Plan by France's parliament. The arrival of a socialist government in power in Germany had impressed the democratic Frenchman. Yet Poincaré was no dewy-eyed idealist. He secured the private assurance that the payment of France's enormous war debts to the US ($6,847,105 including interest), was conditional on Germany continuing to pay reparations to France.[16] Then he set about persuading his reluctant parliament to accept the agreement. He summoned up all his strength and gave one of the best speeches of his career. On 21st July the Young Plan was ratified by the French parliament by eight votes.

Wall Street soared again as The Hague Conference convened to iron out the final issues. The presence of the French troops in the Rhineland was only symbolic to the British but their removal was of the utmost importance to the German military. The stock market climbed to the stratosphere as the Allies agreed to remove the occupation troops from the Rhineland, five years ahead of schedule. Paul Schmidt, Foreign Minister Stresemann's interpreter, recorded this 'unforgettable afternoon'. Both men 'hoped that a new age had come, one in which France and Germany would truly become good neighbours'.[17] However, German Nationalists like Alfred Hugenberg had other ideas and they were about to cause mayhem.

On Friday 31st August the Young Plan was agreed at The Hague. Dr Schacht won acceptance that its implementation should be retrospectively effective from Sunday 1st September even though it was not due to be ratified until the following spring.

On Thursday 5th September *The New York Times* recorded a sudden downturn in the stock market on the 4th. It declared: 'The most obvious explanation ... would be that the pace of advancing prices during the past three weeks has been ... so regardless of the money market position, as to inspire a growing sense of caution even among convinced speculators for the rise.'

After the market continued to fall, the editor of *The New York Times* consoled its readers: 'The money market is guarded against old-time panics, both by the country's accumulation of gold and by its fund of available foreign credits.' But the 'foreign credits' started to disappear and money soon became scarce and tight. In September the financial empire of the fraudulent British financier, Clarence Hatry, collapsed with large losses.

In the 1930s some pundits would blame Clarence Hatry for the Wall Street Crash but there was another explanation. Since raising its interest rates in April, Germany had been buying gold from London in quantity since June, triggering purchases by France and other countries.[18] On 25th September, *The Times* commented:

'An event of much more importance than the Hatry affair ... was the further loss of gold reported by the Bank of England. Withdrawals on this scale are unprecedented, and it is as well to remember that the present gold reserve is nearly £16,000,000 below the level recommended after the Great War.'[19]

After Britain returned to the Gold Standard in April 1925 *The Times* had cautioned: 'This means that the Bank of England must use the weapon of the rate in the event of a persistent export of gold.'[20] Unfortunately, in view of 'the persistent export of gold' in large amounts to Germany and then to other worried countries, in September 1929 the Governor of the Bank of England, Montagu Norman, had no option but to raise interest rates.[21]

Montagu Norman himself would be blamed for the 1929 stock market crash because he had to raise interest rates at this critical time. The removal of the German funds from the American stock market would also have an impact.

On 2nd October Dr Hilferding, the German Finance Minister, promised to enact legislation to counteract the previous high tax on moderate incomes, which was supposed to have encouraged capital flight from the country. The German money started to leave Wall Street.

But it was not only tight money, and the departure of German cash which caused anxiety on Wall Street, a prominent politician also had an influence on the market. Machiavellian, bespectacled Alfred Hugenberg, had already sent a letter to prominent Americans in the spring with a plea for a generous new reparations agreement, in order to 'save Germany from Bolshevism'.

Yet, after the Americans listened to Hugenberg's warnings and gave generous terms to Germany in the new agreement, Hugenberg produced a pernicious new petition, backed by all his five hundred newspapers and put the minority leader, Adolf Hitler, in a prominent position on the petition's committee, which would give Hitler enormous publicity and have a dire effect on the American stock market.

Hugenberg's petition asserted that the German President and all his cabinet should be tried for treason for agreeing to pay any war reparations at all, on the grounds that Germany was guiltless of starting the First World War. If his petition gained sufficient votes, the government would have to hold a national referendum on it.

Stresemann had been a right-winger all his life, but he recognised the threat Hugenberg's petition posed to the peace and prosperity of the German nation. One of the last acts of his life was to get the executive of his People's Party, the DVP, to pass a clear resolution opposing Hugenberg's petition. But he could do no more. His biographer, Antonia Vallentin, described Stresemann at Geneva:

'A marked man stood there in the shadow of death. His suit flapped about his shrunken figure ... His breathing came so hard that his sudden coughing often drowned out his words ... One could almost hear the fevered beating of his heart'. One week later he was dead.

In a book dedicated to Stresemann's memory called *Germany's Role in the New Europe,* Dr Koch-Weser gave an outline of the sort of ambition that he felt that Stresemann would have had for Germany. He envisaged the demolition of economic barriers in Europe, which would have opened extensive sources of raw materials on the one hand and provided markets and an unrestricted field of activity for the enterprise of Germany's abounding and capable population on the other. Koch-Weser believed that the only practicable means of securing this peacefully would be through the formation of the United States of Europe. But it was the militarist, Hugenberg, who was controlling matters now, not Stresemann.

Alfred Hugenberg

On 13th October 1929 the German socialist coalition government felt itself sufficiently threatened by Hugenberg's propaganda campaign to issue an official proclamation that Hugenberg's petition was a 'monstrous attempt to incite the German people against the government and to annihilate the ten-year good-will policy of the republic with Germany's former enemies'.

On 17th October 1929, counting on Hugenberg's petition began. It was scheduled to take two weeks. *The New York Times* believed that Hugenberg would gain the necessary four million votes to trigger a national referendum on his petition because he could count on Hitler's 800,000 votes, and those of other extremist parties, if some of his party's 4.4 million faithful fell by the wayside. It reported selling on Wall Street. There had been a move to 'force' stocks down. On 18th October *The New York Times* again predicted that Hugenberg and Hitler's petition would succeed because it had opened up the 'war guilt' issue.

On 21st October 1929 'perpendicular' falls were recorded on the American stock market remarking 'The outstanding feature of the past week's Berlin money market was the rapid descent of the dollar exchange in favour of the mark.'

On 24th October 1929 Wall Street collapsed and 19,226,400 shares were sold. The American stock market was hit by a devastating crash as it became apparent that Hugenberg's rejection of reparations payments threatened not only the payment of the Allies war debts but that Hugenberg and new friend, Hitler, were capable of defaulting on all America's loans. The paper loss in October and November 1929, at $26,078,000,000, was equal to the entire wartime increase in the American national debt.

Most of the German money that had been on Wall Street, and escaped before the crash, was not sent back to Germany but was lodged in Switzerland and France.[22]

The American stock market continued to plunge until the national referendum on Hugenberg and Hitler's petition was turned down by the German people on 22nd December. The Allies and America breathed a sigh of relief. Yet, as Harold James writes in his book *A German Identity*: 'It was the joint DNVP and Nazi sponsored plebiscite against the Young Plan that took the Nazis back into the centre of the political scene.'[23] When the economic climate worsened the following year and the German people were asked to pay the reparations out of their diminished pay, they would flock to Hitler.

America was still firm in its belief that it could trust Germany. Wall Street staged a rally in the spring of 1930 in the conviction that the Socialist German coalition government would ratify the Young Plan and the reparations would continue to be paid.

On 12th March 1930 foreigners breathed a sigh of relief after the Young Plan was ratified. However, on 30th March the Socialist coalition resigned en bloc after President Hindenburg intimated it was time for it to depart.

Nevertheless Wall Street continued its upward path for another month. On 12th April 1930 *The New York Times* wrote enthusiastically:

'One of the most significant commentaries on the current securities market ... is that the demand for our securities from foreign sources continues unabated. The magnet of the New York Stock Exchange is attracting investors throughout the world.'

Yet, it seemed that foreign investors were more fickle than American investors, or perhaps they objected to Republican talk of 'rushing' a new tariff bill through Congress. The market paused mid-April. Then it started to fall. By 29th April *The New York Times* had to relate of 'unrelieved selling pressure ... The widest break in the year to date'.

168

Most Americans could not conceive that it was their friends the Germans who had stolen their money and were taking them for a ride. In 1919 President Woodrow Wilson had told an astonished British official at a reception at Buckingham Palace during the peace conference: 'You must not speak of us who come over here as cousins, still less as brothers; we are neither.' But the British could not believe that Wilson was not their best friend. Likewise in 1929 Woodrow Wilson's former aide, and now President, Herbert Hoover, and his administration refused to accept that their German 'friends' had caused America such a devastating loss.

CHAPTER EIGHT

The Pan-Germans Pave the Way for Hitler and War

It was often said that Americans woke up in 1930 with a massive hangover from the heady party days of the late 1920s. They could not understand why everything had gone so drastically wrong. So why did it? The reason is that they put their trust in the German people in the 1920s, but the German people were not in charge. The Pan-Germans, who now called themselves the Nationalists, were in control and they were determined to tear up the Treaty of Versailles and impoverish America so that she would not interfere when they returned to war.

Former Pan-German Hugenberg, plunged a dagger into America's heart when he caused the Wall Street Crash. Then he and his friends were ready to turn their attention to the German Social Democrats, who maintained that Germany should pay its reparations and achieve its aim of securing 'a place in the sun' through cooperation with the international community. Meanwhile the machinations of Hugenberg's fellow Pan-German Gustav Krupp in Russia were about to cause a major agricultural depression, which would come to be known as 'the Dust Bowl' in America.

The German Social Democrats were the first to come under fire. There was a gap in the nation's finances because Alfred

Hugenberg's powerful anti-Republican party, the DNVP, had refused to vote funds for the country's Unemployment Insurance Act in the spring of 1929, even though it had been responsible for the legislation in the first place.

In December 1929 Hugenberg declared that the Social Democrat coalition's plan to raise a loan to cover the gap in the nation's finances was the 'last desperate act of a political system which has turned into a runaway pump'. Scurrilous head of the Reichsbank, Dr Schacht, sharpened the attack.

Schacht asserted that the socialist coalition had accepted alterations to the recently negotiated Young Plan reparations deal, which he would never have agreed to; moreover that it had failed to carry out vital reforms to the nation's finances.[1] He forced Minister of Finance, Rudolf Hilferding, to resign. Efficient, moderate General Gröner described Hilferding as 'stuffy', but 'a really decent fellow' and 'a great financial pundit'. Nevertheless Hilferding was impelled to depart. After Hitler came to power Jewish Herr Hilferding would escape from Germany, but he would not evade the Gestapo's clutches. In the Second World War he would be found dead in his cell in the Gestapo dungeon of La Santé in Paris.

Although the 1929 Young Plan report declared that the new Young Plan Reparations agreement 'makes possible an immediate resumption of the tax reduction programme',[2] Schacht quickly said that taxes must go up not down! Indeed, he asserted that a huge pot of gold must be created to restore confidence and ensure the payment of the war reparations.[3]

In March 1930 Heinrich Brüning, who would soon be nicknamed *Hungerkanzler*, was installed as German Chancellor. He was no admirer of Hugenberg or Hitler, but he was an enemy of the Treaty of Versailles and an ardent admirer of his President, Paul von Hindenburg.

Aged ex-Field Marshal Paul von Hindenburg, who the Allies originally intended to indict after the First World War, had kept

171

a low profile since becoming President in 1925. However, on 30th June 1930, when the Allied troops were withdrawn from the Rhineland under the terms of the Young Plan, Hindenburg forced the socialist authorities in Prussia to revoke their ban on Germany's ex-war veterans' organisation, the Stahlhelm, which boasted a membership of nearly a million men.

The Stahlhelm war veterans then marched through the Rhineland in an ugly display of force, with their flag, the hated imperial standard of the Prussian monarchy, black and white with an iron cross in the left corner and the Hohenzollern eagle flying in the centre, prominently displayed. Their march provoked intense anger in France but this was ignored by the German press, which merely used the occasion to call for the return of the Saarland.[4]

Devoted ex-soldier and financial expert Heinrich Brüning, who won both the second and first class Iron Cross in the First World War, was an advocate of 'austerity'. However, although the *Hungerkanzler* Brüning reassured foreign bankers that his purpose in adopting this policy was to return Germany to sound money after the alleged excesses of the former socialist administration, he disclosed to his friends in the unions that his real purpose was to rid Germany of war reparations and debts.[5]

Brüning looked upon the German citizens as soldiers, who must suffer so that Germany could regain its place 'in the sun'. So he kicked off with a poll tax, added taxation and reductions in wages, while increasing the tariff on wheat to twice that prevailing on world markets to protect his country from the imminent deluge of Soviet wheat which would soon be hitting world markets.[6]

The bewildered German people were also faced with paying the reparations, which the railways and industry had formerly taken care of. The German people did not know exactly which country started the First World War but their university

172

professors and teachers maintained that Great Britain was the evil genius behind it.[7] So when the elections were held in September 1930, they gave their support to Adolf Hitler, who had featured so prominently on Hugenberg's so-called 'Freedom Bill' Committee against paying any reparations in 1929, while Hugenberg himself campaigned against the territorial aspects of the Treaty of Versailles, as Sir Horace Rumbold noted with alarm in his report to Foreign Secretary, Arthur Henderson:

'The snowball of "revision" continues to roll down the electoral slopes and as it rolls, it is gathering speed and size. It may now indeed be said that the first electoral campaign which has taken place in Germany without the shadow of the Rhineland occupation has brought out into the open, through one party or another, all that Germany hopes for and intends to strive for in the field of external affairs.'[8]

Hitler scored a great success in the September 1930 elections. The Nazi paper, *Der Angriff*, commented triumphantly on the Nazis' success: 'As the wolf bursts into the flock, so we come' while *The New York Times* observed chillingly: 'In some quarters fears are expressed over the possibility of Adolf Hitler and Dr. Alfred Hugenberg combining to form a party of revenge.'

While Hugenberg was creating mayhem on Wall Street in 1929, his former employer and fellow Pan-German Gustav Krupp, was busy in the Soviet Union.

Gustav Krupp's greatest nightmare had been for the Communists to gain power in Germany. The Communists' aim was to control the 'means of production'. He felt that Socialism was the slippery slope towards Communism and was determined that neither Socialists nor Communists would grab hold of his business, which had taken generations of his family to build up (and was arguably now the biggest company in Europe). So he had an idea. When helping the 'evil' Bolsheviks achieve power in Russia in the First World War, Gustav Krupp and his friends remarked that 'politics have always been utilitarian, and will be so for a long time'. In 1928 the Bolsheviks were nearly bankrupt. The Soviet 'economy had almost no reserves at its disposal, either financial or material'[9] so Krupp sensed an opportunity. He would help Stalin for his own evil ends.

Small, sallow, pock-marked Joseph Stalin was born with gangly legs, a shrivelled left arm and darting yellow eyes. He made his reputation by robbing banks and extorting money from factory owners in order to raise funds for the Bolsheviks. However, he was a master tactician and after Lenin's death had gradually been able to out-manoeuvre all his rivals.

He proceeded, step by step, in lulling his victims into a false sense of security before delivering the fatal blow. The execution would be swift but the planning process could never be rushed. An embrace from him was often the prelude to a sudden fall. By 1928 the man who would later be called 'Genghis Khan with a telephone' not only had chilling power over his own party in the Soviet Union but also over the Communist Party in Germany.

Krupp agreed to help Stalin create giant farms like his own 50,000 hectare concession in the North Caucasus so that Stalin could sell wheat abroad to pay for the modernisation of his armaments industry, and the heavy industrial base to support it; but he had two conditions, firstly that he and his German industrial friends had to be paid in hard currency, and secondly, that even if the Communists were engaged in bloody warfare against the Nazis on the German streets, they must always vote with Hugenberg's DNVP and Hitler's National Socialists in the Reichstag, instead of with their former friends, the Social Democrats.

Krupp's terms were a bitter pill for Stalin but eventually he capitulated. On 28th August 1928 the Russian Foreign Office issued a statement to the German government stating that it wished to 'renew negotiations, as long as journalists are not involved' and on 1st September 1928 the Soviets used the cloak of universality to denounce the German Social Democrat Party, declaring: 'Have our relationships with the Social Democrats changed or not? ... Does this imply any practical conclusions? Yes it does ...'[10]

The deal with what the Soviets called the '*Russlandsausschuss der deutschen Industrie*' was signed on 22nd December 1928.[11] Gustav Krupp agreed to help Stalin create giant farms like his own in the North Caucasus[12] while Stalin undertook to ensure that even if the German Communists were engaged in bloody warfare against the Nazis on the German streets, they would always vote with Hugenberg's DNVP and Hitler's National Socialists in the Reichstag. [13]

The deal was signed in December 1928. Stalin became a valued customer in the depression years 1929 to 1933, buying not only anti-tank guns, howitzers, firing mechanisms and all kinds of munitions,[14] but also the secret of making the precious steel to protect tanks from attack, and the heavy engineering plants to modernise the Soviet Union's antiquated industrial infrastructure. Indeed, by 1931 over 50 per cent of all Stalin's imports came from Germany.[15] German goods continued to flood into the Soviet Union in 1932. By 1933 Krupp and his heavy-industry friends would not only have saved Stalin from bankruptcy but given him the industrial base to survive a Great War.

In return Stalin maintained his immense hold over the German Communist Party. In June 1929, October 1929 and July 1930 the Communists faithfully voted with Hitler's NSDAP and Hugenberg's DNVP. In the September 1930 elections, they alleged that the 'treacherous, corrupt' Social Democrats were 'the conscious agents of French and Polish imperialism' because they supported paying war reparations.[16]

In the spring of 1931, after Stalin's personal intervention, the Communists reluctantly joined forces with Hugenberg's DNVP and Hitler's National Socialists to support the dissolution of the last bastion of democracy in Germany, the Prussian state Landtag (parliament).[17]

Meanwhile, with Krupp and his friends help, Stalin dispensed with the services of his unruly kulak peasants and produced quantities of wheat for export to pay for his goods in hard currency.[18]

Stalin had always hated the kulaks and was happy to find a means of getting rid of them. After the heads of the households were shot, their dependents were crammed into 'death trains' headed for the 'icy North'. Meanwhile the Soviet Union's precious wheat travelled in trains and ships across the Atlantic Ocean to the unsuspecting continent of North America, where it was sold at 'slave labour' prices on the world's already overprovided wheat markets in 1930 and 1931.

The effect on the US farming economy was devastating. All of a sudden America's wheat was totally uneconomic. Farmers tried to expand their production in 1931 to make up for the fall in prices, but prices sank even lower in 1931 than in 1930 and production withered in the exhausted ground. Drought compounded the continuing disaster. Winds whipped across the plains, raising billowing clouds of dust. The dust contained the top soil holding the nutrients that fertile crops depended on. Marginal land was soon semi-permanently depleted. Banks depending on agriculture went bankrupt up and down the country. For many farmers, and those who were dependent upon them, it was worse than being wounded in a war. Thousands of gaunt, unemployed ex-farm labourers descended on the cities in search of work and food, but America could not blame Stalin for the low price of wheat because the Soviets had called their success in selling it 'A triumph of Communism over Capitalism!' Therefore the farmers themselves were blamed.

Joseph Stalin

Americans could not believe that Germany had helped Stalin destroy their wheat market. They were horrified at Hitler's electoral success in 1930 and to discover that the faith that they had put in Hugenberg and other prominent figures in Germany had been misplaced. Worried about the fate of their loans,[19] they turned to the one German they had put their trust in in recent times, former Reichsbank President, Hjalmar Schacht.

Dry, bespectacled Schacht did not reassure them when he spoke at a dinner discussion with John Foster Dulles at the Foreign Policy Association in New York. On the contrary, firstly he promised another crisis over the reparations, and secondly he declared that now that the Allies had withdrawn their troops from the Rhine, there was nothing Americans could do about it.

However, the magician Schacht managed to give Americans another enemy to blame in the event of them not receiving the return of their cash, the Allies! He declared:

'We have made these payments (the reparations) so far entirely out of borrowings, and it is astonishing to see how the payments for import surplus, the payments on reparation and the payments on interest are exactly equal to what we have borrowed in the meantime.'[20]

This misleading statement could be taken two ways. The Americans erroneously chose to believe that it meant that America had lent 'poor' Germany the money to pay its 'huge' reparations bill to the Allies. They were full of sympathy with their German cousins, weighed down with onerous 'unfair' reparations.

Yet Schacht was actually saying something much more sinister. He was saying that though France and Britain may have forced Germany to pay reparations through 'deliveries in kind' and tariffs (the 'input surplus'), plus the value of the trains, ships, land and buildings that Germany surrendered at

178

the end of the war, Germany had always been resolved not to pay any monetary war reparations at all. So it had borrowed exactly the same amount from America as the Allies had asked in total in reparations over a great many years under the terms of the Young Plan – with the intention of not repaying it.

Meanwhile, *Hungerkanzler* Brüning continued with his policy of 'austerity' in Germany, putting pressure on the whole world economy. In the autumn of 1930 he tightened the economic screw in Germany even further by ignoring parliament and ruling by decree. German unemployment insurance premiums were hiked to 6 per cent and salaries were slashed for members of parliament, the civil service, the Reichswehr and the railways, leading to salary reductions everywhere.

On 24th January 1931 frugal ex-warrior Brüning confronted an angry crowd with the explanation that 'ardour in financial and economic matters' was vital as this is the only way to reduce the 'tribute burden' of the reparations.[21]

In its review of the Leipzig Trade Fair on 4th April 1931 *The Economist* revealed that German industry had diverted all its production into exports, declaring:

'In pre-war days, when Germany was a lending and investing country, it was estimated that about ten per cent of the total production was exported ... But according to recent investigations by the Institute for Konjunkturforschung, the share that export bears to total sales varies as a rule between twenty and fifty per cent ... These figures reveal the gradual conquest by German industry of foreign markets.'

America had slapped on a tariff on all imports in 1930 in response to Japanese and German competition. The tariff had hit Britain and France's exports hard, but not Germany's exports because its heavily rationalised industry had merely reduced wages.[22] While the quantity of world trade would remain stationary in 1930, Germany's share doubled. In 1931 Germany would become the world's leading export country.[23]

WORLD TRADE IN 1931.

THE preliminary estimates of the foreign trade of the principal countries during the past year have now been published. The figures show that the economic storm which was raging over the world in 1930 had grown into a devastating hurricane by 1931 :—

VALUATION OF MERCHANDISE TRADE.
(In millions.)

Period.	Net Imports.		Domestic Exports.		Balance.
	Value.	Percentage change on previous Year.	Value.	Percentage change on previous Year.	Export Surplus (+) Import Surplus (−).
			FRANCE.		
	Francs.	%	Francs.	%	Francs.
1929	58,221	...	50,139	...	− 8,082
1930	52,344	− 10·1	42,829	− 14·6	− 9,515
1931	42,199	−· 19·4	30,421	− 29·0	−· 11,778
			GERMANY.		
	Rm.	%	Rm.	%	Rm.
1929	13,447	...	12,663	...	− 784
1930	10,393	− 22·7	11,328	− 10·5	+ 935
1931	6,721	− 35·5	9,205	− 18·8	+ 2,484
			ITALY.		
	Lire.	%	Lire.	%	Lire.
1929	21,665	...	15,236	...	− 6,429
1930	17,325	− 20·0	12,115	− 20·5	− 5,210
1931	11,620	− 33·0	10,040	− 8·3	− 1,580
			SWITZERLAND.		
	Francs.	%	Francs.	%	Francs.
1929	2,724	...	2,098	...	− 626
1930	2,565	−· 5·8	1,763	−· 16·0	− 802
1931	2,251	− 12·2	1,349	− 23·5	− 902
			UNITED KINGDOM.		
	£	%	£	%	£
1929	1,111	...	729	...	−· 382
1930	957	−· 13·9	571	− 21·7	− 386
1931	798	−· 16·6	389	− 31·9	−· 409
			UNITED STATES.*		
	$	%	$	%	$
1929	4,399	...	5,241	...	+ 842
1930	3,061	−· 30·4	3,843	− 26·7	+ 782
1931	2,090	−· 31·8	2,424	− 36·9	+ 334
			CANADA.*		
	$	%	$	%	$
1929	1,299	...	1,208	...	− 91
1930	1,008	−· 22·4	905	− 25·1	−· 103
1931	628	− 37·7	609	− 32·7	−· 19

* Includes transit trade.

In March 1931, Brüning abruptly announced a customs union with Austria, in direct contravention with the terms of the Treaty of Versailles. The French were horrified that Germany had so little respect for the Treaty. They withdrew their short-term loans from Austria in order to persuade her to abandon the plan. As Austria paid no attention to their pressure, depositors started queuing up outside Austria's beleaguered Kreditanstalt Bank.

Germany then said that its banks were under pressure too, additional increases in taxes were published, and *Hungerkanzler* Brüning, came hot-foot to England to enlist her help in saving the German people from the 'intolerable burden' of paying the war reparations.[24]

During Brüning's visit to England, Governor of the Bank of England Montagu Norman, advised by his old friend Hjalmar Schacht, declared that the crisis affecting the Kreditanstalt Bank was threatening the financial security of the Austrian nation and that all south-east Europe was on the brink of collapse.[25] One week later Britain tried to rescue the Kreditanstalt Bank, although by doing so it risked its own financial equilibrium.

The French were not impressed. Aware that the German industrialists had given Stalin a substantial loan in April,[26] the French argued that Germany was not poor but recalcitrant. The launching of the pocket battleship *Deutschland* in May was a further cause for alarm. They tried to persuade Germany to abandon its plans to build a second pocket battleship. Yet the only crumb of comfort that Germany gave them was that 'credits for a third battle cruiser will not, at this juncture, be allocated'.[27]

In June 1931 the financial situation in Germany seemed to get worse and worse. Soon the panic spread to German savers. On 7th December 1929 *The Economist* estimated that German national savings had reached the handsome total of

£1 billion,[28] but since that time their savings seemed to have evaporated. Gold and foreign exchange flooded out of Germany and panic reigned. On 20th June, President Herbert Hoover of America, who had fed the starving German people after the war, generously offered Europe a one-year moratorium on the payment of reparations and war debts. However, as no foreign exchange controls were imposed, German money continued to quit the supposedly 'sinking ship'.

Montagu Norman maintained his friendship with Schacht. British Prime Minister Ramsay MacDonald was equally pro-German. Dark-haired, illegitimate son of a maid servant, MacDonald had managed to reach the top of the Labour Party through his strength of character and organisational ability. A pacifist during the First World War, he travelled up and down the country, drawing crowds with his soft but compelling voice. Since 1918, he had become increasingly antagonistic towards Britain's historic enemy, France, eventually writing wryly in his diary in 1931: 'Germany needs help but the French act as a freezing mixture ... Again and again let it be said: France is the enemy; we shall pay with all our honour for that war.'[29]

On 3rd July, the Nordwolle, one of Germany's largest textile concerns, collapsed. Unfortunately its collapse affected the finances of the Danat Bank. The Danat Bank's failure caused a run on all the German banks and savings institutes, which had been starved of funds by the Reichsbank. Only later would it be discovered that the Danat Bank's collapse originated not from insolvency but from an order from government.[30] Its action was a calamity for German savers and caused consternation abroad but it had a silver lining. America decided to help.

On 21st July, a conference was called in London at which the German government managed to secure agreement to a 'Standstill' of the repayment of most of the 'banking credits in Germany expressed in foreign currency' for a six month period; naturally after the six month period the agreement would be renewed.

Keynes had described the German negotiator at the Versailles peace negotiations, Dr Melchior, as 'exquisitely clean, very well and neatly dressed' and almost professed himself 'in love with him'.[31] Now Dr Melchior was entrusted with telling America and the Allies, in the nicest possible way, that Germany was reneging on its debts. He remarked disgustedly to his colleague Hans Schäffer:

'What we have just experienced is the destruction of the capitalistic system. Yet the system depends on the strictest observation of the rules. This is the first time I have had to refuse to fulfil an obligation ... simply because the state required me to sign. The capitalist system in Germany will not survive such a deviation from its rules. For the deviations will constantly increase, and the system will accordingly dissolve.'[32]

Economic historians such as Guido Giacomo Preparata in his book *Conjuring Hitler: How Britain and America made the Third Reich* have alleged that the Bank of England engineered its banking crash in 1931. We can safely assume that this was the case. We can also presume, in view of Norman's close friendship with Schacht, that there was collusion with Germany. It is so much easier to get away with staging a banking crash, in the wake of another crash, than to do it on one's own and expose one's weakness to all.

In 1925 Britain had been inveigled into going onto the Gold Standard by Schacht and Benjamin Strong at too high a rate, but the Gold Standard had merely brought Britain misery and unemployment. Schacht was telling all and sundry that he intended to bring 'chaos' to the world system until Germany was allowed to abandon reparations payments.[33] Norman was sympathetic.

Norman was hoping that President Hoover's moratorium 'on all debts arising from the war', would soon be made permanent. In the meantime, although Britain had asked her workers to take yet more pay cuts, her exports were shrinking, and she was finding it impossible to compete on world markets. Indeed, after Germany's banking collapse, a run was immediately launched against sterling.

On 13th July 1931 the British released the Macmillan Report, which asserted that Britain was failing its industrial base. The report precipitated a crisis. On 29th July the Bank of England put its interest rate up 'only a point or two', which was deemed totally inadequate. That same day Montagu Norman, who suffered from permanent ill-health, collapsed during a meeting at the Treasury and disappeared, incognito, on a ship to Quebec. France and America offered funds to help the beleaguered country, but the money was belatedly and wastefully used by Norman's subordinates.

On 15th September, five hundred Scottish sailors mutinied because of a pay cut. That was the final straw and on 19th September, Britain deserted the Gold Standard. Nearly two dozen other nations followed Britain's lead.[34] Two days later Montagu Norman's ship docked at Liverpool and on 28th September he was back at the Bank of England, allegedly 'utterly bowled over on discovering the terrible truth' that Britain had devalued while he had been away.[35] He escaped all censure for the banking crisis.

At first American opinion seemed sympathetic to Britain's action. J P Morgan declared the devaluation to be 'a hopeful and not a discouraging event'. Other bankers declined to give their names but were quoted as saying, 'It was the correct move'; 'We had on our hands a patient who had to undergo an operation to save his life ... now the operation is over and we are feeling relieved.'[36] But then there was a terrible run against the dollar. Over the next five weeks European banks converted $750 million into gold, expecting that the United States would be the next to devalue. Naturally, as it had become an article of faith that Germany was poor, the French and the British were blamed for the run on the dollar.

The outflow came at a critical time of mounting US bank failures precipitated by the farming crisis. At the start of 1931 the Federal Reserve Bank of America had $4.7 billion in gold reserves. Nevertheless, by law, every $100 in Federal Reserve notes had to be backed by at least $40 in gold, and the remaining $60 by prime commercial bills. So, although America was still sitting on a mountain of gold, government paper was not allowed to be used to help in the crisis.[37]

In September 1931, Germany also had gold and foreign currency reserves to cover over 40 per cent of the value of the notes it had in circulation.[38] The only difference between Germany and America was that Germany had neatly (either temporarily or permanently!) divested itself of all its debts.

Gustav Krupp was unanimously elected Chairman of the executive board of the Reich Federation of German Industry[39] while *The New York Times* noted hopefully:

'It is held by many economists … that the very large export surpluses now being realised every month in foreign trade will keep Germany on the direct and natural way to recovery, and it is strongly argued that the one necessity is to follow the same road, even if additional sacrifices should prove to be inevitable.'[40]

The Americans did not realise that Brüning's aim in pursuing his deflationary policy was not to nurse Germany's recovery but to persuade the desperate German people to abandon democracy and vote for dictatorship under a Hohenzollern monarch.[41] Hugenberg also hated democracy, but he wanted an entirely different sort of dictator to the Kaiser. He felt that a 'man of the people' like Adolf Hitler would be much more likely to win the hearts of the German population. And he had the support of the coal cartel, which included Gustav Krupp, Albert Vögler and other powerful industrialists among its members, which had placed a royalty on every ton of coal in order to finance the Nazi party.[42]

So Hugenberg had plenty of money to organise a rally to woo the middle classes at one of the few places where the wearing of Nazi uniforms had not been forbidden, the little mountain spa of Bad Harzburg. Bad Harzburg was festooned for the occasion with flags in the old imperial colours, and fourteen generals, three princes, the military veterans association, the Stahlhelm, the former Pan-German Heinrich Class and Dr Schacht also attended.

Although the alleged purpose of the rally at Bad Harzburg was to engineer the fall of Heinrich Brüning's government, the occasion gave Hitler the opportunity to reassure the middle classes that he was a responsible person. He declared repeatedly, 'We are protecting Germany and the rest of the world against Bolshevism.' These words were just what the middle classes wanted to hear.

The German middle classes, like the British, were terrified of Communism, and with good reason. Stalin had allowed Russian kulaks of German origin to emigrate before he began his mass evacuations. The press relayed their horrific stories of Soviet atrocities against the kulaks and of the desecration of the Russian Orthodox churches to an appalled German public. The good German burghers turned to Hitler to protect them against the 'Bolsheviks' and to help them get back to work.

Germany was faced with huge unemployment because of *Hungerkanzler* Brüning's policies. However, the German government was in a better position to help the jobless than most of its neighbours because, besides the fortune in gold sitting in the Reichstag, it had a social-welfare system unsurpassed anywhere except in Britain, and amenities that commanded the wonder of the world.[43] It was also powerful enough to support ailing industries. In 1931 and 1932 the

Deutsche Bank continued to finance struggling car maker, Daimler-Benz because its Chairman, Emil Georg von Stauß, main board director of Deutsche Bank, and friend of Hermann Göring considered that Daimler-Benz's capacity for making war material was critical to the revival of Germany's armaments industry. BMW was also supported in order to guarantee Germany's ability for future military production.[44] In 1931 Dr Carl Duisberg, head of the supervisory board for I G Farben Executive, had sketched some of his ideas for the future in a geo-political book by General Haushofer:

'Only an integrated trading-bloc, stretching out from Bordeaux to Sofia will enable Europe to gain that innermost economic strength which is necessary to uphold her leading position in the world .... The longing for a thousand year Reich cries for a new approach. For such a purpose we can use the mirage of a pan-Europe.'[45]

Meanwhile the Nationalists, who formerly called themselves the Pan-Germans, continued with their policy of impoverishing the workers because they had managed to thwart the military from staging a coup in 1920 by staging a general strike.

In May 1932 the Communists, the DNVP and Hitler's National Socialists proposed a motion of no confidence in Brüning's cabinet because he declined to dismiss General Gröner, who had refused to lift the ban on Hitler's paramilitary organisation, the SA. Within one month of the ban eventually being lifted, 99 people were killed and 1,125 wounded in sickening violence.[46] On 30th May Brüning announced his entire cabinet's resignation.

In June 1932, a year after the German banking crash, the Hoover moratorium expired and there was another conference on the reparations. As Germany had nearly 6,000,000 unemployed, it was offered 90 per cent off its payments, but that was still not enough for Hitler. There was an election coming up and he used the issue in his election campaign. He won a massive majority in the 1932 elections with his crusade against the German people being forced to make any more reparations payments.

Hitler had a good propaganda issue to help his campaign but there were still many people in Germany who voted against him. Indeed, if the Social Democrats and Communists had joined forces at the polls, their votes would have matched Hitler's. Yet Stalin's deal with Krupp was still in force so 'At Moscow's order, the German Communist Party pronounced the Social Democrats enemy no.1'.[47] Only a few months later Hitler achieved supreme power. Coincidentally, after this, a new flight from the franc began.[48] The German money which had been squatting in France streamed back to Germany.

Gustav Krupp von Bohlen und Halbach

Former Pan-German Gustav Krupp, was said by witnesses to have been violently opposed to Hitler before he became Chancellor. However, once Hitler was ensconced in power, Krupp became, in the words of steel tycoon Fritz Thyssen, 'a super Nazi'.[49] Gustav Krupp had already prepared himself for the task. He later recalled, 'After the assumption of power by Adolf Hitler I had the honour to report to the Führer that Krupp stood ready, after a short warm-up, to begin the rearmament of the German people without any gaps of experience.'

The company expanded rapidly to over 100,000 employees and in August 1933 the Nazi salute became compulsory in all his factories. Those who refused to use it were classified as work shy and sent to concentration camps for re-education. Huge portraits of the Führer hung in Gustav's forbidding mansion, Villa Hügel, and every administration office was linked to Gestapo headquarters so that any employee overheard 'sniping at the regime' could be sent there for questioning.[50] Gustav contributed generously to Nazi propaganda in other countries too, designating members of his foreign sales force as members of the government's network. They estimated the industrial potential of possible enemies, including the United States, and forwarded their appreciation to Berlin.[51] In 1935 General Morgan, who had been British Military Representative on the Inter-Allied Council in Germany between 1919 and 1923, was astonished to find on his visit to Germany, that 'the great armament factories' were 'working night and day in triple shifts'.

The Americans were horrified by Germany's unemployment before Hitler. They still felt genuine warmth towards the land of so many of their forefathers. Germany seemed to be in dire straits in 1932 – and they were in dire straits too. They couldn't quite understand what had happened to their wonderful country. America in the 1920s was fizzing with wealth and happiness. According to one historian, 'during the second half of the 1920s the United States, with about three per cent of the world's population, accounted for forty-six per cent of its total industrial output. During the same period it produced seventy per cent of the world's oil and forty per cent of its coal.'[52]

Yet by 1932 America looked like a country which had been struck by a hurricane. In his book *In the Time of the Americans* author David Fromkin described how the Depression hit America:

'Between a quarter and a third of the entire workforce lost their jobs. Fifteen million Americans were out looking for work. In their ranks were not only farmers and factory hands but also professionals who had thought of themselves as insulated from economic distress. People who only a couple of years before had been lawyers or civil engineers or bankers or architects wandered round in a daze, hopeless and defeated, wondering where to sleep or to get food.' Industrial production had halved since 1929 and nearly 80 per cent fewer homes had been built.[53]

Americans did not blame Germany for their troubles. Their anger was directed at the Treaty of Versailles, which they had never ratified, and against the Allies for charging the 'enormous' and 'iniquitous' reparations ordered by the Treaty, which allegedly were responsible for condemning the German people to unemployment and misery similar to their own. Amos J Peaslee of the American Courier Service summed up American sentiment in the early 1930s when he maintained that America '... was almost a unit in laying the blame for all the world's troubles on the Versailles Treaty'. But he also professed his astonishment that in actual fact Germany had paid 'no' reparations'![54]

The Americans could not believe that the German hierarchy would throw their citizens out of work with the express purpose of tearing up the Treaty of Versailles and returning to war. Many Americans were of German extraction and felt that Germany was their close friend. Yet Hitler called America 'a deeply lazy country full of racial problems and social inequalities'. Other prominent Germans were also anti-American. In his book *Germany Plots with the Kremlin,* T H

Tetens wrote: 'The historic truth is that the German ruling class, industrialists, aristocrats, army officers and diplomats, have always viewed, with great apprehension, the United States as the chief antagonist and menace for Germany.'[55] So they continued to take concrete steps to impoverish America so that she would not interfere in any new war in Europe.

America was still reeling from the Great Depression in 1933. She had always regarded Germany as a Triple A customer. She had a large balance of payments surplus with Germany and held 40 per cent of Germany's long-term debt.[56] Unfortunately this made her uniquely vulnerable to German economic assault.

Cotton was America's chief export. Germany had been America's best customer since 1923. When Germany's imports of cotton halved in 1932, newspapers pointed out that if Hoover's moratorium on the payment of reparations was made permanent, it might be a small price to pay for the restoration of their market.[57] Yet although demands for reparations were abandoned in 1933, America's hopes for receiving a good price for her cotton were dashed.

Germany decided that it needed its foreign exchange for rearmament. It therefore offered only German beer and wine in payment for America's quality cotton. Cotton growers were not amused. Since the American government could not conjure up another large customer for their produce, they were faced with disaster. The handsome and infectiously self-confident new President, Franklin D Roosevelt, was landed with the problem. He instituted the American Adjustments Administration bureau, which paid landowners to leave land idle. Yet a vast expanse of 2.5 million hectares of quality cotton-growing land had to be ploughed up and crops left to rot because of the loss of trade with Germany. Another 'dust bowl' had been created, this time in America's cotton-growing area.

In 1934 Hitler appointed Schacht to become Minister of Economics. After unlocking the door to the banks, which held the astonishing 40 per cent cover for Germany's bank notes, Schacht decided on a policy of spending, but only by the state and the armaments manufacturers. He allocated so-called Mefo notes to the armaments manufacturers, and encouraged them to use them to massively expand their production, while he defrauded all Germany's creditors. As his former friends in America held the most German loans, they were naturally the worst affected.

On 9th April 1934 Schacht told Germany's medium-term and long-term creditors, 'A moratorium seems inevitable.' He declared that it was unnecessary to call an international conference 'to establish the complete incapacity of Germany to make transfers ... since the facts are clear to everybody'.[58]

On 14th June 1934 he declared a moratorium not only on Germany's long-term and medium-term debts, but also on the Dawes and Young Plan loans, which had been offered to Germany as sweeteners to persuade it to accept the agreements.[59]

America still believed that Germany was poor. The countries she was really irate with were the Allies. Small savers in America had lent the Allies money in the First World War, in the expectation that Germany would be defeated and the money repaid. Yet, contrary to their wishes in the mid-term elections on 5th November 1918, Germany had been given an Armistice. Then supposedly draconian war reparations had been imposed. Now, when US citizens most had need of the money, the French and the British were reneging on their debts.

Britain originally owed America £938 million in war debts, but she had doggedly continued to pay while receiving negligible cash sums from Germany. Meanwhile she had let all the Allies off their war debt payments to her many years before. In 1931 President Hoover had explicitly recognised the connection between the war debts owed to America and Germany's war reparations when he gave Germany and the Allies a moratorium on all debts payable from the war. So the British were confidently expecting that when America let Hitler off paying reparations that she would agree to the Allied war debts being cancelled too.

Indeed France said that she would never have accepted the 1929 Young Plan Reparations agreement except on that basis. The restoration of France after the First World War alone had cost £830 million and she had received practically nothing towards it. She was acutely worried by Hitler's arrival in power and was running out of money to complete the Maginot Line of fortifications.

Yet hundreds of American banks had gone bankrupt since Hoover's Moratorium and the Americans were seeking someone to blame. When the Allies refused to pay their war debts any longer, the impoverished Americans passed the infamous Johnson Act, forbidding any new loans to nations that had not repaid their First World War debts while Randolph Hearst's *New York American* declared of Britain's decision to abandon payment: 'Someday this will be regarded as the most tragic mistake in England's history.'

The Allies' war reparations demands have always been regarded as extortionate so it is worthwhile looking at how much Germany actually paid in reparations. The headline figure was the modest sum of £1,038,000,000. Yet as the Dawes and Young Plan loans had not been repaid, only £938,000,000 was actually received by the Allies before the Second World War, most being credited in the form of land, ships, colonies, etc., rather than in actual cash. The Czech economist G Borsky, in his book on the reparations called *The Greatest Swindle in the World*, estimated that the actual amount of cash that Germany had paid in total between

1919 and 1933 was £153 million net in cash reparations, or under £11 million a year.[60]

Meanwhile the American historian, Stephen A Schuker, assessed that Germany received a net inflow of funds from America since the First World War of 'no less than 17.75 milliard Reichsmarks,' (approximately £850 million) or 2.1 per cent of national income for the whole period from 1919–1931 and concluded: 'In price adjusted terms, this sum approached four times the total assistance that the United States government would provide to West Germany between 1948 to 1952 under the much-heralded Marshall Plan.'[61]

In the 1930s the Americans complained that the British were robbers for not paying their war debts. But who were the robbers here, the British or the Germans?

After the First World War, the Allies had felt too weak to enforce Articles 227 and 228 of the Treaty of Versailles, under whose provisions the Kaiser and all the rest of the major war criminals were to have been tried. The war reparations were the Versailles Treaty's final sanction to prevent Germany from returning to dictatorship, re-arming and going back to war. But, ultimately, the Allies were as unsuccessful with the reparations as they were with the trial of the Kaiser, the Generals and the politicians who masterminded the First World War.

After another war the Nazis would declare, 'Those dollar diplomats and cowboys are too untalented to cope with the problems of world politics.' Yet, the 'dollar diplomats' had never come across villains like 'the Prussians' before. If President Woodrow Wilson had not intervened at the end of September 1918 the German army on the Western Front would have been crushed, but Wilson's aim was to secure 'Peace without Victory' and that is what the well-meaning President managed to achieve. Germany spent the enormous sum of 48,911 billion Reichsmarks on re-arming in the seven years before the Second World War.[62]

194

The Allies and America were drifting farther and farther apart but Germany wanted to make sure that America stayed isolated, so it decided to transfer its purchases of cotton to Brazil, where there were lots of Nazi sympathisers. Between 1933 and 1938 Germany doubled her share of cotton imports from Brazil. The Brazilian economy thrived, but an economy needs cash too and Germany only paid in compensation marks, which had to be spent on German goods. Brazil desperately wanted to buy German armaments but lacked the money to pay for them. So in the end she decided to 'suspend the service' of her American loans in 1937[63] before signing a £8,280,000 armaments contract with Krupp in 1938.[64] American unemployment fell between 1934 and 1937 but after this new blow it shot up again.

America held over half of Germany's defunct long-term loans, Britain's share was 11.5 per cent. Yet Montagu Norman maintained his faith in Dr Schacht. Like so many Britons he was terrified of Communism. In 1934 Norman declared: 'Hitler and Schacht are the bulwarks of civilisation in Germany and the only friends we have ... If they fail, Communism will follow in Germany, and anything may follow in Europe'. In 1937 he became godfather to one of Schacht's grandchild. In 1938, after Germany's invasion of Czechoslovakia, Norman knowingly authorised the transfer of the Czech gold from the No 2 account with the Bank for International Settlements to the No 17 account, which was managed by the German Reichsbank.[65] Only a little while later Germany invaded Poland.

Was Montagu Norman a fellow traveller, a German agent or merely a fool in 1939? That is for a biographer to decide. Meanwhile, we can at least draw two conclusions, firstly, that Germany caused the Great Depression and secondly that Hitler and Stalin were nourished by Krupp and the Pan-Germans.

CHAPTER NINE

Germany and America's Aims at the End of the Second World War

After Hitler achieved office, the pre-First World War Pan-Germans, Heinrich Class and Alfred Hugenberg, became NSDAP members of the German Reichstag. Class remained a back-bencher but 68-year-old Hugenberg became Minister of Economics and Agriculture.

Hugenberg was not in his position for long. At the World Economic Conference the foreign press revealed that he had written a document disclosing his ambition to colonise Russia.[1] Stalin's suspicions about Germany were confirmed when trusted diplomat Maxim Litvinov told him that Schacht had told a French diplomat that Germany intended to divide up Ukraine with Poland.[2] Britain and France were alarmed, Stalin halted his friendship with Germany and Hugenberg lost his job.

Yet although Hugenberg had to relinquish his news agency, the Telegraph Union, because of the embarrassing revelation that he wanted Hitler to grab Ukraine, he was able to keep most of his extensive media interests, which could be relied upon to take a Nazi view of events.

Austria and Czechoslovakia were stepping stones to Ukraine so one would presume that Hugenberg approved of Hitler's decision to invade them in March 1938 and 1939. Hugenberg had also called for the 'annihilation' of the Polish population as early as 1899, so he must also have been happy with Hitler's invasion of Poland. Yet he should have been careful in his choice of words; Hitler was liable to take terms like 'annihilation' literally. The historian Ian Kershaw, in his study of Hitler, *Nemesis*, declared of Hitler's invasion of Poland:

'The treatment of the people of the newly conquered territory was unprecedented, its modern forms of barbarism evoking, though in even more terrible fashion, the worst barbaric subjugations of bygone centuries.'[3]

In January 1940 Hermann Göring decreed that a million Poles, including women, were to be recruited to work in Germany, three-quarters of them in agriculture. They were to be identified with the letter P, to be barred from all social contact with Germans, and also have their wages slashed to twenty-five Reichsmarks a month. As there was resistance it was decided to break the backbone of the Polish people. The authorities started with a programme of political murders before adopting a more comprehensive system of genocide. Selective food rationing was also introduced. By the autumn of 1940, the Germans in the cities got 2,600 calories a day, the Poles 938, and the Jews 369. By the spring of 1941 the Jews were dying and the Wehrmacht was reporting incidents of skilled workers collapsing at their workbenches.[4]

Beyond Poland lay Russia and the riches of Ukraine and the Caucasus, whose raw materials the German industrialists had appropriated in the First World War. But first Germany wanted to deal with France and Britain.

France's ownership of the Longwy-Briey iron ore field made an invasion of France essential, given the necessity of iron to make Germany's weapons. It was true that the Nazis had developed the vast low-grade iron ore deposits at Salzgitter. However, prominent Nazi Albert Vögler, who had funded Hitler's electoral campaign with a donation of half a million Reichsmarks in 1932,[5] had announced in the First World War that Germany would fight for 'a further ten years' to retain Longwy-Briey. So the invasion of France would be a priority.

France did not want another invasion. She was far poorer than outsiders believed as much of the loose change in French banks in 1932 had been German. After the money returned to Germany in 1933,[6] and Schacht became Hitler's Minister of Finance, Schacht adopted a fraudulent trading system, with the result that German manufacturers ordered a multitude of French goods and then refused to pay for them in cash. French and other European manufacturers lost a fortune before a barter system was organised.

France was surrounded by predatory Fascists in Italy, Spain and Germany. The French people become poorer, fearful and divided – ideal conditions for German spies, trained in the time-honoured methods of Bismarck's Wilhelm Stieber, to make mischief. France had tried to protect herself by creating the Maginot Line along her border with Germany but her borders with neutral Belgium and Luxembourg remained open to countries which did not respect international law and were happy to march into other people's countries – like Prussia/Germany!

France was not the only western European country to be robbed by Germany's system of trading in the 1930s. Soon most countries had to adopt a barter system when dealing with Germany. In 1936 Schacht instituted his so-called 'Drang nach Südostern'. In this brilliantly conceived deception, he offered to pay the south-east European countries – Greece, Hungary, Yugoslavia, Romania and Bulgaria – 30 per cent above the world price for their agricultural produce. They were naturally delighted at such an opportunity and offered to underwrite the deal by advancing the money to the producers and waiting for Germany to repay them. Schacht's next move was to sell the commodities to Rotterdam or London, either at the ruling market price or even below it. His third step was to inform his south-east European creditors that he was wholly unable to find the foreign exchange in the amounts required but that he was prepared to pay on his own terms in certain lines of manufactured goods – particularly armaments.[7] The weapons would be ready and waiting for Germany when it occupied their countries in the Second World War.

After Germany's invasion of Norway and Denmark, the German guns roared into life again on 10th May 1940. The Belgian fortifications on the river Maas were seized and German Army Group B marched towards the Maas River. The bulk of the French army, backed up by the British Expeditionary Force, marched rapidly north. Yet their prompt action was a prelude to catastrophe. While the British and the French were hurrying north, Germany's Army Group A was hurrying west through the hilly, thickly wooded region in south-eastern Belgium called the Ardennes, towards the Maas bridges between Dinant and Sedan. At 8.30 p.m. on 20th May the advanced guard of the Second Panzer Division arrived at Abbeville, where the river Somme flowed into the sea. The entire Dutch and Belgian armies, the British Expeditionary Force and the pick of the French army were trapped between the German armies. Although 370,000 men from the British army escaped by boat from Dunkirk, it was an immense victory for Germany.[8]

The German army seized 314,878 French rifles, 5,017 artillery pieces, 3.9 million shells and 2,170 French tanks. It also seized 4,260 train engines and 140,000 wagons from France, Belgium and Holland.[9] The German firms who worked the Longwy-Briey iron ore fields in the First World War reclaimed control of the mines but they had to share them with Hermann Göring who grabbed the biggest prize, the Wendel mining and steel conglomerate.[10] The Nazis also appropriated 81,000 tons of copper, plus substantial amounts of tin, nickel, petrol and oil,[11] plus great quantities of fish from Norway, dairy produce from Holland and Denmark, and wheat from France.

Hitler could look on his army's military success in Europe with satisfaction. Former Pan-German Heinrich Class, had always wanted, 'by hook or by crook', to create a great Germanic-led bloc in Europe called Mitteleuropa. France, Belgium, Luxembourg and the Netherlands all had important steel industries. They were also sophisticated manufacturers of cars, armaments, planes, electronic and consumer goods. Austria, Polish Silesia, the Czech Protectorate and northern Italy also had important industrial centres. By 1940 the European bloc that Germany had defeated, or coerced into joining, would have a combined GDP greater than either the United States or the British Empire.

Success bred success. As news of Germany's victory against France was heard throughout Europe, Romania stopped her oil deliveries to Britain and delivered them to Germany instead. Mussolini altered his 1939 position and declared war on Britain and France. General Franco shifted Spain's attitude from neutrality to that of a 'non-combatant'. Even Switzerland made positive noises and allowed her high-precision tools and twenty millimetre anti-aircraft guns to be sold exclusively to Germany.[12]

But all was not roses in the Mitteleuropa garden. Germany was an occupying force. It did not charge 'reparations' because the word was tainted. So it decided to charge 'occupation costs' instead. Its principle victim, France, bore the heaviest load. The French maintained that the twenty million Reichsmarks per day demanded of them was enough to feed an army of eighteen million men. As France had no cash, she handed over her shares in Romania's oil industry, her interests in Mines de Bor in Yugoslavia (Europe's largest copper mine), in payment. Cruellest of all, Germany continued with a twist to the barter economic system it had adopted in the 1930s. Young National Socialist civil servant, Dr Gustav Schlotterer, explained how the Nazis used the system to defraud defeated Europe:

'Our tendency is to use sleight of hand, guile and possibly violence to get the European states to sell their goods to Germany, but to leave their credits, when they build up, in Berlin.'

Exporters were encouraged to sell vital commodities to Germany but were paid not by the Germans but by their own governments, who had to raise taxes from their own citizens to pay their exporters. The Germans did sell goods in return, at high profits, which could be credited against imports, but the gap between what western European countries sent to Germany and the goods they received in payment got larger and larger. By 1944 the French government was owed 8.5 billion Reichsmarks.[13]

Germany had managed to appropriate a huge amount of French raw materials for nothing, and France would have to heap more and more taxes on its citizens in order to pay its unhappy producers. Meanwhile, although the 1,100,000 French who were forced to work in Germany were not paid slave wages like the Poles, they still received a third of the wages of Germany's allies, the Italians.[14] It was no wonder that although the Germans at first behaved with strict propriety in the western European countries which they occupied, after a while they had to bring in the Gestapo. The men who had consented to act as Germany's tools, Quisling in Norway, Mussert in Holland and Laval in France, became almost universally loathed.

The Armistice with France was signed in the same railway carriage as the one in which the Armistice was signed on 11th November 1918, and Hitler spent an afternoon sightseeing in Paris. He only had to polish off Britain now before turning his attention to Russia.

In the First World War the big economic associations were convinced that Germany could bring Britain to heel through the use of unrestricted submarine warfare. They threatened to withdraw war finance unless the policy was adopted in 1917. Yet Germany's determination to use unrestricted submarine warfare finally persuaded President Woodrow Wilson to declare war against Germany on 2nd April 1917 and Hitler was worried that 'unrestricted submarine warfare' would draw the US into the Second World War too.

Germany was not allowed to own or build submarines after the First World War. However, in 1935 it decided to build a new submarine force under the command of former First World War U-boat ace, Karl Dönitz. By the beginning of the Second World War, Dönitz had a large quantity of U-boats, including some already at sea, ready for action.

Dönitz had a brilliant new way of using his U-boats – in 'wolf packs'. Wolf packs consisted of a number of submarines spread out across the ocean to detect enemy ships. When one spied a convoy, it reported its position and tailed it, with the other submarines regrouping ahead of the convoy. At a signal, preferably at night, the 'wolf pack' closed in, overwhelming the convoy's anti-submarine escort ships.

On 3rd September 1939, two days after Hitler invaded Poland,[15] head of the German fleet, Grand Admiral Raeder, called for unrestricted submarine warfare. On the same day, the British liner, the SS *Athenia* was torpedoed. However, it transpired that there were twenty-eight Americans among the hundred and twelve passengers who lost their lives.[16]

Hitler was dismayed. He did not want history to repeat itself and America to become involved in his new war. He forbade attacks on all passenger ships, whatever their nationality. Nevertheless Admiral Raeder still advocated an all-out submarine war against England, straight away, declaring: 'Even the threat of America's entry into the war ... must not give rise to any objections. The earlier and the more ruthlessly we commence ... the shorter the duration of the war'.[17]

On 4th November 1939 President Roosevelt announced America's neutrality and delineated 'combat zones' in the vicinity of Britain and France out of bounds to American ships. That gave the German submarines an area they could safely operate in. But Hitler was still worried about giving the US an excuse to declare war.

By the summer of 1940 the U-boats were a real threat to Britain. Between June 1940 and March 1941, the U-boats sank over two million tons of British shipping[18] and continued with deadly success until the Enigma cipher was broken. Winston Churchill, who had returned to his First World War position as First Lord of the Admiralty, would later disclose that 'the only thing that ever really frightened me during the war was the U-boat peril'. But Hitler did not give the production of U-boats sufficient priority at the start of the war. Instead, after the British turned down his offer of an imperial partnership, he ordered the invasion of Britain to go ahead.[19]

It was lucky that Hitler's so-called 'Operation Sea Lion' involved a battle for the skies, and a sea crossing, before the Panzers could roll across Britain's green and pleasant land, as the evacuated British army had to abandon all its military equipment at Dunkirk. But Hitler would have to move fast. Three days after General von Kleist secured his great victory against France, President Roosevelt proposed the construction of the world's largest military-industrial complex, capable of supplying the US with 50,000 aircraft a year, and available to Britain on Lend-Lease.[20] Admiral Raeder consoled the Führer that the cost to Britain would be high. In his view the British Empire would not crumble but would have to submit to radical alterations, which would result in it giving America equal power.[21]

The former Pan-Germans, who became the Nationalists and were now part of Hitler's administration, had never contemplated the invasion of Britain in the First World War and there were many arguments against it in 1940. For a start the German navy had already been depleted in battle. The invasion of Norway had been expensive in shipping terms because the Oslo garrison destroyed Germany's newest heavy cruiser, the *Blücher*, and the Royal Navy inflicted damage on the *Gneisenau, Scharnhorst, Lützow, Nurnberg* and the *Leipzig*. So Raeder dryly told Hitler that the invasion of Britain could only be contemplated after air superiority had been achieved.

Although the German air force had some wonderful fighters, like the Messerschmitt 109, many believed that the Luftwaffe needed a much larger and more powerful fleet of bombers and long-range fighter escorts to deal the killer blow against Britain. In July 1940, the Luftwaffe focused on bombing coastal shipping convoys and ports like Portsmouth; in August it concentrated on RAF airfields and attacking the hangars repairing and preserving the precious Spitfire and Hurricane planes. Finally, after an alleged Allied provocation, Hitler decided to bomb British cities, even managing to hit Buckingham Palace on 10th and 13th September. Yet by October, Britain's days of fear and anguish were over. The Battle of Britain had been won by Britain's brave air force, helped by pilots from Poland, Czechoslovakia, New Zealand, Australia, Canada, South Africa and Belgium, and volunteers from neutral Ireland and America. The situation continued to be worrying but the threat of invasion had faded. Hitler turned his attention to Russia.

Before invading Russia, Hitler took the precaution of concluding a Tripartite Pact with Italy and Japan. He encouraged the Japanese to invade Singapore, asserting that the

American fleet was too puny to intervene, hoping that America's fear of Japan's predatory intentions would keep her preoccupied in the Pacific.[22]

The Tripartite Pact did not intimidate Roosevelt. In fact it had the opposite effect. In November 1940, after Roosevelt was re-elected for a third term, he immediately embarked on a massive expansion of his armaments programme. Germany's anti-Semitic embassy in Washington had only one explanation:

'As an exponent of Jewry ... Roosevelt wants England to go on fighting and to prolong the war ... until the armaments effort of the United States is fully in gear ...'[23]

Yet Roosevelt had made a measured response to the threat of war against his country. Although he reassured American fathers and mothers before his re-election for a third term by saying, 'I have said this before, but I shall say it again and again and again: Your boys are not going to be sent into any foreign war.'[24] His decision to vastly increase his armaments would be fully justified when Germany's ally, Japan, invaded Pearl Harbor on 7th December 1941.

In 1939 Japanese Minister of Foreign Affairs, Yosuke Matsuoka, stated that the influence of American citizens of German origin was so strong in the US that it was most unlikely that America would go to war against Germany.[25] German-American farmers in states like Wisconsin, Minnesota and North Dakota, which had paradoxically been the hardest-hit by Stalin's deluge of wheat in the Great Depression, did not know of Krupp's assistance to Stalin and were reluctant to send their boys to fight against the land of their forefathers in the Second World War. However, Japan's attack on Pearl Harbor was an affront to the American nation, which even they could not tolerate. When Germany and Italy declared war on America on 11th December 1941, and the country was faced with war on two fronts, they were happy that Roosevelt had prepared the country for the challenge.

Hitler's Tripartite Pact with Italy and Japan was eventually enlarged to include Hungary, Romania, Slovakia, Bulgaria, Yugoslavia (after a month lost in war), and Croatia. Then Hitler was ready for his grand scheme, the invasion of Russia.

Hitler has been condemned for his decision to invade Russia. He had such a large European empire in 1941 that people could not imagine why he wanted to venture further. Yet Hugenberg was obviously in favour of the invasion and if one looked at the First World War map of the German 'New Order' in the East in summer 1918, one can see why.

Although Germany was tactful enough not to call the areas it had conquered in Russia in 1918 'Empire' to avoid upsetting President Woodrow Wilson, it was apparent that it controlled a vast area. It called Ukraine and Crimea 'territories of closest economic involvement with Germany', Poland and Lithuania 'territories of direct German influence', Estonia, Livonia and Georgia 'areas of German settlement', while Finland and Romania were termed 'territories of political and economic connection with Germany'. The Province of the Don Cossacks and the Kuban were named spheres of influence, with raw material bases demanded by Germany; finally Azerbaijan and Armenia were said to be 'closely connected with the Central Powers'.[26]

This empire had been easy to snatch from the Bolsheviks in 1918. So in theory the unloved Soviet Union should be easy to invade again. This was certainly Hitler's opinion.[27] But unknown to Hitler and the rest of the German people, heavy German industry had been supporting the Bolsheviks. Former Pan-German and present Nazi supporter, Krupp, had persuaded the German government to cancel all Germany's wartime loans at Rapallo in 1922 so that the German army could train in Russia,[28] with the quid pro quo that the Soviet army could be trained by Germany. Krupp also undertook to help Stalin modernise the Soviet army's equipment in 1928 when the friendless Bolshevik empire had only ninety-two tanks.

Although the German steel and armaments concern of Rheinmetall concluded the agreement to provide the Soviets with anti-tank guns, howitzers and machine guns, the most significant contract was concluded with the firm of Krupp on 17th June 1929. Under this agreement Krupp provided the technical know-how to some of the largest enterprises in the Soviet Union – Barrikad, Zlatoustovskii, Krasnyi Putilovets, Krasnow Sormove and Elektrostal. This led to a significant improvement in steel casting in open-hearth furnaces, including those needed for military production of carbide and specialised steel,[29] which could be used in the manufacture of tanks. In 1928 the Red Army had only 92 tanks. By 1932 it had 1401.[30] By the 1940s Stalin was able to create a formidable modern army with tanks that could beat the Panzers.

Krupp had supported Stalin because he was a ruthless individual who could be relied upon to persuade the German Communists to vote with Hugenberg's DNVP and Hitler's NSDAP in the Reichstag. But it appeared that Hitler knew nothing of Krupp's assistance for Stalin's armaments industry. He was consumed with hatred of the Communists and believed that the hapless citizens dwelling in the Soviet Union needed wiping from the face of the earth.

In 1912 Pan-German Heinrich Class, who became part of Hitler's administration in the 1930s, wrote in his book, *If I were the Kaiser*: 'Since we have broached the question of evacuation (of native populations) in passing, so to speak, it is perhaps not out of order to speak of it publicly on occasion.'

In the Second World War, Hitler declared that Russia was populated by 'Untermensch' Slavs, ruled by 'Jewish Bolshevik' masters. Through his invasion he hoped to kill two birds with one stone, slaughtering or enslaving the majority of the Russian population and wiping out the Jews. Over a million

Jews were slaughtered even before the Final Solution massacres started.

Hitler called his plan to invade Russia 'Operation Barbarossa'. On 22nd June 1941, over four million soldiers of the Axis powers invaded the Soviet Union along a 2,900 km front; a month later 'the Final Solution of the Jewish question' was authorised by Reichsmarschall Hermann Göring. It would kill six million Jews.

Hitler originally stated, in his Directive 34, that his war aims were to take the Crimea, the Donets Basin in eastern Ukraine and the Caucasian oilfields. These aims were remarkably similar to Germany's objectives in the First World War. However, after the German army's striking successes in the summer of 1941, the great tank general, Heinz Guderian, wanted to march to Moscow.

The Führer was reluctant to accept Guderian's plea for a march on Moscow. 'My generals,' he declared, 'know nothing about the economic aspects of the war'. The land around Moscow was not rich in minerals. It was Ukraine's iron ore, manganese and coal in the Donets Basin, that the German armaments makers coveted and the armaments factories which used them. Stalin hastily moved his armour plate mill from Mariupol to beyond the Ural Mountains, even though the fighting was still hundreds of miles away. The sprawling tube-rolling mill at Dnepropetrovsk was also dismantled and 283 major industrial enterprises rapidly evacuated from Ukraine.

Meanwhile Guderian's superiors, Generals von Bock and Halder, put Guderian's proposal to march to Moscow to Field Marshal von Brauchitsch. Hitler surprised them by agreeing to fly to von Bock's headquarters at Novy Borisov to discuss the way forward.

During the German army's successful First World War invasion, it bypassed St Petersburg and never went near Moscow. However, Hitler interviewed Generals von Bock,

Halder and von Brauchitsch separately about the prospects for taking Moscow and changed his mind.[31] The siege of Leningrad started in September 1941 and the battle for Moscow started in October.

The Abwehr estimated that the Soviets had two hundred combat-ready divisions at the start of the war and came in for criticism when the German army faltered. The number of Soviet divisions seemed much higher than they had told him but this was because Stalin had organised the home front into a paramilitary organisation, with thirty-six million members, called Osoaviakhim (30 per cent of whom were women), whose specialities were harassment, night attacks and guerrilla activities. Loaded on to convoys without front-line training, they were taken to combat areas, tipped out and dispatched headlong against the superbly disciplined soldiers of the Wehrmacht. Machine gun squads brought up the rear to prevent 'unauthorised withdrawals'. The resulting casualties were appalling.[32]

In Operation Barbarossa the German forces captured over three million Soviet prisoners of war, most of whom would be deliberately starved to death as part of Hitler's 'Hunger Plan' to diminish Eastern Europe's population.[33] Yet neither Leningrad nor Moscow would fall into German hands and the carnage was only just beginning. In 1942 the Axis powers launched a summer offensive to seize the oilfields of the Caucasus and to occupy the Kuban steppes.

By the end of the 1930s Gustav Krupp became senile. His son Alfried took control. Alfried Krupp had a hawk-like nose, sunken cheeks and a sardonic mouth. His eyes were flat and faded, and his manner with strangers, wary. He had enormous self-control and soon would preside over a vast slave empire.

In the First World War the Allied soldiers who became prisoners of war were treated like slaves. Some of the British prisoners of war in Germany were sent to Angersee, Mitau,

Wainoden and Libau prisoner of war camps on the Eastern Front, where they were overworked, deliberately starved, denied food parcels and suffered from frostbite. Conditions for those imprisoned on the Western Front were equally bad, with guards using 'shocking barbarity'.[34]

In 1925 the Geneva Convention came into force, which set a minimum standard that applied to the Allied and American prisoners of war in the Second World War. The Germans did not, however, apply the same rules to the Soviet prisoners of war.

In 1942 Alfried Krupp attended a session of the Central Planning Board in which it was decided to impress 45,000 Russian civilians into the steel plants Germany owned or had conquered, 120,000 prisoners of war and 6,000 civilians into the coal mines, and to set the medical standards for recruiting the Russian prisoners of war lower than those required of Germans employed in the coal mines. He also had work for foreign saboteurs and Jews.[35]

Alfried was short of labour. He thought that the 'Final Solution' was wasteful. He told the Führer that every party member favoured the liquidation of 'Jews, foreign saboteurs, anti-Nazi Germans, gypsies, criminals and anti-social elements' but he could see no reason why they should not contribute something to the Fatherland before they died. Therefore, in theory, one could call him 'the saviour' of at least a few of the Jews, who managed to survive the rigours of Auschwitz and elsewhere. But it did not appear like that to them.

After new arrivals had been issued with wooden clogs, Krupp blankets stamped with the three interlocking shields and the firm's prison uniforms the segregation began. Jews, at the bottom of the totem, wore yellow cloth tags, with the heads of the Jewish girls shaved to form grotesque designs. Russian slaves wore white initials SR and the Poles were painted with a big P. Names were forbidden, individuals were known only by their numbers. They were put to work constructing a manufacturing plant for automatic weapons at Auschwitz.[36] When the Russians were taken to Germany it was decreed that they 'must be strictly segregated from the German population, other foreign workers, and all prisoners of war. They were to be accommodated in closed camps from which they could only leave under armed guard, to go to their place of work'.

On 14th March 1942 the tool shop supervisor complained that the rations given to the Russians were so inadequate that they were getting weaker by the day. He asserted that with so little nourishment they were too feeble even to be able to tighten a turning part; if care was not taken to change the feeding arrangements, 'their employment, and all the expense connected with it, would have been in vain'.

Krupp was one of the few firms whose SS contract permitted it to make its own arrangements for feeding slaves, thus enabling it to cut its allotted four marks per diem payments to Himmler. I G Farben was also allowed to make its own arrangements, but Farben slaves were at least given the full ration, with supplementary meals provided for men assigned to heavy duty. Alfried ignored both the Führer and the army and the German population's call for better conditions for the Russians. At the Nuremberg trials the eminent Washington attorney Drexel A Sprecher, would declare that 'Alfried's exploitation of slave labour was worse than that of any other industrialist, including I G Farben.'[37]

By 1943, with the help of slave labour, Krupp sales reached an all-time peak, surpassing the record year of 1939. Alfried was the king of the continent's greatest industrial empire, no one in Europe could challenge him; he held seven high offices in the government and the National Socialist Party, each of which entitled him to immediate access to Hitler. Indeed the Führer even allowed Krupp to call his company 'a State within a State'.[38]

Things were not going so well on the battlefront however. Neither Moscow nor Leningrad fell into German hands, and the Germans experienced a terrible defeat at Stalingrad. With the failure of the final large offensive at Kursk, the German army was on the retreat. The Eastern Front caused 95 per cent of all the army's casualties between 1941 and 1944.

Germany was on the retreat on the Western Front as well as in the east. The Allies won a decisive victory at the second battle of El Alamein in the autumn of 1942 and in September 1943 they invaded the Italian mainland. Soon the American and Allied invasion of Normandy would commence. Then the Americans would attack Germany. This time the Americans would insist on the German army's 'unconditional surrender' if the Soviets didn't get to Berlin first.

By 1943 Hugenberg could see the writing on the wall for Hitler but all may not have been lost for Krupp and his friends. Their use of 'slave' and indentured labour had made them potentially much richer than the Allies after the Second World War. Despite their shattered cities, they felt that there was still hope for the future.

On 10th October 1944 there was a meeting at the Rotes Haus, the famous old hotel in Strasbourg, which was in German hands. Among those present were representatives from Krupp, Rheinmetall, Messerschmitt, Volkswagen and other major industrial concerns. SS Obergruppenfuhrer, Dr Scheid, who presided, outlined how the Nazi empire could survive after defeat.

He stated that all the industrial material in France should be evacuated to Germany immediately. From then on German industry should realise that the war could still be won if it took steps in preparation for a post-war commercial campaign. Each industrialist should make contacts and alliances with foreign firms, but this should be done individually and without attracting any suspicion.

As examples, Dr Scheid cited the fact that patents for stainless steel belonged to the Chemical Foundation Inc. and the Krupp Company jointly. US Steel Corporation, Carnegie Illinois, American Steel and Wire, National Tube, etc., were thereby under an obligation to work with the Krupp concern. He also cited Zeiss Company, the Leisa Company and the Hamburg-American Line as firms which had been especially effective in protecting German interests abroad and gave their New York addresses to the industrialists.

The German industrialists were already increasing their patent registrations[39] and placing their funds in neutral countries abroad, especially in Spain and in Switzerland through the offices of the Basler Handelsbank and the Schweizerische Kreditanstalt of Zurich. Dr Scheid also stressed that the ground must be laid for borrowing considerable sums from foreign countries after the war.

Following this meeting a smaller pivotal meeting was held, presided over by Dr Bosse of the German Armaments industry, and attended only by representatives from Krupp, Hecho and Rochling. At this meeting it was stated that, although the war was practically lost, the Nazi party would continue fighting until a guarantee of the unity of Germany could be obtained.

One week later, on 18th October, Adolf Hitler officially announced the existence of the *Volkssturm*[40] comprising the elderly from all walks of life, those previously considered unfit for military service, former industrial workers and teenagers. Each Nazi party district leader, or *Gauleiter* was to be in charge of instilling the *Volkssturm* with fanaticism. Newspapers would spread the word, not only of the Red Army's atrocities but also of atrocities committed by the Americans (with their black troops portrayed as the culprits) and the members of the *Volkssturm's* fighting spirit would also be stiffened by the Hitler Youth and regular soldiers. On 16th September Hitler had already declared that 'every block of houses in a German city, every town, must become a fortress on which the enemy is either bled to death or in which its defences are buried beneath (the rubble) in man to man combat'. [41] By February 1945 even women and girls were conscripted to join and given instructions on the use of small-arms, bazookas, machine-guns and hand-grenades.[42] The *Volkssturm's* losses were appalling. The German military historian, Rüdiger Overmans, concluded that approximately 1.23 million German military personnel (including *Volkssturm* men, who suffered more than 50 per cent of the entire losses) would die in the final four months of the war. This represented an average of 300,000 deaths per month, the highest average of the war. [43]

Industrial representatives at the Red House were also told that they should increase post-war exports and prepare themselves to finance the Nazi party, which would be forced to go underground. The government had accumulated large reserves from appropriating gold, raw materials, foreign reserves and 'occupation costs' from invaded countries. From now until the end of the war it promised to allocate large sums to the industrialists so that they could establish a secure post-war foundation in foreign countries.

The armaments factories were also asked to create small high-tech research bureaux which could be absolutely independent and have no known connection with the factory. They would receive plans and drawings of new weapons as well as documents which they would need to continue their research. They were to be established in large cities where they could be most successfully hidden, as well as in little villages near sources of hydro-electric power, where they could pretend to be studying the development of water resources. The existence of these research institutes was to be known only by a few in each industry and must not be allowed to fall into enemy hands.[44]

The V-2 rocket was the world's first long-range guided missile. Twelve thousand forced labourers had reportedly been killed bringing it into production. It managed to hit targets in London, Antwerp and Liège. When Germany collapsed, teams from the US, Britain and Russia raced to capture the key manufacturing sites. However, the research that the Americans and the Russians were most interested in was Germany's nuclear weapon development programme.

In 2005 a book would be published by a German historian claiming that Germany tested a 'small atom bomb' in 1945. This claim was vehemently refuted in the press, but it was widely believed that 'during the last months of the war, a small group of scientists working in secret under the nuclear scientist Kurt Diebner, and with the strong support of the physicist Walther Gerlach' built and tested 'a nuclear device'.[45]

Germany would exact a huge price from America for not developing its own nuclear weapons during the Cold War.

Meanwhile, Alfried Krupp managed to jettison his war bonds, to cash in his claims for war damages and to collect his outstanding debts from the Reich. Altogether 162,000,000,000 marks of what would become worthless paper[46] was sold off as Alfried squirrelled his cash abroad. Other industrialists were encouraged to do likewise.

At the end of the First World War, with the German army facing defeat, the Allies and America started to look out for their own interests. In 1918 President Woodrow Wilson did not view the British as his cousins, nor did he share Britain's view that the British Empire had been a force for peace in the world. So he advocated the principle of 'self-determination' for nations, believing that the nations which had formally been part of the British Empire could stand on their own two feet.

Wilson's principle of 'self-determination' on the basis of language has become the basis for countless nations, large and small, to achieve their dream of statehood since that time. However, in the 1920s, the doctrine merely prevented states like Bavaria from escaping from Bismarck's Reich, while gnawing away at the power of the multilingual British and French Empires.

In 1945, with the approach of peace, Americans remembered that the British did not repay all their war debts after the First World War and blamed them and the 'iniquities' of the Treaty of Versailles (which they had not ratified) for their misery and unemployment in the 1930s. They did not know of the magnitude of the suffering that Germany had inflicted during the Second World War, not only upon the Jews but also upon its millions of slave labourers from Russia, Ukraine, Poland and the rest of Europe. They also conveniently forgot that had they supported the Allies in enforcing the payment of war reparations, their war debts would have been paid.

Some Americans even actively disliked the sanctimonious British and believed, like Harold Russell (who would portray a vet who lost both hands in the war in the film *The Best Years of our Lives*), that 'The Germans and Japs had nothing against us. They just wanted to fight the Limeys [a derogative term for the British] and the Reds.'

So, whereas in 1940 Admiral Raeder envisaged Britain having to share its empire with America after the Second World War, with Britain as the junior partner, many Americans believed by 1945 that the British Empire was past its 'sell-by' date. It was high time that the British and other European empires were extinguished altogether under the principle of 'self-determination'. Hopefully the United Nations could take over Britain's role as guardian of the peace.

The Germans, on the other hand, did believe in empires. That was why they had started two world wars, to achieve Mitteleuropa and Lebensraum. Despite the ravages brought about by Allied bombing, the country could yet rise like a phoenix from the ashes after the Second World War, if it were allowed to keep the coal-rich Ruhr.

In 1942 Reich Minister for Economic Affairs Walter Funk (who would later be indicted at Nuremberg), stated his ambition for a Mitteleuropa-type empire in Europe, declaring: 'Only on the foundation of such a European economic area can Europe really win the battle against Bolshevism and Americanism.' That eventually would become Germany's ambition.

In 1945, the Soviet army came crashing through the Berlin suburbs. The poor Russian soldiers were astonished at the wealth they saw there. The abandoned furniture, well-stocked libraries and pavements neatly planted with trees, begged the question as to why the German army had invaded 'impoverished downtrodden Russia'[47] in the first place. They responded with enthusiasm to Stalin's encouragement 'to rape and pillage' their country's former tormentors. Allegedly two million German women were raped and tens of thousands committed suicide after the Russians invaded.[48] The German military/industrial leadership had been preparing to lay all the blame for the carnage and atrocities of the Second World War on Hitler alone, but now there was another monster to share the blame – Stalin.

CHAPTER TEN

Who Won the Peace after the Second World War?

In October 1918, at the end of the First World War, the *Boston Herald* pleaded for President Wilson to demand the German army's 'unconditional surrender', asserting: 'Unconditional surrender is not alone the sole course for us, but it is the best for our enemies. The German people and their rulers must trust to the magnanimity of the Allies. The hour of reckoning has come, and the reckoning cannot be a matter of bargain and sale.'

On 7th May 1945, at the end of the Second World War, America and the Allies secured the German army's 'unconditional surrender'. The Americans now felt that they could give Germany the sort of magnanimous peace that they believed the Allies failed to give at Versailles, but a lot of water had passed under the bridge since the *Boston Herald* made its plea for a magnanimous peace in 1918.

Germany was not weak or the victim of injustice after the Treaty of Versailles, but strong and recalcitrant. Equipped with a powerful industrial base, propaganda, guile and ruthless economic manipulation, the German military/industrial clique managed to reduce their enemies to poverty and live to fight another day. Adolf Hitler elevated being 'German'

218

and part of the 'Master Race', to the status of a religion and not only killed people on the battlefield but systematically tried to exterminate the Jewish race, and millions of Poles, Russians and gypsies too. Was there any hope for Germany after its soldiers were defeated?

In 1944, Chief of the Intelligence Division of the German High Command, Admiral Canaris, told his superiors that there was still hope for Germany, even after a crushing military defeat, because of the good will felt towards them among Republican Americans. However, he also felt that Germany could do a deal with Russia, declaring:

'We must assume that the Slavs will do everything in order to retaliate against the harsh treatment we have inflicted upon them. In spite of everything, no effort should be spared to stir up ... political animosity inside the Anglo-Saxon countries which would enrage the Soviets ... In the event of a negotiated peace, or should we be defeated, Germany would have everything to gain – in the long run – by joining the East.'[1]

German heavy industry had a long association with the Bolsheviks. In 1918 the German leadership declared: 'The Bolsheviks are a very evil and antipathetic people. Nevertheless, politics have always been utilitarian and will be so for a long time.'

In the 1920s it assisted Lenin in return for Lenin allowing the German army to secretly train on the Russian steppes. In the 1930s it helped Stalin modernise his economy and armaments system, in return for his help in persuading the German Communists to vote for Hitler. Germany and the Soviet Union were also partners in dreadful crimes between 1939 and 1941. German school leavers had been fighting and dying in the last desperate battles of the Second World War, but the country's industrial leaders were still confident about the future. Despite the bombing of Germany's cities, the country remained the world's third-strongest industrial power through its use of slave labour and the organised looting of occupied countries. It had also secreted vast sums abroad through bearer shares in holding companies, which could only be traced with immense difficulty.[2]

A political deal with the Soviets was not a serious option but it could be used as a negotiating tool. Admiral Canaris thought that Germany should concentrate on securing a favourable deal with America, declaring: 'There is great fear in the USA of Bolshevism. The opposition against Roosevelt's alliance with Stalin grows constantly. Our chances for success are good, if we succeed to stir up influential circles against Roosevelt's policy', of allying America with the Communists.[3]

By 11th May 1945, Otto A Friedrich, wartime Deputy Reich Plenipotentiary for Rubber, and soon to become an influential spokesman for West German industry, wrote confidently in his diary, 'the latent tension between Russia and the Western powers provides us with the opportunity to work our way up to the status of a new subject.'[4]

President Roosevelt died on 12th April 1945. On 8th May new American President, Harry S Truman, had a very special celebration for his birthday. VE Day was the public holiday to mark the 'unconditional surrender' of the Nazi forces in Germany.

In contrast to Roosevelt, who came from a wealthy, privileged background, Harry S Truman was a plain-speaking man from Independence, Missouri, who spent much of his youth as a dirt-poor farmer on family land that was later repossessed by the bank. A snappy dresser, who always wore a double-breasted, light-coloured suit, he disliked the 'snobbery' of the smooth Ivy League officials, particularly those from the Foreign Service (who might have been more pro-British!). He called them 'the men in striped pants'.[5]

The British were 'America's least trusted ally' after the Second World War. Americans disliked Britain's high-profile empire and accused Britain of sucking the life-blood out of Germany with her reparations after the First World War. Some even believed that the Treaty of Versailles, which they had never ratified, had been responsible for Hitler and the Second World War. And to cap it all, Britain had refused to continue paying her war debts in the 1930s, when Americans were in most need of the money.

In the autumn of 1945 John Maynard Keynes, who had been elevated to become Lord Keynes, was sent to America to secure a loan for Britain. Lord Keynes insisted that without help, and a lot of it, 'we have not a hope of escaping what might be considered, without exaggeration, a financial Dunkirk'.[6]

Keynes believed that he would be warmly welcomed in Washington, even though his impertinent and incorrect comments about President Woodrow Wilson being 'led by the nose' by British Prime Minister Lloyd George, at the Versailles Conference[7] had been bandied about in the 1920 American Presidential elections and grated on Americans ever since. Indeed, Keynes's statement that 'The poor President would be playing blind man's buff' at Versailles could have been one of the reasons why the Americans were so insistent on blaming the Allies rather than President Wilson for the defects of the Treaty of Versailles!

Keynes asked for an interest-free loan of $3.5 billion. However, he ultimately agreed to pay $3.75 billion at two per cent interest over fifty years, with the small print revealing that Britain must forego its system of 'imperial preferences' which bound the empire together, in order to secure the money. Keynes also accepted that the repayment should be fixed in dollars and that sterling must become a freely convertible currency within a year of the loan being agreed. Britain was aghast at the terms.

Lord Beaverbrook, a tough negotiator, who was Canadian by birth and a firm believer in the Commonwealth, contended that Britain did not need the loan. He argued that Canada and the rest of the empire could provide the raw materials that Britain required and nearly caused a constitutional crisis between the Lords and the Commons over the issue.[8]

Another problem was Keynes' undertaking to repay in dollars. A nation at the centre of an empire like Britain could not wipe out its savers and indulge in a Great Inflation like Germany. However, every country had to have a little inflation after a World War. It would have been more sensible for Keynes to advise the Socialist government to bow to the inevitable, and devalue the pound in 1945, before going cap in hand to America. As it was, there would soon be a 'run on the pound', leading to a 30 per cent devaluation of sterling in 1949. So the American loan would become increasingly costly.

Truman was acutely suspicious of Britain but looked forward to meeting America's other major wartime ally on the Western Front – Joseph Stalin.

The Second World War had aged Stalin. At sixty-seven years old he looked shorter than his five feet four inches and had developed a paunch that was not entirely hidden by the baggy trousers and grey square-cut tunics that hung loosely around his body. He lost his temper more frequently and his formerly amber eyes lit up in a 'flash of menace and fury' when he heard something which displeased him. However, he still had a phenomenal memory and was a formidable negotiator.[9]

Truman's meeting with Stalin was a disappointment. He summed up his experience in a letter he penned for his Secretary of State, Dean Acheson:

'Russia had no program except to take over the free part of Europe, kill as many Germans as possible, and fool the Western Alliance. Britain only wanted to control the eastern Mediterranean, keep India, oil in Persia, the Suez Canal, and whatever else was floating loose.

'There was an innocent idealist at one corner of that Round Table who wanted free waterways, Danube-Rhine-Kiel Canal, Suez, Black Sea Straits, Panama, and a restoration of Germany ...' and other European and Asian states.

'But a large number of agreements were reached in spite of the setup – only to be broken as soon as the unconscionable Russian Dictator returned to Moscow!'[10]

It would be easy for America to destroy Britain's empire, although America would actually diminish her own power and influence in the process. However, Truman quickly discovered the threat that Stalin posed. By July 1945, Stalin effectively controlled the Baltic States, Poland, Czechoslovakia, Hungary, Bulgaria and Romania, and was busy installing Communist regimes in his new empire. Although he aimed to quell postwar internal dissent over the post-war shattered state of Russia by mass liquidations if necessary, in the newly occupied countries he applied a softly-softly approach. In East Germany local mayors could be 'bourgeois' or Social Democrats, but their deputies must be 'loyal and report to the Communist Party' while in Poland he told Premier Gomulka, 'You must move towards Socialism not directly but in zigzags and roundabout ways.'[11]

On 10th May 1945 Truman signed the US occupation directive JCS. The integrity of the German Reich would be respected, and states like Bavaria forced to stay glued to Prussia, but the US occupation forces were ordered to take 'no steps towards the economic rehabilitation of Germany'. However, sentiment soon altered. The Potsdam Conference merely agreed upon 'the elimination or control of all German industry that could be used for military production' and turned a deaf ear to France's plea that the Ruhr should be internationalised.

Although the Ruhr was only about fifteen miles wide by forty long, it contained almost all West Germany's coal mines, also nearly all its iron and steel industries and a large proportion of its engineering plants, including Krupp at Essen. Coal was still the energy source of the age. Whoever owned coal could potentially become immensely wealthy. Germany had traditionally been one of the world's largest coal and coke exporters,[12] but for now restrictions were placed upon coal production and distribution.

Stalin's retribution in occupied Eastern Germany was swift. Between 1945 and 1946 the Soviet Union took half a billion dollars-worth of factories and equipment from its zone as war reparations. The skilled technicians and managers of the plants were taken to Russia too. Under the Potsdam Agreement Stalin was also allowed 10 per cent of the war reparations taken from the Allies' zone in return for sending coal, wood and food from the bread-basket areas of East Germany.

In 1946 Stalin stopped delivering coal and agricultural goods to the West.[13] American opposition to him increased. In 1946, the American Joint Chiefs of Staff declared that 'the complete revival of German industry, particularly coal mining is now of primary importance to American security'. After the war German coal production had plunged. All the countries dependent on German coal in Western Europe were thrown into darkness; but now production was allowed to crank up again. Sixty-six-year-old Secretary of State, James F Byrnes, who had been accused by Truman of 'babying up to the Soviets'[14] reassured the West Germans: 'Our Security forces will probably have to remain in Germany for a long period. I want no misunderstanding. We will not shirk our duty. We are not withdrawing. We are here to stay.'[15]

Encouraged by this turn of events, German heavy industry spokesman Otto A Friedrich, raised the question as to whether it would not be better for Germany 'to come out openly *in favour* of the West's political aims and to clarify, slowly but determinedly, the preconditions of such an alliance, and to put demands accordingly'.[16]

The human tragedy of the war in Germany was immense: bombed-out cities, millions of homeless, sickness, hunger and despair. Yet, William I Clayton had reported to the US Senate that there had been a 'flight of capital in anticipation of defeat' and that the Nazis 'have made strenuous efforts to move abroad assets of all kinds', while Senator Kilgore asserted darkly that Germany not only was 'the third largest industrial economy', but also was 'better prepared to implement her plot for world conquest than she was at the end of World War I'.[17] German industrial capacity was estimated to be 11 per cent higher in 1947 than in Hitler's Reich in 1936.[18] When German industry's funds were finally repatriated they could help power Germany to greatness again.

Daimler-Benz, which employed thousands of slave labourers during the war, had been shattered by Allied bombing, but Volkswagen had suffered only surface damage and Krupp was poised to export household goods.

In 1937 Volkswagen had the largest press shop in Europe and 2,700 of the finest specialised tools. Three Allied bombing raids against the strategically vulnerable Volkswagen plant at Wolfsburg had resulted in only superficial damage. A clever scheme in which the roof was deliberately damaged in non-essential areas to give the aerial appearance of destruction, deceived the Allies. With the help of British military engineers it was soon in production again, and was allowed to become the sole supplier of vehicles to the occupation authorities.[19]

Soon, however, the British were subject to odium in the German press. In 1945, 69-year-old, wiry, Catholic Rhinelander Konrad Adenauer was asked by the Americans to resume his former Weimar Republic job as Burgomaster of the City of Cologne. A few months later he was dismissed by the British authorities. Sir John Barraclough, a Midlands industrialist who, as 'Brigadier Barraclough', did the actual sacking, wrote in his own defence:

'The devastation in Cologne was almost indescribable. Public transport was non-existent. Electricity and gas supplies had broken down. The navigation channel of the Rhine, one of the main arteries of communication, was completely blocked. The sewers were open. Thousands of Germans were starving. Hundreds of thousands of refugees were moving on the roads. I arranged a meeting with Adenauer. We met in the office of the local commander in Cologne ... Although I was impressed by his personality, I freely admit that I did not realise that I was face to face with a man who was to become one of Europe's leading politicians ... I did my best to impress upon Dr Adenauer the desperate urgency of the problems facing us, and appealed to him to cooperate. His immediate reaction was to show me an album of drawings entitled 'The Cologne of the Future', or something to that effect. Apparently he thought it impracticable to rebuild the city on the existing site. His plan was to build a new Cologne outside the boundaries of the old city. We talked for the best part of two hours, but made no progress. Surrounded by the chaos I have described, here we had the senior paid administrative official with his head well in the clouds. With great reluctance, I decided that for the good of his own people he would have to go.'[20]

Dr Adenauer made much of the iniquity of his removal from his position. He voiced his animosity towards the British, and to Social Democracy and in no time at all he was made Chairman of the Conservative Christian Democratic Union, the second-largest political party in Germany. The Americans were happy with Konrad Adenauer's political advancement. Dr Adenauer was a Conservative. There was not a whiff of Socialism about him. Meanwhile the 'Reds' seemed to be creeping up all over Europe. The American Republican party not only objected to Britain's overseas empire, but also to the new British Labour government's socialist policies at home.

The Labour government had imaginative social-welfare plans, including instituting a National Health Service. However, its ambition to nationalise the key industries of the post-war economy, such as the Bank of England, the fuel and power industries, inland transport, and iron and steel, brought horror into American Republican industrialists' hearts. They were frightened of 'Reds under the bed' at home and warmed to 'der Alte' (the old one), as Adenauer was affectionately called, with his resolute anti-socialist rhetoric and his firm stance against Communism.

President Truman had been shocked by his meeting with Stalin. He consulted his Russian expert, the patrician George F Kennan.[21] Kennan had investigated Stalin's great purge between 1936 and 1938, and believed that the only solution to stop Stalin taking over the whole of Europe was to determine a demarcation line that the Soviets could not cross without risking war.

On 12th March 1947 Truman made a pledge to support Greece and Turkey from falling into the Soviet sphere, stating that it was 'the policy of the United States to support free people who are resisting attempted subjugation by armed minorities or by outside persons'.

In June 1947, Secretary of State George C Marshall proposed to widen America's assistance to allocate his so-called Marshall Plan funds to all the devastated regions of Europe, the major clause being that they should use the money to buy goods from America.[22]

The Marshall Plan was a brilliant concept to help the poor countries of Europe, without impoverishing the United States. America's goals were to rebuild war-devastated regions, remove trade barriers, modernise industry and make Europe prosperous again.

One of her gnawing anxieties had been to avoid the dreadful unemployment she suffered in the 1930s and to guarantee a trade surplus with the rest of the world. As all the European countries were penniless, she decided to give them grants with the proviso that they used their dollars to buy American goods.

Every country benefited from the Marshall Plan but Britain was granted the greatest largesse. However, in practice the clause in the Marshall Plan that Britain should purchase its raw materials (except oil), from the US was a further nail in the coffin of Britain's trade with its traditional suppliers in Canada and the empire.

26 per cent of the Marshall Plan was allocated for Britain, 18 per cent for France but Germany had not been forgotten either. It was to receive 16 per cent of the funds. However, General Marshall was frustrated. The ungrateful Germans were creating difficulties. He declared: '(German) recovery has been retarded by the fact that two years after the close of hostilities a peace settlement with Germany and Austria has not been agreed upon'.[23] Otto A Friedrich and his friends in heavy industry had 'come out openly in favour of the West's political aims and (were putting) slowly but determinedly, the preconditions of such an alliance'.

Meanwhile inflation soared in Germany and the human toll of German misery mounted. Trainloads of penniless people fled from the Communist zone to the West, clinging to the roofs of trains and between the carriages. Although Germany's breadbasket areas were in Soviet-occupied Poland and East Germany, desperate people streamed to the Ruhr to seek work away from Communist oppression. Faced with little food and stacks of extra mouths to feed, the British set the daily ration at 1,125 calories in their zone of occupation.

The British were blamed for their inhumanity in setting the daily food ration so low. In 1947 Europe had one of its vilest winters in a century. In the early months of the year, they were accused of reducing the German peoples' rations to between 700–800 calories per day for those not engaged in heavy labour. It was alleged that if the German population did not actually die of starvation on that amount of food, it would perish from disease and malnutrition.

The British had had their own meagre food rations slashed since the war ended. The average adult allowances of food was down to thirteen ounces of meat, one and a half ounces of cheese, six ounces of butter and margarine, plus one ounce of cooking fat, two pints of milk and one egg a week. However, stirred by the writings, amongst others, of the left-wing publisher, Victor Gollanz, Britain dug into its empty pockets to buy extra food for Germany. Chancellor of the Exchequer Hugh Dalton was persuaded, extremely reluctantly, to spend £82 million to feed the starving German people but he declared of the gift: 'What we are doing amounts, essentially, to us paying reparations to the Germans.'[24]

Millions of Americans, from Quakers to trade unionists, also rose to the challenge to feed the German people. The first shipment contained 2.8 million packets of cheese, coffee, flour, sugar, cocoa, chocolate and powdered milk but the situation was still dire. The currency reduced to waste paper in value while hundreds of thousands of people allegedly died from starvation.[25] Indeed, John Hynd, the British Labour Party Minister responsible for Germany, later declared: 'It was a matter of days whether twenty-three million people were going to starve in the streets.'[26]

Eventually, recently elected Director of Economics, Ludwig Erhard, solved the problem. In June 1948 the Reichsmark was removed and replaced by the Deutschmark. Suddenly people could buy delicacies that they had only dreamed of in the past three years. Bakeries produced and displayed delicious cakes, and vegetables, butter and eggs appeared in the shops. More goodies appeared the next day and the next – clothes and hardware, even silk stockings.[27] It was a miracle! Or had it been contrived in order to wipe out Germany's internal debts 'and teach the German people how to work'?

In 1950, the Madrid Geo-Political Centre (a Nazi think tank operating in exile after the war in Spain), revealed in its secret *Madrid Circular Letter* that it sent to influential like-minded people in Bonn and elsewhere in the world, that the malnutrition and cold that the German people suffered in the Ruhr in 1947 was not due to the inhumanity of the British occupation authorities but was a deliberate ploy of the industrialists and their Nazi friends. It declared:

'In order to bring the Americans back to reason ... we organised chaotic conditions in a thorough and systematic manner ... The peasants were delivering next to nothing to the cities; no coal was brought up from the pits, the wheels of industry were not turning, the people came near to starvation; the monetary systems were disintegrating – there was nothing for the Yankees to do but to give in and abandon the Potsdam programme.'[28]

The adoption of the Deutschmark in June 1948 and the arrival of the Marshall Plan a month later had far reaching results for the Soviet Union. Although Marshall Aid was available to all the devastated areas of Europe, Stalin was not happy for any his satellite states, which included Poland, Hungary and Czechoslovakia, to receive it. Many people believed that it was the Communist economic system, rather than the armaments and heavy industrial base that Germany had sold Stalin – and Stalin's giant will – that had enabled him to triumph over Hitler. He had promoted the benefits of his economic system to the rest of Europe and nations were considering adopting it – but the small print of Marshall Aid disclosed that it would only be available to countries with an 'open-market capitalist system'. So Stalin forbade Eastern Bloc countries from accepting Marshall Aid.

Naturally this made Stalin highly unpopular, especially in Czechoslovakia, where he had to resort to supporting a brutal *coup d'état* in 1948 in order to maintain order. The arrival of the Deutschmark was an even greater, permanent threat to his new empire. It had been blessed by the Americans. They had even printed the bank notes. The Deutschmark's arrival would mean a massive exodus of funds from the impoverished Soviet area of Berlin to the American and Allied zones.

The day after the 18th June announcement of the Deutschmark, Soviet guards halted all passenger trains and traffic on the autobahn to Berlin. On 22nd June the Soviets announced that they would introduce a new currency in their areas of occupation in Germany, the Ostmark. On 25th June the Soviets stopped supplying food and coal to the civilian population in the non-Soviet sectors of Berlin.

The Americans declared: 'We are convinced that our remaining in Berlin is essential to our prestige in Germany and in Europe ... it has become a symbol of the American intent.'[29]

It was a brave decision. By 1948 there were only 31,000 American combat troops left in West Germany and only 8,973 American, 7,606 British and 6,100 French troops in West Berlin. Meanwhile the Soviets had one and half million troops surrounding the city.

America and the Allies decided to defy the blockade by flying food and coal into their beleaguered sector of Berlin. Aircrews from the Anglo-Saxon countries, America, Britain, Australia, Canada, New Zealand and also South Africa, flew 200,000 flights in a year to the city.[30] Eventually, Stalin gave in. The Soviet blockade was lifted a minute after midnight on 12th May 1949 and the trains started running again. Germany shared the costs with America and Britain.

America had won a great victory for the Deutschmark, for West Germany and for capitalism. West Berlin remained part of West Germany, 160 kilometres inside East Germany's borders.

Between 1945 and 1946, the Western Allies, but primarily America, had contributed $700 million to their zones of occupation in West Germany.[31] Between 1948 and 1951, under the terms of the Marshall Plan, the United States gave about $12.5 billion to all the Western European countries in grants and favourable loans.[32] No one in Western Europe should ever forget the assistance that America gave them after the Second World War.

In 1949 73-year-old Konrad Adenauer was elected Chancellor of Germany by one vote over Kurt Schumacher, his Social Democrat rival. The American leadership breathed a sigh of relief. Schumacher had excellent qualifications to become Chancellor of Germany. He had spent over ten years in Nazi concentration camps before and during the war, and had labelled the Communists, 'red-painted Nazis'. However, since the war he had campaigned against Allied and American propaganda to impose 'collective guilt' on the German people for the Nazi atrocities against the Jews,[33] and advocated the nationalisation of heavy industry, on the grounds that its funding enabled the Nazis to achieve power. The Americans smelled a whiff of Socialism about Schumacher's campaign so they backed Konrad Adenauer instead.

Adenauer was a devoted Catholic and Rhinelander and always impeccably dressed, despite his age. During the Second World War the Nazis accused him of having formerly advocated separatism for the Rhineland and locked him up in a Gestapo prison, where he had to endure listening to the screams of those being tortured. Eventually, Adenauer's soldier son managed to secure his release. Adenauer declared that there were two Germanys: 'the Germany which is fundamentally based on the Roman cultural inheritance, and the Germany of Prussia, which imposed its own will'.

In the years before Adenauer's election he had made many memorable comments, including telling the British that the greatest mistake they had made was 'at the Congress of Vienna, when you foolishly put Prussia on the Rhine as a safeguard against France and another Napoleon', and that 'Prussianism in its turn culminated in National Socialism'. After he became Chancellor his tone slightly changed because he had to represent all the people in his party, including the former Nationalists (and Pan-Germans), who were in heavy industry, and those who were former Nazis.

After being imprisoned twice, Adenauer did not believe post-war Nazis to be a serious threat, despite the fact that his denazification law of 1951 pardoned 792,176 people, including 3,000 functionaries of the SA and SS, who participated in deporting victims to prison camps, and 30,000 other Nazis sentenced for murder. One could not lock people up for ever. Besides, Adenauer concluded, there were able people, who he could use, among those indicted.

Adenauer had a simple formula for former Nazis whose services he wished to use in government. He was willing to have them in his administration, but it was made clear to them that if they crossed him they could expect their case of denazification to be re-opened. Indeed his aide, Hans Globke, had been largely responsible, in 1935, for the official commentary on the infamous Nuremberg Laws, which classified people as Jewish if they had three or four Jewish grandparents or Mischling (mixed race) if they had one or two. The law prohibited the two groups from marrying a German and deprived them of German citizenship.

Globke was, however, exonerated at his denazification trial on the grounds of the 'administrative pressure' put on officials who were not members of the Nazi party. Indeed, Adenauer denounced the denazification process on the grounds that it sought to punish all the millions of unfortunate Germans who had lived under the Nazi regime and were now Christian Democrat voters. He viewed the Nazis as a small criminal gang, who were now all conveniently dead, with the mass of their supporters being people whom Hitler had tricked into following him. For this reason he insisted that a memorial day should be set aside for the victims of National Socialism, provided that it included all the Germans killed by Allied bombing and the German soldiers fighting in the Wehrmacht and in the Waffen SS.

The only German soldiers that Adenauer failed to mention were the members of the country's 'Dad's Army', the *Volkssturm*, which consisted not only of the old, but former industrial workers, the very young and the injured. The *Volkssturm* was raised in the last few months of the war, when the military situation looked hopeless. Over 600,000 died.[34]

By 2013 the British historian Richard Overy, would revise down the figure of civilians killed by Allies' wartime bombing from 600,000 to 353,000,[35] with *Der Spiegel* concluding that no more than 18,000 to 25,000 were killed at Dresden.[36] These were still huge numbers, compared to the roughly 60,000 British civilians killed by German bombing. The British have felt guilty about the bombs they sent to German cities ever since.

Nevertheless, the Allies were certain that the Germans would have obliterated their cities if they could. Indeed, many emaciated forced labourers and slaves were hanged at the V2 armaments camps at the Dora-Nordhausen-Mittelwerk complex as late as March 1945 for trying to thwart the missile programme to destroy Allied and American cities. If Adenauer wanted to include the German military and Waffen SS in his memorial, he should have included the *Volkssturm* and the Allied military and civilian casualties too, and the six million forced labourers and slaves who worked and died in the Nazi's huge factories and underground complexes, including those who were hung in March 1945 for trying to prevent the destruction of American cities.

Truman ended the war against Japan in August 1945, when he dropped atom bombs on Hiroshima and Nagasaki, but America was still alarmed by the spread of Communism in Asia. All too soon South Korea became under threat from Communist North Korea.

Korea had been jointly occupied by Russian and American troops after the Second World War, when the war with Japan was still raging and the plan was to occupy the Japanese home islands. The Russians and the Americans were able, without difficulty, to agree on the 38th parallel as the demarcation line between north and south, pending the creation of a single Korean government. Russian and American occupation troops were subsequently withdrawn but the country remained divided with the Republic of Korea in the South, supported by America by virtue of an election sponsored by the United Nations, whilst a Soviet-supported Democratic Republic of Korea ruled the North.

Neither of the Korean governments was happy with the situation. They both wanted control over the whole peninsula. One of the reasons that Americans had withdrawn their troops from South Korea, was the fear that South Korean President, Syngman Rhee, might drag them into a war they did not want. However, America's decision to withdraw its troops may have given Rhee's North Korean counterpart Kim Il-sung the wrong signal, that America would allow North Korea to grab the South without intervening. The situation was discussed between Stalin's Foreign Minister Molotov and China's Mao Zedong. Stalin approved of the idea of America being dragged into a war in the East. He now had a vast empire in Europe but his country was still ravaged by war and he was desperately short of money. A war in Korea would remove the pressure against him in Europe. Kim Il-sung was told that according to information coming from the United States '... the prevailing mood is not to interfere' and the green light was given to Kim Il-sung to invade. Kim Il-sung boasted: 'The attack will be swift and the war will be over in three days.'[37]

President Truman was not keen on becoming involved but the reputation of the United Nations was involved. On 19th June 1950 John Foster Dulles, who would become Secretary of State in 1953, reassured the South Korean parliament: 'You are not alone. You will never be alone, so long as you continue to play worthily your part in the great design of human freedom.' Unfortunately his words did not deter the North Koreans. On 25th June they invaded South Korea and the Korean War began.[38]

By November the Americans thought that they had won the war. However, China's Mao Zedong had other ideas. He wanted Stalin to give him the sort of military and heavy industrial base that German heavy industry had given Stalin during the Great Depression, and he was prepared to expend the lives of countless Chinese soldiers in North Korea, and suffer severe military reverses, in order to persuade a reluctant Stalin to let him have it.[39]

America was faced by war in Korea and Stalin in Western Europe. US High Commissioner in West Germany, John McCloy, was horrified. America was not prepared for another war on the Western Front. According to the *Nazi Madrid Circular Letter*: 'Russia had used the five years' interval since the end of the war to strengthen her military preparedness in an extraordinary manner', whereas the United States and the western coalition had neglected their military establishment.

It was not only the Ruhr's coal, steel, machinery and chemicals that were needed in this emergency; McCloy wanted thousands of German troops to help hold the line in Europe. Adenauer was quick off the mark. On 29th August 1950, without even consulting his cabinet colleagues, he declared his readiness, 'in the event of the formation of an international West European army, to make a contribution in the shape of a German contingent'.[40]

The French were horrified. The last thing they wanted was a renewed German military presence on their soil. However, in September 1950, Secretary of State, Dean Acheson, told France's Foreign Minister, Robert Schuman, bluntly that if France wanted American troops to remain on French soil the US government had 'to have an answer now to the possible use of German forces in Europe'. And the French had to accept 'the whole package'.[41]

It seemed that part of 'the whole package' was related to the problem of Germany's war reparations payments. The Ruhr industrialists were accompanying their protests against paying war reparations with a savage propaganda campaign against the Allied dismantling of West Germany's heavy machinery, declaring that the Allies' attempts to secure reparations were motivated by feelings of revenge.[42]

So the demands for First World War reparations were reduced and the Second World War reparations slashed until the distant day when Germany was unified. In October 1950 America, Britain and France issued a joint declaration to the effect that

'The three countries agree that the plan (for reducing Germany's debts) includes an appropriate satisfaction of demands towards Germany so that its implementation does not jeopardise the financial situation of the German economy through unwanted repercussions nor has an excessive effect on its potential currency reserves. The first three countries are convinced that the German federal government shares their view and that the restoration of German solvability includes an adequate solution for the German debt which takes Germany's economic problems into account and makes sure that negotiations are fair to all participants.'[43]

Germany's pre-war debt amounted to 22.6 billion marks including interest. Its post-war debt was estimated to be 16.2

billion. The sums demanded were slashed to 7.5 billion and 7 billion, and America and the Allies were only allowed to enforce payment if the German economy was growing.[44]

Although the major powers agreed the deal, it continued to cause anger and anxiety in the war-torn countries of Europe. How could one explain to the millions who had suffered in the Second World War, and were still suffering from its after-effects, that they were going to receive little or nothing in the way of compensation, while Germany seemed to be getting off scot-free? The only way forward for America was to return to the fable of the horrendously large reparations charged to Germany by the Allies after the First World War, whose 'iniquity' allegedly led to the rise of Hitler and the Second World War.

As the secret primary source material remained locked in the Prussian and Austrian state archives, no one could actually prove who was responsible for the First World War. So, blame was heaped on the Allies for helping to instigate the First World War and causing the Great Depression and the rise of Hitler through their onerous and unjust war reparations claims. This legend would gradually lead to a guilty feeling by the Allies that they had been unfair to Germany.

America was still so anxious to get West Germany on-side that she gave the country extra concessions. West Germany did not automatically have to pay its debts if it was not prospering. To the astonishment of the historian and political scientist Éric Toussaint, the creditors also accepted that Germany could pay its debts in its national currency, and that although other Marshall Aid recipients had to buy American goods with Marshall Aid cash, West Germany could manufacture the goods itself, and then sell them abroad to achieve a positive trade balance. This was a major blow to British, French and American exporters, who up till now had furnished over 40 per cent of West Germany's imports.[45]

The Allies would be made to pay their war debts until the twenty-first century, while Germany's post-Second World War reparations were slashed until the distant day when the country was reunified.[46] Meanwhile, American President Wilson's 1923 prediction that unless adequate war reparations were charged Germany would conquer the world industrially would come true again after the Second World War. West Germany's economic recovery would become the wonder of the world in the 1960s, while the countries that had been occupied, raped and maltreated by Germany during the war, laboured under hardship and debt.

The French realised that they were in a desperately weak position compared to Germany. When a high French official referred to the delicacy of French opinion over the German re-armament issue, John McCloy wrote dryly: 'I think the time has come to tell these people that there is no other opinion than US opinion and that US opinion is getting damn delicate itself.'

It was clear that America had no respect for France's susceptibilities and that weak Britain could not help her either. France had been invaded three times, in part because of the iron ore fields that she possessed. So French Foreign Minister, Robert Schuman, eager to promote his Coal and Steel Community, swallowed the legend that we all 'slithered into war' in 1914 as the only way forward for France's economic survival.

Originally France had a different idea. Civil servant, Jean Monnet, came up with a scheme to turn the area spanned by the German coalfields east of the Rhine into an International State, supervised by America and France. When this was rejected, however, Monnet wrote to Schuman that the only solution was 'through the creation of a federation of the West'. Schuman's aim was to make war between European Member States impossible by creating a single market. No longer would Germany have to invade France in order to secure the iron ore from Longwy-Briey. France would also have peaceful access to German coal without having to send her troops into Germany. Schuman and Monnet were credited with the concept of the European Economic Community, which has grown into the European Union.

Adenauer's first choice to handle the negotiations for the Schuman Plan was the banker, Hermann Abs, who spoke fluent Dutch, French and English. However, Hermann Abs was not only on the board of Deutsche Bank throughout the war but was also on the supervisory board of I G Farben, which built its largest-ever plant, at the cost of twenty-five thousand deaths, near the death camp at Auschwitz. So Adenauer decided instead to use a Professor of Law called Walter Hallstein to draw up the Schuman Plan with Frenchman Jean Monnet.[47]

In 1942, the Germans toyed with the concept of a European Economic Community, with Germany running the show. Reich Minister for Economic Affairs, Walter Funk, declared: 'Seen this way, the creation of a European economic area that is immune to Europhobic influences and relies on the cooperation of its people, also represents an act of European self-determination.' Dr Philip Beisiegel, director of Hitler's Labour Ministry, seconded Funk's view, saying: 'The European Economic Community is in no way yet a sure fact, rather a political aim ... We have to differentiate between the present needs under the circumstances of war and those of a future peaceful order, which will look very different from the wartime organisation.'

Indeed, the *Madrid Circular Letter* intimated that the Germans and Americans had already discussed the project, declaring: 'These considerations resulted in a plan – first formulated secretly in Washington and later openly discussed, aiming at the creation of a united Europe as a bulwark against Russia with the proviso that a strengthened and rearmed Germany be incorporated in such a combination.'

One would imagine therefore that West Germany would have been keen on Schuman's plan. Yet West Germany drove a hard bargain over sharing its resources with France, Italy and the Benelux countries and for providing America with the forces to defend Europe from Soviet aggression. Schuman also planned to create the world's first international anti-cartel agency so that a firm like Krupp would not be able to create 'a state within a state' in Europe. The German chemical industry responded with a thunder of opposition, alleging that the anti-IG Farben fanatics in Frankfurt and Washington had struck a new blow at Germany. IG Farben's many prominent American supporters also rose in a swarm to support Germany and IG Farben.[48]

The American government was in a difficult position to negotiate with West Germany on the future of the European Coal and Steel Community, or indeed on any other point, because it was so anxious for the reluctant German people to provide a force of half a million men on the Western Front to contain Stalin.

In 1950 in the *Madrid Circular Letter,* the Nazi editor posed the question: 'How should Germany proceed diplomatically in the present situation? ... We have to undo the shame of the judgements motivated by revenge (Nuremberg War Crimes Trial etc.) which the victors executed on the military and civic leaders of the Third Reich. The offerings which the Americans could make in this respect would cost them nothing. To save a few dozen brave men from the gallows and to free a few hundred from the prisons, should not prove too difficult to accomplish if the Bonn Government would take a resolute stand. To obtain such a token of friendship from the Yankees, we could even give them some promises. But there is a difference between mere promises and such commitments as would bind us irrevocably ... The Yankees need us today more urgently than ever before ... Those dollar-diplomats and cowboys are too untalented to cope with the problem of world politics. The struggle against the American bossing of Europe will become Germany's main task in the future.'[49]

So the German negotiators demanded a further quid pro quo for providing an army, that America commuted the death sentence on SS war criminals. At the end of 1950 more than two dozen men were still in the death cells in Germany, waiting for a decision on their fate. They consisted of the SS unit which had committed the notorious Malmédy massacre of eighty American prisoners of war in 1944, and the commanding officers of the various SS special task forces who had carried out the brutal mass executions of several hundred thousand Jews, Poles and gypsies in the occupied East in 1940 and 1941.

A huge petition was organised against imposing the death penalty for the SS murderers. Thousands of letters and telegrams arrived from all over the world pleading for their lives. The Christian Aid committee in Munich, which contained leading churchmen and politicians, flooded the High Commissioner's office with telegrams and petitions imploring that he commute the sentences against the 'red jackets' still facing the death sentence. At the same time McCloy's 'mail became heavy with threats against his life and that of his family'.

On 9th January 1951 High Commissioner McCoy received a delegation from the President of the Bundestag, Dr Hermann Ehlers, and other prominent dignitaries representing each of the political parties. They told a no doubt astonished McCloy that West Germany had abolished the death penalty and 'they want no more blood spilling in Germany'. Germany had decided to become a pacifist country.

By the end of January 1951, Commissioner McCloy gave in to Germany's pressure to let off their war criminals. He commuted the sentences of all but seven SS special task force officers.

242

Meanwhile, also under the terms of the agreement, immensely powerful Ruhr magnates, who had employed thousands of slave labourers, had their prison sentences reviewed without fanfare, and were released quietly from custody in small groups. At the end of the first week in January 1951, America allowed all the I G Farben personnel who had been convicted of responsibility for their employees' beatings, starvation, abuse, and murder of inmates, at Buna-Werke, Fürstengrube, Auschwitz and elsewhere, out of prison. Former board member, Fritz ter Meer, who would later become Chairman of the supervisory board of Bayer, again told reporters as he walked out a free man, 'Now they have Korea on their hands, the Americans are a lot more friendly.'

On Saturday 3rd February 1951, Alfried Krupp led twenty-eight other freed prisoners, including four former generals, out of jail. But the news had got out. Alfried heard 'a great shout' and discovered that he had 'become a national idol'.[50] He would soon be privately acknowledged as the richest man in the European Economic Community.

The industrialist Friedrich Flick, who was convicted as a war criminal for plundering the Jews' factories in Germany and Eastern Europe, and of 'enthusiastically' using slave labour at Daimler-Benz and in other parts of his huge armaments combine, was also released in 1950. Much of his property was returned to him, including his 39 per cent holding in Daimler-Benz.

VW and Daimler-Benz received the warm breath of government and banking support to start manufacturing again. They lost no time in entering into a variety of patent, research, and marketing and sales agreements with other core manufacturers to protect themselves and their partners from competitive American subsidiaries.[51] The Americans had wanted to get the wheels of German industry turning again – but it came at a price.

On 18th April 1951, the Treaty of Paris was signed by France, West Germany, Italy, Belgium, the Netherlands and Luxembourg, forming the European Coal and Steel Community. Meanwhile allowing so many Nazis out of prison was bound to give the old guard confidence.

In September 1951, Minister of Transport Dr Seebohm, addressed a mass meeting of the Sudeten Germans at Stuttgart, denouncing the 'monstrous crime the victors ... committed against Germany, Europe and the whole world'.[52] In 1952, 10 per cent of West Germans thought that Hitler was the greatest statesman of the century, and in 1953 13 per cent said that they would welcome a return of the Nazi party. On 15th January 1953 Dr Werner Naumann, whom Hitler had nominated as the successor to Goebbels, was detained with several other Nazis for trying to undermine the democratic government.[53]

Worryingly, the plot appeared to have had international backers and been instigated by a vast, well-resourced, Nazi network reaching from Düsseldorf to Cairo, Madrid, Buenos Aires, and Mälmo in Sweden.[54] The evidence about the conspiracy was compelling but the Americans did not want the incident to be highlighted when West Germany was the lynch pin of their fight against Communism. And Adenauer eventually would solve all America's worries by winning a huge electoral victory on 6th September. Meanwhile the West German negotiators decided to press on with demands for economic and political concessions while America was weak.

To an outside observer, West Germany had won the war. Although the German people themselves were poor, the country had eliminated its internal debts and had been absolved, until the distant future, from paying its external debts, on the grounds that it was too poor to pay and was no more responsible than any other country for starting the First World War. It was, the negotiators claimed, the Allies' war reparations and the notorious lone ranger, Hitler, who were responsible for the Holocaust and Second World War!

The American people believed that the British had behaved callously towards West Germany in 1947 and were open to German propaganda that told them the country was still poverty-stricken. Under the American CARE aid programme, cartons holding clothing, medicine, tools, agricultural and scientific equipment continued to flood into West Germany until the mid-1960s, even though it had become one of the most powerful countries in the world.

CHAPTER ELEVEN

How Reunification was Achieved

'*Die Stunde null*', zero hour. That's what the Germans called it. Everything was to start afresh from the moment peace was declared. In fact, zero hour could more accurately be said to have begun after the start of the Korean War. According to Frederick the Great's maxim: 'Money is like a sorcerer's wand'. Without it one could do nothing. With it one could invade one's neighbour's territory, or secure the return of one's own. The task of reunifying Germany would take forty years.

In 1950 the authors of the *Madrid Circular Letter* declared: 'The Americans have lost the peace, the Cold War and their entire future but they are not yet aware of it.' That may not have been a fair comment but it deserved scrutiny, if only because of its anti-American rhetoric at a time when America believed that West Germany was its best friend. America was appeasing the country by throwing money at it, in the same fashion as in the 1920s. Meanwhile the German industrial hierarchy was making plans to trade with the Soviet Union,[1] while calling on America and NATO to defend their country against the Communists.

Some 70 per cent of the German people were opposed to any rearmament. Yet Adenauer was determined that West

Germany should re-arm and the Americans, faced with the Korean War, were desperate for them to re-arm too.

In 1950, French Prime Minister René Pleven proposed reluctantly that the European Defence Community (EDC) should be formed from the armies of Italy, France and the Benelux countries, with the addition of a contingent from Germany. The French people were unhappy at the thought of the EDC in any shape or form if it meant German re-armament. Nevertheless, Adenauer gained a new friend to support him. In January 1953 the arch enemy of Communism, John Foster Dulles, became US Secretary of State.

Dulles had a rigid mind-set. After the First World War he clung to Keynes's 1919 view that the Treaty of Versailles would 'reduce Germany to servitude' and was still busy lending Germany money to make amends even after Hitler came to power. After the Second World War, Dulles's moral outbursts were against Communism everywhere. Stalin had conducted a bomb test in 1949. The stage was set for the Cold War.

In November 1953 Adenauer announced that the US deployment of nuclear weapons in West Germany was essential for its defence. Only a few days' later people were astonished to see 280 mm nuclear-capable cannons 'make their journey down the Rhine amidst a fanfare of publicity'.[2]

Adenauer also pushed for the European Defence Community to be ratified. At a NATO Council meeting on 14th December 1953, Dulles stated that if the EDC was not ratified by the French parliament, the United States would 'face an agonising reappraisal of its foreign policy'. Dulles' words infuriated the French press. In August 1954 the French National Assembly voted against allowing the motion to ratify the European Defence Community onto its agenda. That killed the EDC.[3] Adenauer later complained in his memoirs, 'In France, in Britain, everyone was pressing for disarmament while we in the Federal Republic stood for rearming.' Nevertheless, Adenauer could depend on America while Dulles was Secretary of State.

Aggressive monster Stalin died in 1953 but he left his henchmen behind. Despite the Soviets being over-extended financially, having an industrial base a third of the size of America's, a faltering agricultural sector and a struggle in keeping up with the arms race, Dulles maintained that 'Soviet military threats and subversive efforts created an intolerable sense of insecurity.'[4]

No one could disagree with those sentiments, especially not Adenauer. He was eager and able to help in a concrete way by re-arming, and his country had the resources. When the German mark was stabilised in 1948 the Americans allowed it to be fixed at a very advantageous level against other currencies. It was soon apparent that it was seriously undervalued. In the couple of years since the 1953 elections, the economy had grown at an average of over 7 per cent a year and by 1955 the balance of payments surplus would be a whopping DM3.07 billion. To those with inside knowledge Germany seemed already to have won the Second World War, but there was still a huge chunk of the Fatherland, torn away by Stalin in the East, which needed to be reunited with West Germany, either by chatting up the Soviets, or else by using America. Adenauer favoured using America.

America was desperate for West Germany to join NATO. In April 1949 the First NATO Secretary General, Lord Ismay, defined NATO's aims as being 'to keep the Russians out, the Americans in, and the Germans down'.

Yet 'the Germans' were no longer 'down'. In fact they seemed to have the upper hand. So securing West Germany's acquiescence to becoming part of NATO meant more arduous negotiations and a final new concession by America and its Allies, which would come back to haunt them.

Although West Germany promised 'never to have recourse to force to achieve the reunification of Germany', it extracted a pledge from the Western Allies that 'the achievement through peaceful means of a fully free and unified Germany remains a fundamental (NATO) goal'.[5] On that condition it finally joined NATO on 9th May 1955.

The significance of the deal would soon become apparent. West Germany promised not to use force to secure reunification itself but it expected America to threaten to use force on its behalf. 'The achievement through peaceful means of a fully free and united Germany' would soon mean a huge build-up of nuclear weapons in America and the Soviet Union, which would cost America a fortune and cause anxiety to the whole world.

Adenauer was happy in December 1956 when a NATO military committee stipulated that there should be twelve West German divisions on the Eastern Front, all equipped for nuclear warfare.[6] Although Adenauer told the pacifist German people that he favoured arms control and disarmament negotiations; privately, however, it was soon apparent that he was intent on securing nuclear weapons for the Bundeswehr.

After a French devaluation, the European Economic Community developed successfully. West German industry pursued its traditional path of subsidising the European Economic Community's agriculture in order to sell its industrial goods. Its initiative was tremendously successful and provided the basis for a lasting friendship. Small French farms flourished with just a few cows, Italian hills were clothed with olives. Wine producers were also encouraged to multiply their production, while an outlet for their wine was found in the former beer drinking countries of Britain and Northern Europe. Tariffs were lowered throughout the EEC but each country continued to run its own economy.

Adenauer's main preoccupation, however, was still with East Germany. He asked Walter Halstein to draw up what became known as the Halstein Doctrine. This asserted that West Germany had the exclusive right to represent, not just West Germany, but the entire German nation and that there would be 'serious consequences' for any state that recognised East Germany. This was a threat to the Soviet Union.

New Soviet President Nikita Khrushchev, who had started life as a poorly educated peasant, now became chief of the threatening but impecunious Soviet Empire. Blustering, yet aggressively insecure, he was appalled by the carnage that nuclear weapons could create but equally determined not to divulge the information to the Americans. He claimed that he was turning out missiles 'like sausages' when in fact he had far fewer than he made out and his missiles lacked the precise guidance to arrive at the right destination.[7] In November 1958 the Soviet Union proclaimed that all Soviet rights and duties in East Berlin were being handed over to the East Germans and therefore that the Allied troops should be withdrawn. Khrushchev told the Polish leader, Wladyslaw Gomulka, 'There will be tensions, of course' but 'War will not result from this'. His aim was to achieve international recognition of East Germany (GDR).

On 10th January 1959, Khrushchev followed up his note with a proposal to all the countries that had fought Germany in the Second World War, suggesting a peace conference to discuss the solution of the two German states, accompanied by a draft peace treaty, to be signed by both states, or a confederation, offering Germany to be united as a neutral country.

Dulles was dying of cancer but he was keen to call Khrushchev's bluff by threatening nuclear war; yet Adenauer could not secure Britain or France's cooperation for a hard line.[8] At last, in May 1959, the conference that Khrushchev had been working for occurred with a delegation from East Germany (GDR). To Khrushchev this constituted de facto recognition of East Germany – but he had achieved recognition only just in time. The Soviet Union was impoverished. It could not give East German citizens the quality of life that West German citizens had come to expect. In July 1961 thirty thousand refugees poured into West Berlin.

In early August 1961 new American President John F Kennedy reflected, 'Khrushchev is losing East Germany. He cannot let that happen. If East Germany goes, so will Poland and all of Eastern Europe. He will do something to stop the flow of refugees. Perhaps a wall.' His prophecy was correct. In the early hours of Sunday 13th August 1961 East German workers erected the barbed wire barricade that was the precursor to the Berlin Wall.

There was no doubt that the Soviet economy was faltering. Adenauer's strategy of building up Western military strength until the Soviet Union either collapsed or negotiated over the future of East Germany on his terms had so nearly worked – yet the strategy was no longer tenable. The Wall was there, East Germany was being recognised as a country and, now that Dulles was dead, Adenauer could no longer count on the US threatening to bomb it into submission. Khrushchev had secured a success.

Moreover, although his country's economy was ailing, and his droves of missiles a fiction, Khrushchev was determined not to let the rest of the world know of the poor state of the Soviet economy. Russian engineers had made an improved anti-aircraft missile. On 1st May 1960, they used it to shoot down a U-2 espionage flight and capture the pilot, Francis Gary Powers. In 1962 in response to America's Bay of Pigs invasion of Cuba and the presence of America's Jupiter missiles in Turkey, Khrushchev agreed to Cuba's request to place nuclear missiles in Cuba.[9]

The crisis evolved swiftly. In response to Cuba's request for missiles to defend itself, Khrushchev sent missiles to Cuba with a range of 2,000 miles. The world was aghast and the crisis deepened. Eventually, after a worrying stand-off the Cuban missiles were removed and the US secretly agreed to dismantle Jupiter missiles in Turkey and Italy. A hotline was installed between the White House and the Kremlin and connections between the two countries improved.[10] Nevertheless, it was a public relations disaster for Russia. The American people became increasingly alarmed not only by Communism but also by the threat of a Russian-inspired nuclear war.

Adenauer was a strong man. He warned his Minister for Foreign Affairs, Heinrich von Brentano in 1955, 'I keep in my hands, the leadership in European affairs, affairs with the United States and the Soviet Union.' But occasionally Adenauer's ministers stepped out of line. His Defence Secretary, Franz Josef Strauss, was a heavy-weight from Bavaria with unlimited ambitions. By 1962, he was in trouble. He success-fully sued the editor of the newspaper *Der Spiegel*, Rudolf Augstein, for libel over the newspaper's allegation that he was a threat to democracy, his lust for power was inexhaustible, and that he was planning a nuclear war. *Der Spiegel*'s editor spent 103 days in prison but eventually Strauss had to resign, complaining that he had been treated like a 'Jew who had dared appear at a Nazi party convention'.

The idea that European nations owed a measure of repara-tion to West Germany for asserting that it was solely respon-sible for the First World War, and burdening it with unfair and onerous reparations at the Treaty of Versailles afterwards, helped reconcile the nations of Europe with their former foe. Friendship blossomed in the new environment. Then German Professor Fritz Fischer's book called *Griff nach der Weltmacht* (Grasp at World Power) in German, and *Germany's Aims in the First World War* in English, was published, threatening to destroy their spirit of solidarity. In his introduction to the book, Hajo Holborn of Yale University wrote:

'Through long labour he (Fischer) has collected from archives in West and East Germany and Austria a tremendous range of unpublished material ... proving beyond any reasonable doubt that the Chancellor, Bethmann Hollweg, was determined to use the Austro-Serbian conflict to break the "encirclement" of Germany ... at any price, even that of a great war.'

Fischer revealed how Sir Edward Grey, again and again, tried to get Germany to mediate between Austria and Serbia to avert the looming European war after the Archduke Ferdinand's murder, after Austria sent Serbia an almost impossible to accept Ultimatum, whose wording, Fischer revealed, had already secretly been agreed with the German leadership. In desperation, on 27th July, Germany's ambassador to Britain, Lichnowsky, pleaded for Germany to publicly support Britain's efforts to avert the war, declaring, 'If we rejected every attempt at mediation the whole world would hold us responsible for the conflagration and represent us as the real warmongers. *That would also make our position impossible here in Germany, where we have got to appear as though the war has been forced on us.*'

However, Chancellor Bethmann Hollweg managed to deceive both the German people and his friends in Britain into believing that his country had no bellicose intent by refusing to allow Generals Moltke and Falkenhayn to declare a 'state of imminent war' until he had prodded Russia into a general mobilisation of its armed forces, insisting on 28th July, 'It is imperative that the responsibility for any extension of the conflict to Powers not directly concerned should under all circumstances fall on Russia alone.'

Fischer's book caused uproar in West Germany but elsewhere reaction was muted. The European Economic Community was reliant on German funds to keep the Community marching forward and America wanted West Germany to keep protecting the world against Communism. Both in Europe and America the German people and its leadership were now regarded as good friends and neighbours.

Yet Fischer's *Germany's Aims in the First World War* opened up some awkward questions. How did Germany get away with causing so much misery and bloodshed in the First World War? And why had it caused its citizens such suffering and unemployment in its Great Inflation when it had emerged from the war in a far better state than the Allies and paid practically 'no' 'actual cash' in reparations? Was its economy really as weak as it made out in the 1920s when its coal mining industry was massacring the British coal mining industry? Or could it actually have caused the 1929 Wall Street Crash and been responsible for the Great Depression?

America and the Allies decided to sweep the issue under the carpet. Meanwhile West Germany was prepared to bide its time and subsidise the European Economic Community. It knew that he who paid the piper ultimately called the tune. It also realised that if – and when – the Berlin Wall came tumbling down, not only East Germany, but the whole of Eastern Europe would fall under its sphere of influence.

In 1963 Adenauer finally resigned at the ripe old age of eighty-seven. In October his former Minister for Economics, Ludwig Erhard, became Chancellor of West Germany. Heavy-jowled, cigar-smoking Ludwig Erhard was not fooled by Khrushchev's attempt to put nuclear missiles on Cuba after America's abortive attempt to destroy Fidel Castro's regime. The German industrialists had told Erhard of Russia's threadbare existence behind the Iron Curtain. The Soviet Union had a powerful military machine, but in every other area its economy was weakening and it was running out of cash. As he drove through Berlin with Mayor Willy Brandt, Erhard asked the astonished Social Democrats, how much 'would it really cost for Russia to concede the GDR to us?'

Cool economist, Ludwig Erhard amplified his scheme. West Germany would deliver industrial plant and equipment for the development of Siberia in exchange for a 'phased programme' involving 'the (Berlin) wall, reunification, self-determination and freedom for Germany'. He also told American diplomats about his plan but they did not believe that Russia would accept it.

Erhard was not to be deterred. He went to a barbeque at President Lyndon B Johnson's Texas ranch at Christmas in 1963. Johnson related: 'Erhard was all over me. He was ready to go in the barn and milk my cows if he could find the teats.' But Johnson was not prepared to meet Khrushchev, and in the meantime the British, French, Italians and Japanese provided the Soviets with cheap loans.[11] They did not like the Soviet regime but they had become accustomed to and even happy with the Berlin Wall, which restricted the clout of their powerful West German neighbour.

By the mid-1960s the German Air Force was allowed to train with the US Seventeenth Air Force in handling, arming and delivering nuclear weapons. Erhard believed that he could use America's nuclear arsenal to force the ailing Soviet Union to the negotiating table, or even hopefully to collapse the whole Soviet edifice in Eastern Europe.

In 1963 West Germany reputedly offered two billion dollars towards the creation of a five billion dollar multilateral nuclear force to confront the Soviet Union.[12] The Soviets protested, asserting that the money would allow West Germany to wield undue influence over America's nuclear weapons policy.[13] Erhard told the Bundestag on 10th November 1965:

'We have repeatedly made it known that we do not desire national control of nuclear weapons. We should, however, not be kept out of any nuclear participation simply because we are a divided country. The partition of Germany is an injustice. It must not be augmented by another injustice by

255

making it more difficult for us – rendering substantial contributions to the Western Alliance – to defend ourselves against the threat from the East.'

Neither the Europeans nor the Americans realised the menace behind these words. West Germany was asserting that America must keep her nuclear arsenal in Western Europe the equivalent size to the Soviet Union's, otherwise West Germany's promise only to use nuclear power for peaceful means was no longer binding.[14]

America obviously believed that West Germany was capable of producing a nuclear device in the 1960s because an atom bomb had already been made in Germany before the end of the Second World War.

In 2005, Mark Weber in the magazine *Nova* would declare of the device: 'At best this would have been far less destructive than the atomic bombs dropped on Japan. Rather, it is an example of scientists trying to make any sort of bomb they could in order to help stave off defeat.'[15] Other authors, however, would assert that Germany's atom bomb programme was much more advanced at the end of the war but that it lacked an effective delivery system to send it to America. However, the scientists had got as far as testing a new A 10 rocket called the 'Hammer of Thor', which they intended to fire at major cities in the US, such as Washington, Boston, New York and Philadelphia, and four test rockets had already been launched by the end of the war. [16]

Thousands of half-starved slave labourers had worked on producing the V-1 buzz bomb and the V-2 rockets in the Harz Mountains, some of whose parts were envisaged to go into the A10 'Hammer of Thor' rocket. Over a hundred were accused of sabotage and strung up to hang in March 1945, in the final weeks of the war. Just a little time later Himmler gave the directive that that the slaves working in the Dora/Nordhausen complex of concentration camps should be herded into one of the subterranean factories and gassed, but there was not enough time to carry out the order. The Americans arrived and found about five thousand corpses in varying states of purification. However, one thousand of the starving slave labourers, their filthy prison uniforms hanging 'loosely on their shrunken bodies', were rescued from the stinking decomposing scene of carnage.[17]

Some of the scientists working on the nuclear programme were also saved, de-briefed and employed by the Americans, others were taken to an uncertain fate in Russia and 62 were murdered by the SS. Nevertheless, America knew that Germany had enough knowledge to make good its threat to produce an atom bomb by the 1960s and to send it to its chosen destination (in America!).

West Germany eventually signed the Nuclear Non-Proliferation Treaty with the international community on the understanding that it could export nuclear energy for peaceful use, even if it was not allowed to produce nuclear weapons itself. It did, however, reiterate at the eighteen-nation disarmament committee meeting in Geneva in May 1967: 'Those who are the first to contribute have the right to expect the community of nations to rectify any resultant one sidedness.'

By 1967 the Deutschmark was declared to be the world's most 'stable' currency – a euphemism for saying that it was the strongest. The next month a grand coalition was formed under Germany's new President, Kurt Georg Kiesinger. Suave, good-looking Kiesinger was a controversial figure because of his Nazi past. He had spent the war in the propaganda section of the Nazi Foreign Ministry, rising quickly to become the department's connection with Joseph Goebbels's Ministry. After the war he was interned briefly before being released. In 1951 Kiesinger became a member of the CDU executive board. In 1967 he became Chancellor of West Germany.

West Germany maintained a confrontational attitude towards the Soviet Union, but its hard line had no effect in achieving reunification. Indeed, in 1968, when Czechoslovak leader Alexander Dubcek tried to loosen the reins of power and give more freedom to the Czech people, East Germany, Poland and Hungary supported the Soviet Union's action in sending tanks into Prague. Meanwhile a young French woman called Beate Klarsfeld attracted public attention world-wide when she appeared in the Berlin Convention Hall, shouted out 'Nazi Kiesinger' and slapped him in the face. Later she said in explanation: 'Kiesinger and his colleagues are turning Germany into a revengeful, expansionist nation that ignores the consequence of world war and demands atomic weapons. So long as Kiesinger and his accomplices remain in power all the people who suffered under Nazism ... will have good reason to be wary of the Germany governed from Bonn.'[18]

Her gesture had a wide impact. A new approach had to be tried. The Russian economy was ailing. West Germany decided to try and woo the Soviets, instead of planning to bomb them into submission. In 1969 Kiesinger slipped out of the picture to be replaced by charismatic left-winger Willy Brandt.

The frugal son of a single parent, Brandt had to flee from the Nazis during the war. In 1946 he returned to Germany as Governor of Berlin. He also wanted the removal of Berlin's barbed wire entangled Wall dividing East and West Germany, but believed in a conciliatory approach.

Brandt's arrival in power gave a fillip to left-wing movements everywhere. Thousands of British university students embraced the Communist ideology while in Germany the violent Baader-Meinhof gang was born. Peace-loving Brandt would forge lasting relationships with his Soviet colleagues but his mission was to secure political concessions from the Soviet Union through economic help.

The Deutschmark had been stabilised at too low a level after the Second World War. The world was awash with West German exports. Deutsche Bank Chairman Hermann Abs campaigned stridently against the revaluation of the Deutschmark but after Brandt became Chancellor he allowed it to be revalued by a hefty amount against the dollar. The country seemed to have secured two major concessions for revaluing its currency, permission to construct a pipeline to the Soviet Union to meet its energy requirements, and finance so that German industry could help modernise Brazil.

America had been fighting Communism in Korea and Vietnam and her economy was flagging. Although the 'Reds' in Russia were her greatest bogeys, it was difficult for her to refuse a plea from her close friends in West Germany. So although Adenauer had been an ardent supporter of the NATO decision to ban the sale of large-bore pipelines which could be used to transport Soviet oil and gas to the West in the early 1960s, a massive new pipeline deal was signed on 28th April 1969, through which Germany would receive fifty-two billion cubic metres of gas over twenty years in return for providing Russia with the pipelines.

Germany did not actually need the gas at this time[19] but the deal led to increased trade and a rapid thaw in political relations. Brandt secured 'Four-Power' access to Berlin and increased human contact between the two sides of the city. However, even though the investment possibilities in Russia and Eastern Europe were exciting, revaluing the Deutschmark would make German exports more expensive. So Germany was offered another sweetener. The US offered loans to facilitate West German business investment in Brazil.

American investors had shunned lending money to Brazil because Brazil had reneged on her American debts in the 1930s and was governed by a repressive military dictatorship in the 1960s. This led to widespread disturbances on the streets and to the kidnap of the US ambassador, Charles Burke Elbrick.

'Then, quite suddenly', Professor Stephen A Shuker, remarked in 1988 in his book *American 'Reparations' to Germany 1919– 1933, Implications for the Third World Debt crisis*, the climate of investment opinion changed.[20] American loans poured into Brazil to facilitate German investment in the country. One of the Generals, Ernesto Geisel, was of German extraction. He would soon become Brazilian President. West German investment in Brazil soared. In the 1970s, the city of São Paolo received the highest level of German investment in any one city in the world, including in West Germany.[21]

British companies were wary of investing in Brazil because of the unhappy labour situation, but German heavy industry was prepared to deal resolutely with shop floor defiance if necessary. Soon after the elections (in 1974) more than two hundred workers at Volkswagen were "put into jail at one time". There were also "innumerable imprisonments", mainly of metal workers, at Mercedes, Phillips, and other factories in São Bernadino and São Caetano. However, Josef Rust, Chairman of Volkswagen's supervisory board, expressed his satisfaction that his company had chosen Brazil for expansion, boasting: 'the returns to the parent company are frightening'.[22] The company agreed to increase the exports from its Brazilian operations from thirteen million dollars to four hundred million dollars. The Brazilian government was overjoyed.

The British and Americans were impressed that the West German economy seemed to be riding out the recession in Europe so well. They were filled with admiration for their erstwhile foe, whose people seemed ever more peace-loving. Nevertheless, West Germany's heavy industrialists and politicians appeared to be less worried about world peace than their electorate. In the mid-1970s a German firm signed an agreement with Brazil for the purchase of up to eight nuclear reactors and plants to enrich and reprocess nuclear fuels,[23] with the 'hot breath' of governmental support.

The Americans were dismayed as Brazil had not signed the Nuclear Non-Proliferation Treaty. They argued that West Germany should have prevented the countries it sold enrichment or reprocessing plants to from making weapons from the plutonium produced. However, the German industrialists' reply was that the International Atomic Energy Agency safeguards were all that could be hoped for.[24] They reiterated their view the following year, declaring that if countries really wanted the nuclear bomb, they would get it anyway.[25]

West Germany's intransigence over the nuclear plants it sold in Latin America upset new American President Jimmy Carter. The American people wanted the nuclear arms race scaled down after the Vietnam War. However, there was a hawkish lobby among the American military; West German politicians were also more bellicose than was popularly supposed.

Carter was bitterly condemned by German right-wingers for his decision not to proceed with the production of neutron weapons. Adenauer's former Defence Minister, Franz Josef Strauss, who had lost his job in 1962 after the left-wing newspaper *Der Spiegel* alleged that he was a threat to democracy and 'planning a nuclear war'[26] declared: 'Doubts about the US capacity to lead are not only permitted but are unfortunately justified ... When the federal (American) government finally pulled itself together enough to approve this weapon, the American President withdrew. In my knowledge of American history since World War II this is the first time an American President has openly and recognisably bowed to a Russian Czar.' [27]

Social Democrat politician Helmut Schmidt now replaced Willy Brandt as Chancellor. 'The firm jaw, the intense grey eyes, the sudden brilliant almost voracious smile' quickly won Schmidt a newspaper vote as 'Germany's No. 1 Sexy Man'.[28]

However, Schmidt was deceitful. When Schmidt was first elected to the Bundestag he had campaigned against nuclear weapons, but he soon lost his idealism. Even though German industry must have known of the weak state of the Russian economy, Schmidt soon expressed his disapproval to his NATO colleagues of meagre American plans for upgrading the US's conventional and nuclear forces to defend West Germany 'with the apparent course of events it suggests concerning limited nuclear options'.[29] After Russia deployed a modern accurate missile called the SS20 to defend its country, Schmidt argued that Soviet missile technology had advanced to such an extent that it would be easy for the Russians to select and knock out essential strategic targets in Europe.[30] He was supported by the hawkish American Committee for Present Danger in America. So, as he revealed in his memoirs, his arguments for the modernisation of America's nuclear weapons eventually prevailed:

'In the summer of 1977 disagreements as to the proper response to Soviet SS20s were added to our other differences of opinion (with the US) ... My efforts had only slight results (the opinion of American National Security Advisor Brezinski was that) ... should the Soviet Union ever threaten the Federal Republic with SS20s, the United States, using its strategic nuclear weapons, would be in a position to counter the threat ... At the outset Carter agreed with his security advisor ... Fifteen months later, however, there was quite a different outcome. They (the Americans) realised that what we call the "grey zone" could not be neglected.'

The Carter Administration eventually accepted the report of a working group of NATO members, which concluded that new intermediate-range nuclear weapons targeted against the Soviet Union would make it crystal clear to the Soviets that an isolated attack on Western Europe would be met by retaliation from American weapons aimed at Russia's heart.

These new weapons were not to be viewed as a counter weight to the SS20, but as a qualitatively new type of deterrent with its own rationale.[31]

The West German people were pacifists at this time. The rapprochement between the German people and their eastern neighbours was deepening. They would have been appalled if they had realised that it was their own government that was pushing America to modernise its nuclear weapons. They didn't even want any more nuclear power plants in Germany, let alone nuclear weapons. On 23rd February 1975 over 30,000 people occupied the earthworks near the tiny hamlet of Wyhl, near the wine growing district of Keiserstuhl in south-west Germany, where planning permission had been granted to build a nuclear reactor.

Schmidt decided that if any nation was to appear bellicose it had to be the US, not West Germany. At a closed meeting on 31st January 1979, Schmidt's divided cabinet eventually agreed that any decision to deploy new intermediate-range nuclear forces had to be taken by the American President alone, and that Bonn would not seek even partial control of any new warheads capable of striking the Soviet Union.[32]

Was it merely West German arguments within NATO that caused the US to change its mind about deploying new nuclear weapons or did the Brazilian nuclear reactor order play a part in their decision? If so, the West Germans continued to use the sale of nuclear technology to Brazil as a bargaining chip right up to the time that the Americans decided to go ahead with their new nuclear weapons project.

In May 1979, one month before Russia agreed to the important SALT II nuclear arms limitation accord, the Brazilians expressed a desire to export their nuclear technology. *Nucleonics Week* reassured its readers that the West Germans continued to have control over the transfer of technology and decision-making in the Brazil-West German nuclear reactor deal, four years after it had been agreed.[33] *Nucleonics Week* repeated the message with greater unease on 30th August 1979, when it carried the headline on its front page: 'Brazil pot boils as German hold on nuclear technology is revealed'.

Finally, in November 1979, *Nucleonics Week* revealed that after Iraq's Industry Minister Hassan Aliyin visited Brazil in August, the President of Brazil's state nuclear agency, Nuclebras, Paulo Noguiero Batista, flew to Baghdad in September to sign a 'protocol' for nuclear cooperation between the two countries.[34] Germany also seemed about to clinch a nuclear reactor deal with Argentina without adequate safeguards.[35]

Perhaps it was the prospect of Brazil (and Argentina) exporting technology that could be used to furnish countries like Iraq with nuclear bombs that finally persuaded Americans that West Germany's pleas about its defence could not be ignored. At any rate, in 1979, America decided on a massive new arms race, despite the fact that the Soviets had just signed the SALT II arms limitation agreement and that the Soviet economy was in its worst state since the Second World War.[36] By 1981 life expectancy in Russia would be declining, 'an unprecedented phenomenon in an advanced industrial society'.[37]

American public opinion stiffened against the Soviet Union in the autumn of 1979 after it was revealed that some three thousand Soviet troops were still stationed in Cuba. So in December 1979, NATO decided to deploy 572 new INF warheads, whilst simultaneously proposing new negotiations with the Soviets to limit their forces.[38] The Soviet invasion of Afghanistan at the end of December 1979[39] further worsened US-Soviet relations. New American President Ronald Reagan was more than happy to continue the nuclear arms modernisation programme which Carter had begun.

Meanwhile, the German public were horrified at the prospect of a possible nuclear war over their country, and public alarm grew about the possible contamination from the use of nuclear energy. So West Germany decided to lessen the pace of its industrial expenditure in Brazil.

The cost of the arms race would eventually cause the Soviet Union's collapse. It was also costly for America. And soon a new headache was added to the cost of producing new nuclear weapons to confront the Soviet Union – Brazil's reluctance to pay its debts. In 1984 Brazilian Finance Minister Ernane Galvêas declared: 'We're not going to pay off our debt, the bankers know it, the official institutions know it, and the governments know it.'

In 1987 Brazil was the world's largest coffee and sugar exporter, the seventh-largest steel producer and the ninth-largest car producer, yet in February 1987 it audaciously declared a moratorium on the payment of interest on its $101 billion debt, most of it owed to American banks. The American stock market crashed and the value of the dollar plunged. People lost money everywhere, including in West Germany.

On 12th November 1988, the fiftieth anniversary of the Kristallnacht Pogrom in which 91 Jewish people were murdered and an estimated 30,000 incarcerated in concentration camps, Herr Philipp Jenninger, the former aide to Franz Josef Strauss, present Speaker of the West German Bundestag and close friend of Chancellor Kohl, gave a speech lauding Hitler's triumphs in the 1930s. He said:

'From mass misery there was something like prosperity for the widest sections (of the population). Instead of desperation and hopelessness, optimism and self-confidence reigned. Did not Hitler just make reality what was just a promise under Wilhelm II – that is to bring wonderful times for the Germans?

'And as far as the Jews were concerned: hadn't they in the past measured themselves for roles that did not suit them? Didn't they finally have to accept restrictions? Didn't they perhaps, even deserve to be shown their place? And above all: Apart from wild exaggerations which were not to be taken seriously, didn't basic points of the propaganda reflect one's own speculations and convictions?'[40]

Herr Jenninger was sacked for his offensive words. Yet he and his friends must have been pleased. The American financial world was taking a battering and the Soviet Union's whole economic structure was about to collapse.

On 9th November 1989 the Berlin Wall crumbled, just a year after Philip Jenninger's speech. By goading America and the Soviet Union into an ever more expensive arms race, Germany had succeeded in securing Adenauer and Erhard's goal of German reunification without bloodshed. It was a monumental achievement. But Germany had played for high stakes and frightened the whole world. Did its actions bode well for the future?

CHAPTER TWELVE

Germany and the
Lehman Brothers Crash

Western European leaders were ecstatic in public when the Berlin Wall fell, but privately they were dismayed. Germany had twice tried to grab a huge empire stretching from the Atlantic to the Urals, at the cost of millions of dead and wounded. Although not a shot had been fired to secure the fall of the Berlin Wall, many quaked at what might lie ahead. German Neo-Nazis paraded in the streets of Berlin and France's Socialist President, François Mitterrand, was gripped by a paroxysm of fear. He warned Mrs Thatcher that unification would result in Germany gaining more influence than Hitler ever had and urged her to publicly oppose heavy weight German Chancellor Kohl's plans for immediate reunification.

At a personal level Helmut Kohl and Margaret Thatcher had not had the warmest of relationships. Kohl complained that Thatcher took exception to him serving her his favourite dish of pig's stomach with sausage and sauerkraut, while she was vexed that he excused himself quickly from their meeting, only to be spotted 'scoffing cream cakes in a nearby teashop'.[1]

Thatcher's plea for a five-year transition period with a lower exchange rate for East Germany before the two Germanys united fell on stony ground. Chancellor Kohl brushed the idea aside and the East Germans supported him. Although they had the fifth-strongest economy in Europe, they had been under the control of the Stasi. The Stasi was one of the largest secret services the world had ever known, with links to Russia's KGB. Kohl offered East Germans freedom, democracy and the D-Mark. East Germany was delighted to be incorporated into a new reunited Germany.

After any honeymoon, however, adjustments often have to be made. For East Germans the adjustments were particularly hard to cope with. They went to the sun on holiday with their precious new D-Marks, only to find that their employers had gone bankrupt when they returned. The D-Mark was too expensive an exchange rate for East Germany's fragile industries. The area soon became an industrial desert, with depopulation and huge levels of unemployment. Former Bundesbank official, Horst Bockelmann, later commented: 'It was not a surprise that the East German economy should collapse. If you wanted to ruin an economy that was the way to do it.'

Britain was also taken for a ride in 1990. Most British people shared the East Germans' joy at the fall of the Berlin Wall and they supported Britain entering the Exchange Rate Mechanism (ERM) in 1990, which meant that the pound would float within a narrow range of the D-Mark. Margaret Thatcher's objections against the ERM were swept aside and her Secretary of State for Environment, Nicholas Ridley, was sent packing after he declared: 'Economic and Monetary Union is a German racket, designed to take over the whole of Europe.' In next to no time Thatcher went too.

Unfortunately, joining the ERM proved to be a disaster for Britain. The Bundesbank urgently needed to attract funds to pay unemployment benefits to all the formerly fully employed East German citizens who were now on the industrial scrap heap. So it decided to raise interest rates to unprecedented levels. The Bundesbank's high interest rates had a devastating effect on the weaker British economy. Britain had to raise her interest rates even higher than Germany's to preserve funds at home, putting a terrible pressure on mortgages and businesses. On 16th September 1992, faced with a crippled economy and massive speculation, Britain bowed out of the ERM on the day that became known as 'Black Wednesday'.

The rise in German interest rates after reunification also had disastrous repercussions in Yugoslavia. The Communist Federation of Yugoslavia was once a powerful country but had decayed ever since President Tito's demise. German high interest rates between 1990 and 1992 squeezed funds from the whole of Europe, bringing the Yugoslavian economy almost to breaking point. Many considered that the Balkan bloodshed in the 1990s was exclusively due to Serbian General Milosevic and his henchmen's excesses, but it seemed that there was another side to the story.

After the fall of the Berlin Wall the Communist system was discredited everywhere. Hopefully, Yugoslavia would soon abandon it too. Time was what was needed at this difficult economic juncture. Yet the Croatians were in a hurry to desert the sinking ship and set up their own republic, and they had a powerful ally – Germany. The Croatian ruling party declared Croatia's sovereignty on 22nd December 1990, six months after the collapse of the Berlin Wall. It asserted that the Croats aspired to democracy, western values and free-market culture, in contrast to the Serbs, whom they depicted as old-fashioned barbaric Communists. This excited the press, especially in America. Yugoslavia was the last bastion of Communism in Eastern Europe. The Serbs were destined to become the sole villains of the Balkan tragedy.

On 25th June 1991, the Slovenian and Croatian parliaments declared their independence from Yugoslavia. German Minister of Foreign Affairs Hans Dietrich Genscher supported their claim with his American counterpart, James Baker.

In December 1991, the European Economic Community heads of state gathered for a crucial meeting at Maastricht to agree a treaty for the future development of the European Community. Before the meeting, EEC members were eleven to one in favour of maintaining Yugoslavia's unity. However, at four in the morning, after heated discussions on European security and a common policy on foreign affairs, Germany managed to force the EEC into recognising Croatia and Slovenia's independence, as a condition of its involvement.[2]

The Maastricht Treaty was signed and a press statement issued, stating that the EEC was united on all major policy matters. A few days later Germany recognised Croatia and Slovenia as independent states, effective from 15th January 1992.

In 2009, aged pro-Serb French General, Pierre Marie Gallois, would allege that the dismemberment of Yugoslavia had been planned by Germany, even before President Tito's death in 1980. General Gallois was the French representative at informal, two-day international seminars, presided over by German Defence Minister, Franz Joseph Strauss, in the 1970s. He declared that it was at these seminars that Germany sought to gain acceptance for the proposal that Yugoslavia was already 'inanimate' and that its structure should be altered after Tito's death.

He would also allege that Germany's purpose was to reward Croats and Muslims, who had supported it during the Second World War, and get its own back on Serbia, which had held up precious German divisions from joining the attacks on Moscow and Leningrad.

In 1992, after Croatia gained its independence, the Serb areas within Croatia's new boundaries tried to exercise their right to self-determination, but the European Community feared that Yugoslavia would splinter further. It refused to acknowledge the Serbs' claim, stating that the areas they lived in were part of the Republic of Croatia. The Serbs foolishly refused to accept the new realities of the situation. This led to four years of conflict, twenty-two thousand deaths and a total Croatian victory.

On 6th April 1992, the anniversary of Hitler's Second World War invasion of Yugoslavia, Germany forced the European Community's recognition of Bosnia-Herzegovina.[3] Britain's Lord Carrington resigned his post as Peace Negotiator. Yet America saw the conflict as a fight for democracy against Communism and threw her might against the Serbs, who then brutally tried to get their own back for the 'Serbian Genocide' in the Second World War.

America could count herself as a winner in the Balkan conflict because Communism was vanquished. Yet Germany was the overall victor. Croatia, Slovenia and Bosnia-Herzegovina were all now members of the UN and certain to vote with Germany on crucial issues. Historical maps also revealed a striking resemblance between the zones of Germany's current political and economic dominance in the region and those of the Holy Roman Empire.[4]

With the fall of the Berlin Wall, the Allies and America expected the payment of the rest of the Second World War reparations, which were due under the terms of the 1953 London Agreement, but President Kohl declared that the costs of reunification were huge and his pockets were empty. Those to whom Second World War reparations were due found themselves in exactly the same position as Germany's First World War creditors in the early 1920s. Germany was large and powerful; if it chose not to pay there was very little they could do to exact payment.

In 2000, in a test case, the Greek High Court obliged Germany to pay twenty-eight million euros in compensation for the massacre at the village of Distomo on 10th June 1944, when a total of 218 men, women and children were raped and killed in revenge for a partisan attack. Yet the German Federal Constitution Court ruled in 2006 that Germany did not have to pay compensation to individuals seeking damages over war crimes. With the exception of compensation paid to forced labourers, no more Second World War reparations have, to date, been paid.

In 1990 President Mitterrand was horrified at the implications of the fall of the Berlin Wall. The German newspaper *Der Spiegel* would later accuse him of having forced an unwilling Germany to abandon the D-mark and adopt the euro as his price for agreeing to German reunification.

German interest rates were climbing steeply even before the Berlin Wall came down and were forecast to rise to the stratosphere in the years ahead. Like Britain, in the early 1990s France was suffering greatly from being tied to the D-mark. Her prize industrial enterprises were also teetering on the edge of bankruptcy. 'We may have the nuclear bomb, but the Germans have the deutsche mark' protested the officials at the Élysée Palace as they watched their economy going into a tail-spin.[5] They were desperate not to quit the European Community like Britain. Their hope was that if all the countries, including Italy, Portugal, Ireland and Greece, adopted the euro it would be a weaker currency.

Mitterrand was bitterly criticised in Germany for forcing it to abandon its beloved D-Mark and to adopt the euro instead. However, German Finance Minister, Theo Waigel, insisted that the adoption of a single currency had always been Germany's ambition. And what better time could Germany have to negotiate than when it had an excuse to put its interest rates up to unprecedented levels? Former Bundesbank President Karl Otto Pöhl, said later: 'I was convinced that we would have to wait at least a hundred years for the euro' – but the French and the Italians were already pleading for Germany to adopt it.

Chancellor Kohl gave his view that the adoption of the euro would be a 'castle in the air' without economic and monetary union. The long hard negotiations for the Maastricht Treaty began.

Kohl was right about the German people's dislike for relinquishing the D-mark. The plans for the euro created uproar in Germany. Both the best selling *Bild-Zeiting* newspaper and the up market *Der Spiegel* voiced the German people's alarm at the thought of any institution except the Bundesbank being in control of their currency.

The Bundesbank had a special place in the German peoples' hearts because of its claim to have preserved the value of the mark after Germany's Great Inflation of 1923. Heart-rending pictures of little old ladies carrying baskets of worthless marks continued to terrify the German people with the thought that another Great Inflation could reoccur in the future. 'Never again' was the Bundesbank's rallying cry, even though Germany had presided over two more hyper-inflations, one in 1948 and the other in East Germany in 1990.[6]

So the Bundesbank prescribed the strictest criteria for aspiring members of the euro, the annual deficit for member countries should not exceed 3 per cent except in exceptional circumstances and governmental debt should not exceed 60 per cent of GDP. The new European Central Bank would be situated in Frankfurt, all the future eurozone banks would be independent and the ECB would become a 'virtual' clone of the Bundesbank.

Watching from the side lines, Karl Otto Pöhl concluded that the French and Italians were ready to agree to almost anything to escape the grip of the D-Mark. Meanwhile Chancellor Kohl decided to give France massive financial assistance to enable it to stay in the ERM. There were strings attached, however, one of which was that a forty thousand strong French- and German-speaking military force was to be formed – out of the control of NATO.[7]

As the 1990s continued, and the arrival of the euro drew near, French worries about Germany's predatory ambitions eased. The costs of unifying the two Germanys seemed to be throttling the German economy. Britain's *The Economist* magazine even labelled Germany the 'sick man of Europe' after the euro arrived (virtually) in 1999.

On 1st January 2002 the euro coins arrived, accompanied by fireworks, champagne and Beethoven's 'Ode to Joy'. German Chancellor, Gerhard Schröder, declared: 'We are witnessing the dawn of an age that the people of Europe have dreamed of for centuries',[8] but the German people remained sceptical.

Indeed there was no joy for them at all in the first few years after the arrival of the euro. Soon over four million German people were out of work. It's no wonder that Katina Barysch still called her 2004 article for the Centre for European Reform 'Germany, the sick man of Europe?' Her title was almost the same as *The Economist*'s in 1999, but importantly it included a question mark. Although Germany had breached the sacred Maastricht criteria with a deficit of more than 3 per cent of GNP, it had become the world's largest exporter, with a hundred billion euro trade surplus in 2003. The only blot on the landscape was its huge unemployment rate of nearly 10 per cent of the population, which would rise to a whopping 12 per cent in February 2005.[9]

One reason why unemployment was so high was because there was no money in the country. The German people didn't trust the euro so they had put their money abroad. Yet when the money arrived in less profitable countries, there were fewer viable options for investment.

Former American President Bill Clinton could speak conversational German, as he had studied it at university. He felt a kindred spirit with the German people after reunification, and had stated, '*Amerika steht an Ihrer Seite jetzt und für immer*' (America stands at your side, now and for ever) to an audience of fifty thousand people at the Brandenburg Gates in Berlin.

Everyone knew that there would be a flight of some cash until the reluctant Germans got used to the euro. The tantalising question is whether Clinton had actually been asked if presently thriving America was ready to accept some German funk money before the euro gained acceptance at home.

In September 1999 *The New York Times* reported that the Clinton Administration was pushing for more lending to low and moderate income borrowers so that they could share in the American dream. The idea was that people would only have to put a few dollars down to buy a house and then repay when the house went up in value. The sub-prime market grew slowly though, with sub-prime mortgages representing only 10 per cent of all mortgages up until 2004.

Then the Federal Reserve raised interest rates because of the cost of the war in Iraq. In 2004 the National Public Radio Correspondent alleged that there was 'a giant pool of money', which was seeking a supply of relatively safe, income generating investments in the US. Unfortunately, however, when the foreign money arrived it was attracted by the sub-prime market. Buoyed up by the 'giant pool of money' sub-prime mortgages swelled to 20 per cent of all American mortgages.

In 2006 the euro was strong but the dollar was still weak and the cost of creating peace in Iraq was high. So America put her interest rates up to over 8 per cent. This was unfortunate because the European Central Bank started to inch up its admittedly low interest rates too. It raised them by a quarter of a per cent five times in 2006. By the end of December the American sub-prime market was looking sick. The New York Stock Exchange tried to restore order.

On 14th March 2007 New Century Financial Corporation, the second-biggest sub-prime mortgage lender in the US was de-listed by the New York Stock Exchange and the Federal Reserve predicted that the next move in interest rates would be downward.

On 14th March and on 13th June 2007 the European Central Bank raised interest rates. The rises had an impact in America. In July, Bear Stearns announced the bankruptcy and liquidation of two large hedge funds that used leverage to invest in Collateralized Debt Obligations backed by sub-prime mortgage loans.[10] On 6th August the tenth-largest retail mortgage lender in the US, the American Home Mortgage Investment Corporation, filed for bankruptcy.

The next day, perhaps understandably, the French bank BNP Paribas announced that it was suspending withdrawals on two of its funds that were heavily invested in the US sub-prime market. Unfortunately, its decision hit Britain's Northern Rock Bank.

Northern Rock, a profitable and solvent bank, had relied for much of its borrowing on the wholesale markets, which had previously seemed to have so much money to spare. Now the wholesale money had vanished and there was a gaping hole in its finances. The press got wind of this drastic development, there was a run on the bank and dreadful pictures were shown in the media of thousands of desperate people queuing up to retrieve their savings. The following Monday the government stepped in to guarantee all Northern Rock's deposits.[11]

On 18th September 2007, American prime interest rates were reduced to 7.75 per cent, in October to 7.5 per cent, in December to 7.25 per cent and in January 2008 they were reduced twice – to 6.5 per cent and 6 per cent – in a desperate attempt to stop the sub-prime mortgage crisis getting out of hand. These measures were followed by further large reductions in interest rates in March to 5.25 per cent and in April to 5.0 per cent.

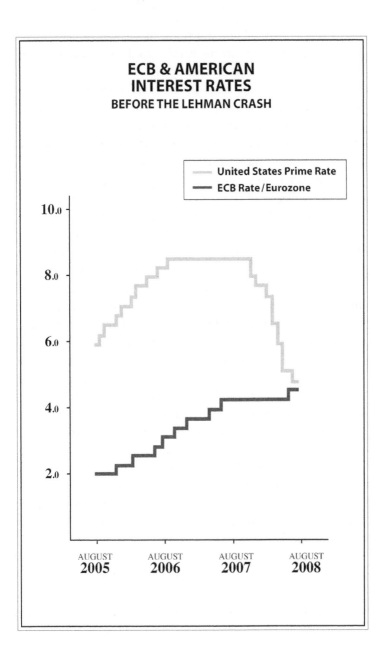

**ECB & AMERICAN
INTEREST RATES**
BEFORE THE LEHMAN CRASH

- - - - United States Prime Rate
—— ECB Rate / Eurozone

10.0

8.0

6.0

4.0

2.0

AUGUST
2005

AUGUST
2006

AUGUST
2007

AUGUST
2008

However, the American sub-prime mortgage crisis continued. In March 2008 Bear Stearns itself agreed to be acquired by J P Morgan Chase & Co in the hope of staving off bankruptcy. There was a full-scale crisis in the banking industry and the New York Stock Exchange teetered on the edge of disaster.

In July 2008 the European Central Bank put interest rates up again to 4.25 per cent, saying that the rise in world oil and commodity prices was inflationary. Two months later the global financial services firm Lehman Brothers collapsed, threatening the collapse of the entire American banking system.

In 2011 the US Financial Crisis Inquiry Commission looked at the unhappy saga before the Lehman crash and concluded that the 'crisis was avoidable and was caused by widespread failures in financial regulation, including the Federal Reserve's failure to stem the tide of toxic mortgages; dramatic breakdowns in corporate governance, including too many financial firms acting recklessly and taking on too much risk; an explosive mix of excessive borrowing and risk by households and Wall Street that put the financial system on a collision course with crisis; policy makers ill-prepared for the crisis, lacking a full understanding of the financial system they oversaw and systemic breaches in accountability and ethics at all levels'.

The US Financial Crisis Inquiry Commission's conclusions sounded pretty conclusive but they contained no historical parallels with previous major stock market crashes and without them a definitive judgement cannot be made.

There have been three huge stock market crashes in the period covered by this book; the stock market crash of 1873, the stock market crash of 1929 and the stock market crash in 2008, and they all bear remarkable similarities: the arrival of a huge new currency, a stock market bubble, rising interest rates – and a horrendous crash!

The 1873 crash occurred after Bismarck's 'Second' Reich, comprising twenty-seven highly disparate states, adopted the

Gold Standard. At first the arrival of the French indemnity in Germany encouraged people to spend. Then interest rates rose and silver was removed from the German coinage. In 1873 there was a devastating stock market crash. Bismarck blamed Austria and Austria blamed the Jews. Europe was plunged into a long depression and the scandals went on for years but eventually Bismarck achieved the economic consolidation of his new Reich.

The stock market crash of 1929 was also associated with the arrival of a large new currency, gold. After Germany returned to the 'gold standard (in effect)' all the major countries gradually returned to the Gold Standard. In 1928 a huge wad of money escaped from Germany to America, spooked by the arrival of Germany's socialist coalition government. In the happy cash-filled economic climate, the German government managed to extricate itself from all the financial controls the French had put on its economy. Then it bought so much gold that Britain was forced to raise interest rates in September 1929. The trigger for the crash came when prominent politician, newspaper magnate and former Pan-German, Alfred Hugenberg, received endorsement for his and Hitler's petition to call upon the German government to tear up the Treaty of Versailles and all its obligations, on the grounds that Germany was guiltless of starting the First World War.

There was no political trigger to the stock market crash of 2008. Yet the economic similarities between the crashes were apparent. A huge new currency, the euro, had arrived, just like the Gold Standard in the 1920s. There was also a mass exodus of cash from Germany, just as happened in 1928 and 1929. Germany was also said to be 'the sick man of Europe' in the early years of the euro, just as it was alleged to be 'sick' in the 1920s because of its huge reparations obligations.

According to the Bank for International Settlements, Germany lent almost one and a half trillion dollars to Greece,

Ireland, Spain, Portugal and Italy before the Lehman Brothers crash. How much of the 'giant pool of foreign money' that arrived in America was German was hard to assess but it was pretty clear that 'wherever parties were taking place, German banks were supplying the drinks'.[12]

Such was Germany's prestige that everywhere German money arrived, money from other sources came too. Indeed, after the German banks put twenty-one billion dollars into Icelandic banks, UK investors, including pension funds and hospitals, could not resist putting thirty billion dollars into Iceland as well.

From January 2006, interest rates in the eurozone started to rise, quarter point by quarter point. The American Federal Reserve Bank raised its rates too. As America had been weakened by the Iraq debacle, American interest rates had to be much higher than the ECB's in order to attract funds. By June 2006, America's interest rates had risen to a peak of 8.25 per cent.

In 2007, the German government decided to cut corporation tax and give other advantages to industry, and to raise VAT by 3 per cent in order to pay for them. Naturally, company bosses were asked by their workers for money in compensation. I G Metall boss Jurgen Peters declared: 'Order books are full, and profits are surging, so they can't fob off workers with cheap pay.'[13]

Yet, after wage increases of 4.1 per cent were agreed with Germany's most powerful union, I G Metall, and dark-haired heavyweight President of the Bundesbank, Axel Weber, insisted that European Central Bank's Governor, Jean-Claude Trichet, must raise interest rates throughout the eurozone in order to curb German inflation.

Statistics later revealed that German wages actually fell in real terms between the year 2000 and 2007[14] and President Sarkozy of France complained bitterly that the euro was already so high in relation to the dollar and the Chinese yuan that it was ruining French competitiveness. Indeed France's bank chief, Christian Noyer, declared flatly: 'There is no concern that (eurozone) inflation will get out of hand. The risk has not increased.'[15] Yet, such was the power of the Bundesbank that the eurozone put interest rates up twice in the spring of 2007, reaching 4 per cent in June.

This must have alarmed the American authorities. They knew that the only way to help their beleaguered home owners was to lower rates. If the eurozone put its interest rates down it could alleviate the desperate problem in the US by allowing the authorities to lower their rates in an orderly manner. However, in October 2007, Bundesbank Chairman Axel Weber declared that inflation was rising in Germany and eurozone interest rates would have to rise at least once more to curb it. Traders began to believe that Axel Weber would be able to enforce his view in European Central Bank summits despite President Sarkozy's opposition and the damage that the high rate for the euro was doing to France's industry. They hedged their bets accordingly.[16]

In November the European Central Bank held interest rates at 4 per cent. Beleaguered ECB President, Jean-Claude Trichet, declared that the present rate of inflation in the eurozone of 2.6 per cent was caused by a spike in oil and food prices and would subside the following year. France's Airbus and its car producers were suffering immensely from the euro's high value and Trichet was annoyed by the traders who had transferred their funds to the euro, calling the euro's 10 per cent rise against the dollar 'brutal'. Nevertheless, Axel Weber declared that inflation in Germany could increase to 3 per cent by the end of December and people believed that he could enforce his view that eurozone interest rates must rise again.[17]

American interest rates came tumbling down in the autumn of 2007 and in the first months of 2008 as experts predicted a

40 per cent chance of the American downturn becoming a full blown recession.[18] What America needed was for Europe to reduce its interest rates too. Yet, tension remained high in the spring of 2008 as pundits predicted that eurozone interest rates would go higher and the price of oil continued to soar. Excluding the spike in the price of oil, alcohol, food and tobacco, eurozone inflation remained at 2 per cent in June 2008[19] but the oil price continued to climb to the stratosphere affecting the statistics.

The price of oil had fallen to $60 a barrel in the early part of 2007 before rising steeply to $90 a barrel in October 2007. On 2nd January 2008 the price for light crude hit $100 a barrel. On 18th April it reached $119.90. On 6th June it rose $11 in twenty-four hours shocked by a rumour of an Israeli attack on Iran.

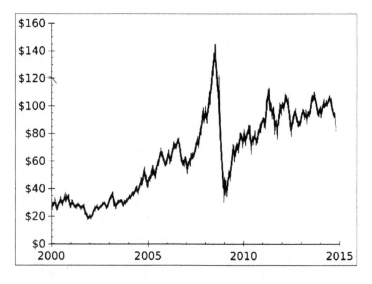

Iranian Oil Minister Gholam-Hossein Nozari declared stoutly that world markets were saturated with oil, and the Saudis promised to increased production. However, on 27th June prices touched $141.71 a barrel for August delivery amid Libya's threat to cut output and the OPEC's President's prediction that prices would rise to $170 by the autumn.[20]

On 3rd July the price for Brent North Sea crude oil for August delivery rose to $145 a barrel. Trichet declared that eurozone inflation had reached 4 per cent. He reluctantly raised eurozone interest rates to 4.25 per cent on 9th July 2008 despite a marked slowdown in the eurozone economy.[21] As American interest rates were only a fraction higher than the ECB's, at 5 per cent, his action immediately drew money back to Europe. Two months later Lehman Brothers collapsed.

Germany admitted no responsibility for the Lehman crash. It did not acknowledge that the escape of funds from Germany after the arrival of the euro could have caused the bubble in world markets, nor that the head of the Bundesbank, Axel Weber, was unjustified in pushing ECB President Jean-Claude Trichet to raise interest rates in 2007 for the entire European Union on the grounds that inflation in Germany was getting out of control (after his increase in VAT caused the workers to ask for higher wages in compensation). Weber also went on record, in December 2007, as saying that the eurozone interest rates would have to raise again, despite the fragile state of the American economy and the hurt that it would cause France's industry.

As the huge surge in the price of oil contributed to Trichet's disastrous decision to raise the European Union's interest rates in 2008, it is worth examining the reason behind the surge. A booming China's voracious appetite for oil naturally affected the oil price. Tensions in the Middle East and Nigeria upset the price of oil as well. However, there was another reason for the oil spike. It was priced in dollars. Oil had been only $60 dollars a barrel in the spring of 2007. When observing that the oil price had risen by a third to $90 in October 2007 the BBC commented that its price was affected by the reducing strength of the dollar against the euro.[22]

If the weakness of the dollar was already affecting the price of oil in the autumn of 2007, it would have affected it far more in 2008 when American interest rates tumbled and the eurozone was threatening to raise rates. If the eurozone hadn't threatened a further rise in interest rates from the autumn of 2007 onwards, the pressure against the dollar might have been reduced, the oil price lower and inflation in Europe less, in which case Trichet might been able to resist calls for the last disastrous hike in the eurozone's interest rates!

The German press's view of the Lehman crash was simple. *Die Welt* declared: 'Greed and stupidity have plunged the market into chaos ... Any economics student in his first semester could have concluded that the American economic model is not tenable', while *Die Zeit* posed the question: 'Is finance-capitalism finished? And predicted the 'end of world domination by the Anglo-Saxon finance industry'.

The American hedge funds were blamed in particular for the Lehman crash. The German leadership had been gunning for the elimination of the hedge fund system ever since 1998, when the American hedge fund LTMC went bankrupt owing $4.6 billion.

In 2005, President of the German Financial Supervisory Authority, Jochen Sanio, went as far as to declare that hedge funds were the 'black holes of the world financial system' and the *Süddeutsche Zeitung* warned that they could trigger another LTMC-size disaster, which would 'threaten the entire financial system of the globe'. After the Lehman crash, Reuters reported that German Chancellor Angela Merkel had indirectly criticised the United States and Britain for thwarting her government's attempts to tighten controls on financial markets before the crash, under the heading 'I told you so'.

Undoubtedly the hedge funds, and other financial instruments, made a bad situation much worse at a critical time but there was no way that the hedge funds alone could have caused such an immense catastrophe. In view of this book's research into the 1929 stock market crash, it concludes that Germany should have admitted its own mistakes in 2008 before ascribing blame.

In 2009 the *Economic Intelligence Unit Survey* expressed surprise that 'the German banking system has been among the worst affected anywhere ... despite the absence of high price inflation and credit growth'. But luckily it appeared that the taxpayers of Europe had come to its rescue.

In writing about the Greek crisis on 23rd May 2012 *Bloomberg*'s editors wrote under the catchy heading, 'Hey Germany: You got a Bailout, Too':

'Irresponsible borrowers can't exist without irresponsible lenders. Germany's banks were Greece's enablers ... According to the Bank for International Settlements, by December 2009 German banks had amassed claims of $704 billion on the so-called PIGS – Portugal, Italy, Ireland, Greece and Spain, much more than the German banks' aggregate capital. In other words, they lent more than they could afford.' At the start of the crisis German banks had 30 per cent of all the loans made to these countries public and private sectors, representing over 15 per cent of the size of the German economy.[23]

But help was at hand for the German banks. The PIGS did not declare themselves bankrupt and refuse to pay their foolish lenders like Iceland had done in similar circumstance. They behaved totally honourably. *Bloomberg* explained:

'When German banks pulled money out of Greece, the other national central banks of the euro area collectively offset the outflow with loans to the Greek central bank. These loans appeared on the balance sheet of the Bundesbank, Germany's central bank, as claims on the rest of the euro area. This mechanism, designed to keep the currency area's accounts in balance, made it easier for the German banks to exit their positions ... In short, over the last couple of years, much of the risk sitting on German banks' balance sheets shifted to the taxpayers of the entire currency union.'

After the 1929 stock market crash, German Chancellor Heinrich Brüning advocated a policy of 'austerity' and a return to sound money. 'Austerity' was Germany's clarion call after the 2008 crash, despite the fact that Chancellor Brüning had adopted 'austerity' in 1930 for political reasons in order to put pressure on Germany's creditors to allow Germany to tear up the Treaty of Versailles, return to dictatorship and to re-arm.

The American economist, Paul Krugman, was censorious of Germany's austerity policy after the 2008 crash in his book *End this Depression Now*, stating: 'While modern conventional wisdom links the rise of Hitler to the German hyperinflation of 1923, what actually brought him to power was the German depression of the early 1930s, a depression that was even more severe than that in the rest of Europe, thanks to the deflationary policies of Chancellor Heinrich Brüning'.[24]

On 7th February 2009 the German authorities decided that the government and Länder would adopt new rules compelling them to eliminate their budget deficits by 2020.[25] Naturally they lost no time in calling upon the entire European Union to adopt the same policy too. Their appeal initially found favour. People remembered Mr Micawber's famous caution in Charles Dickens' *David Copperfield* that 'happiness depends on living within your income' and were full of censure for Americans and southern Europeans who had taken advantage of Germany's previous largesse with loans. It was difficult, however, for the southern European countries to repay their loans because Germany had grabbed their home market and their economies were in a tail-spin. This is why the 'quantitative easing' adopted by the ECB to kick-start the European Union's economy and help the unemployed back into work, had so much less impact in Europe than America.

Germany's unemployment, however, actually fell after the Lehman crash, helped by the return of cash from abroad. The figures for Germany's production and export were most impressive. Although Germany was only the third-largest exporter in the world (as opposed to the largest in 1931), it was the second-richest country in the world and recorded the highest trade surplus, worth $270 billion.[26] Yet in their book *From the Sick Man of Europe to Economic Superstar*, Christian Dustmann and his co-authors gave a depressing reason for Germany's economic success. Those at the bottom of the pile in Germany had seen their wages, in real terms, 'dramatically decline'.[27]

As the German leadership was so tough with the East Germans in 1990, it was going to shed few tears over the travails of the citizens of southern Europe. Germany lent the so-called PIGS (Portugal, Italy, Ireland Greece and Spain), a fortune before the Lehman crash. Afterwards the PIGS never thought about defaulting on their debts, as that would have excluded them from the European Union, which had enriched them for decades before; nevertheless millions became unemployed and extremism grew in their countries.

The Labour Party in France declared: 'The Community project – of Europe – is hurt by the selfish inflexibility of Chancellor Merkel, who only thinks about the savings of the German depositors, the trade balance recorded by Berlin and its electoral depositors.'

In Spain a reporter wrote in *El Pais*: 'Angela Merkel, like Hitler, declared war on the rest of the Continent, this time to make sure of having an essential economic space.'

While in Greece 'Germanophobia' reached its height as desperate young people dressed up in SS uniforms and shouted: 'No to the Fourth Reich!'[28]

Germany's *Der Spiegel* gave a different perspective from the German people's point of view. It wrote of the arrival of the euro: 'And so ... elephants like Germany and France came together with mice like Portugal, Ireland and Luxembourg. Stable, prosperous countries of the north shared their common currency with shaky, underdeveloped countries of the south; mature industrialised nations joined forces with what were hardly more than developing countries.'

In 1992, this was just what Mitterrand wanted for the European Union's new currency – the euro. He felt that southern Europeans must have a weaker currency to survive in the new project. Yet after the arrival of the euro Germany's exports to the PIGS soared while their own industries shrivelled.[29] There were other benefits for Germany. Every time that there was a crisis in Greece, the euro plunged in value and German exports to the rest of the world benefited, but Greece did not receive much thanks.

Apparently when Mitterrand first heard that Chancellor Kohl was bent on immediate German reunification after the fall of the Berlin Wall, he 'threw a small temper tantrum lasting several hours'. It was not only the strength of the D-mark he was worried about. He imagined 'a new superpower rising up on the eastern border of his country ... whose political might would shatter post-war harmony in Europe'.[30]

After the fall of the Berlin Wall, the EU expanded eastwards. Poland, Lithuania, Latvia and Estonia embraced democracy and flourished with the freedom to travel to the West. People in Western Ukraine saw how rich the Poles had become and longed, like them, to take the long march to Germany and England to enrich themselves. However, the European Union was only prepared to offer Ukraine $800 million via the IMF in return for limited Association status and this came at the cost of painful economic reforms. In contrast Russia was prepared to offer twenty times as much and was the largest market for Ukrainian exports – bigger than the whole of the EU put together.[31] So Ukrainian President Viktor Yanukovych turned the EU deal down.

The subsequent genuine Ukrainian protests in Maidan Square in Kiev were hijacked by extreme right-wing Neo-Nazi groups[32] and the elected Ukrainian government was forcibly overthrown. Russian President Vladimir Putin lost no time in occupying Crimea, where the Russian fleet had been stationed for over a hundred and fifty years. He organised a favourable plebiscite among the predominately Russian-speaking citizens and declared it part of the Russian Federation.

The Americans were horrified and they were supported by the British. They called for sanctions against Russia; the Cold War seemed to be starting up again. However, the German reaction was more muted. Although German Defence Minister Ursula von der Leyen immediately called for NATO to station soldiers in the Baltics, and retired General Egon Ramms told the newspaper *Bild*: 'We need compulsory military service. There is no other way for Germany to guarantee national defence within the mutual alliance', [33] much of the press seemed sympathetic to Russia. Former German Chancellor Helmut Schmidt, who had deceived the German people about Germany's intentions in the 1970s, even called the sanctions against Russia 'dumb'.[34] As in the Cold War, Germany on the one side seemed to be encouraging NATO to take a hard line against Russia over Crimea, while on the other aiming to retain its business contacts.

Recently Germany has made more aggressive noises about the Russian-speaking separatist movement in the Donetz Basin near the Russian border, an area that it had coveted in the Second World War. In early May 2015 Germany called for a 'renaissance' of the transatlantic alliance to defend Western global hegemony. It also initiated a debate on NATO's nuclear rearmament, alleging that Russia 'has not only modernised its conventional armed forces … since 2008, but also upgraded its nuclear arsenal'.[35]

By June 2015 Germany seemed to have tired of America and NATO dragging their heels and decided that the Bundeswehr should purchase the MEADS air defence system (largely built in Germany), to replace the American Patriot system. Already the world's third-largest military exporter after United States and Russia,[36] it also decided to develop a new German/French battle tank to replace the German Leopard 2 and a 'weapons capable' drone. Military experts also asked for depleted uranium rounds to counter the new model of Russian tank.

Now the sons of the Waffen SS, who fought on Germany's side in the Second World War in Ukraine, and the sons of the Communists who fought on the Allied side, are fighting a civil war.[37] Corruption and brutality are emerging again as the horrific memories of the estimated seven million Ukrainians killed in the Second World War[38] resurface. In the meantime the Ukrainian economy is in dire straits and many German companies are aching to trade with Russia again. So Angela Merkel is pressing President Poroshenko to secure approval from the Fascists in Kiev's parliament for a constitutional amendment to provide Eastern Ukraine with special status.[39] Hopefully, agreement on this amendment will bring rapprochement between East and West, rather than a new Cold War to pay off old scores.

Conclusions

Does the German hierarchy exercise a benevolent influence over the Brussels bureaucrats and our historic rivals, the French, in the European Union today? Or are we in danger of 'Prussia' seizing control now that reunification has taken place?

After the Second World War, future President Conrad Adenauer told the British that their greatest mistake in 1815, was 'when you foolishly put Prussia on the Rhine as a safeguard against France and another Napoleon' and that 'Prussianism in its turn culminated in National Socialism'. The German people have been our friends for the last fifty years, but unless we face up to the truth about the First World War and its aftermath, Prussianism and even Nazism could return in Germany.

In the early 1950s, when America was faced with war against Communism in South Korea, she wanted German help to defend Western Europe against Stalin. She was willing to abandon securing post-Second World War reparations and let war criminals like Krupp out of prison in order to secure West Germany's help in the all-important struggle against Stalin. So the legend was promoted that we 'all fell into war' in 1914 and that Germany was charged huge and unfair reparations afterwards, leading to Hitler and the Second World War.

Most Americans and many British believed the story and it led to a blossoming of friendship between West Germany and its erstwhile enemies in the European Economic Community. However, when Hamburg University Professor Fritz Fischer at last researched the secret Austrian and Prussian archives, he found conclusive proof that German Chancellor Bethmann Hollweg had imitated Bismarck by egging Austria into war in 1914, while pretending to the British that he was doing his best to prevent it.

When Fischer published his heavy book *Griff nach der Weltmacht* (Grasp at World Power) it struck a discordant note. Although it caused a storm in Germany, it was published in English with the duller name of *Germany's Aims in the First World War* and was ignored by the general public. However this book has unravelled the telegrams which Fischer found and put them into chronological order. They reveal the evil influence Bismarck had on Chancellor Bethmann Hollweg and how Bethmann Hollweg pushed Russia into general mobilisation in 1914 because he believed that the German Social Democrats and the British Socialists would support his contention that Germany was innocent if Russia was labelled the warmonger.

If anyone in Britain blames Germany for starting the First World War today, they blame Wilhelm II, who lost his crown in 1918. Kaiser Bill did make bellicose statements. However, in the view of the militarist clique that surrounded him, he always backed away from war at the last moment. That was why Chancellor Bethmann Hollweg decided to copy Bismarck by spicing up the Kaiser's 'Halt in Belgrade' telegram, while insisting to his ambassador in Vienna:

'*You must carefully avoid the impression that we want to hold Austria back. We are concerned only to find a modus to enable the realisation of her aim without at the same time unleashing a world war, and should this prove unattainable, to improve as far as possible the conditions under which it is to be waged.'*

Bethmann Hollweg's sinister achievement was to prod Austria and Russia into war, even while pretending to the German Social Democrats and to Germany's many friends in Britain that he was a man of peace.

Professor Fritz Stern of Columbia University wrote in his review of *Germany's Aims in the First World War*: 'A book at once scholarly and dramatic; without it neither the history of modern Germany nor the First World War can be adequately understood.'

The book not only reveals how Germany started the First World War but also how much less it cost Germany to fight than the Allies. While Britain exhausted much of its national treasure buying iron and raw materials from America, Germany used France and Belgium's coal and iron throughout the conflict and operated their factories too. Germany also made a fortune out of Russia. In economic terms it won the First World War.

Unfortunately, as America never ratified the post-war Treaty of Versailles, the Allies were unable to bring the Kaiser, Wilhelm II, Chancellor Bethmann Hollweg or Generals Ludendorff and Hindenburg to trial. Research has also unearthed the fact that the Allies secured practically no meaningful cash in war reparations either. Without American backing, demands for 'cash' reparations could not be enforced.

How could the British government tell a million men that their efforts in the blood-filled trenches had been in vain? Impressionable John Maynard Keynes had grown up in 'a pro-German household', which employed German governesses, loved German philosophy and science and disregarded tales of the 'Jackboot'.[1]

Most of Keynes's friends had been pacifists. With the enthusiasm of youth, Keynes decried the Treaty of Versailles as 'abhorrent and detestable' indeed 'one of the most outrageous acts of a cruel victor in civilised history'. Gradually the establishment seized upon his story of poor and suffering post-war Germany, unable to pay large reparations, and eventually they believed it themselves. Meanwhile German history books accused Britain of starting the First World War.

In 1920, members of the former 'Prussian' military/industrial clique tried to reinsert the monarchy the minute that the American troops had gone home, but they were thwarted by the shop floor, who staged a general strike. Germany's Great Inflation eliminated Germany's internal debts, and bankrupted the workers, who were then forced to work longer hours for much lower wages. The Allies 'abhorrent and detestable' reparations were blamed for their misfortunes.

America poured money into Germany after its Great Inflation. Popular legend still relates that Germany used it to pay the reparations, but practically the only cash that Britain ever received during the 1920s was through a tariff on German exports.

The German coal industry made a fortune out of the British miners' strike. 1929 would also be a record year, with output up by 23per cent in the Ruhr and coke and briquette output up 50 per cent. German heavy industry was massacring Britain's all-important coal industry while pushing its friends in government to protest that the country was poor.

In the autumn of 1929, Germany was given a favourable reparations deal in order to persuade it to pay its reparations in cash. However, it then inched up British interest rates by draining Britain's gold reserves, before politician, and newspaper magnate, Alfred Hugenberg, put Hitler on the committee of his petition, stating that Germany should pay no reparations at all as it was absolutely 'guiltless' of starting the First World War. The predicted success of Hugenberg and Hitler's petition caused a disastrous collapse on Wall

Street, as reparations, related war-debt payments and even American loans were now dependent on Germany's good will. The western world was devastated while Hitler received a blast of publicity in time for the 1930 elections.

In 1930 a new Chancellor called Heinrich Brüning came to power in Germany. He was nicknamed *Hungerkanzler* because of his economic policy of 'austerity'. As Germany was such a strong country, his deflationary program affected all the countries on the Gold Standard. Yet Brüning was not implementing his policy for economic reasons, but to gain acceptance for reneging on paying reparations, tearing up the Treaty of Versailles, re-arming and persuading the unemployed and embittered German people to vote for dictatorship.

Brüning wanted the return of the monarchy. However, Krupp and Hugenberg favoured a man of the people like Hitler as dictator. Krupp came to an agreement with Stalin to force the German Communists to vote with Hugenberg and Hitler in the Reichstag, in return for modernising Stalin's armaments industry and heavy industrial base. Stalin sold his wheat at 'slave labour' prices on the world economy to pay for his precious armaments, which had a terrible effect on the American farming economy. Meanwhile the divide between the two left-wing German parties, the Social Democrats and the Communists, eventually enabled Hitler to secure power.

Germany seemed to target the America economy in the 1930s, to deter her from supporting the Allies in another war. American unemployment was huge before the Second World War. However, Americans blamed Britain for their misery, especially after Britain stopped paying her war debts. Britain would be made to pay her Second World War debts until the last penny was paid in 2006.

Although Germany lost the Second World War on the battlefield and its cities were devastated by Allied bombing, Senator Harley M Kilgore, in his report to the American

Senate Military Affairs Committee, claimed that Germany still had the world's third-strongest economy because it had lived off the countries it had conquered. The Americans were so relieved that they had secured the German army's 'unconditional surrender', that they decided to put their faith in West Germany as a bulwark against Communism.

The British people's meagre food rations were cut after the Second World War, but they were still accused of inhumanity because the German people were said to be dying from hunger in the British Controlled sector of the Ruhr. Chancellor of the Exchequer, Hugh Dalton, reluctantly spent £82 million extra to feed them but he declared of the gift: 'What we are doing amounts, essentially, to us paying reparations to the Germans.'

The British continue to be blamed to this day for the West German people's misery after the Second World War. However, as in the 1920s, the German leadership believed that it was imperative to wipe out the value of the currency and 'teach the German people how to work'. They also achieved other ambitions. In 1950, the former Nazi High Command wrote in its secret *Madrid Circular Letter* under the title: 'The War in Korea and World Political Possibilities for Germany and Europe':

'In order to bring the Americans back to reason and away from Potsdam, (peace agreement), we organised chaotic conditions in a thorough and systematic manner ... The peasants were delivering next to nothing to the cities; no coal was brought up from the pits, the wheels of industry were not turning, the people came near to starvation, the monetary systems were disintegrating – there was nothing for the Yankees to do but to give in and abandon the Potsdam programme'.[2] The German mark was stabilised at a very favourable level and Germany was given Marshall Aid.

However, it was after the start of the Korean War that West Germany achieved its greatest benefits. Nazi war criminals were released from prison, West Germany was let off paying war reparations and the idea of a United States of Europe took hold as a means of stopping all the European states from 'slithering into war'.

Although it is popularly supposed that the Frenchman Jean Monnet was the chief architect of European Unity, the Pan-Germans (who counted Gustav Krupp and his former managing director Alfred Hugenberg among their followers) had talked of creating a Germanic empire called Mitteleuropa before the First World War.

Mitteleuropa was envisaged to include much of Europe and the whole of the Austro-Hungarian Empire. It was to be initiated by means of a customs union, which would prepare the way for community-wide legal and political institutions. Finally, if necessary, it was envisaged that force might have to be used to complete the process.

Mitteleuropa was not achieved through the First World War. However, in the Second World War the Nazis wrote of their ambition to create a post-war 'European Economic Community' and the *Madrid Circular Letter* in 1950 revealed that Germany had mustered American support during the war declaring that there were circles in America who 'recognised in the Russian victory a strengthening of Communism, and they feared its complications and the shattering effects it entailed for the capitalist system ... These considerations resulted in a plan – first formulated secretly in Washington and later openly discussed, aimed at the creation of a united Europe as a bulwark against Russia, with the proviso that a strengthened and rearmed Germany be incorporated in such a combination.'

From this we can conclude that the post-war concept of the European Union was initially conceived by Germany, with the support of America, rather than by Jean Monnet of France.

Naturally America wanted West Germany to be part of NATO too, but it drove a hard bargain for becoming a member. It promised 'never to have recourse to force to achieve the reunification of Germany', but it extracted a pledge from the Western Allies in 1955 that 'the achievement through peaceful means of a fully free and unified Germany remains a fundamental goal'. The threat in these words was soon apparent. West Germany would not use force itself, but it expected America and NATO to adopt ever more threatening nuclear weapons to counteract the Soviet menace, even though West Germany traded with the Soviets and told its citizens that America's Star Wars programme was the American President's decision alone. Eventually the Soviet Union went bankrupt, Germany was reunified and Eastern Europe embraced western values. Professor Volker R Berghahn of Columbia University commented:

'Germany, which twice in the first half of the twentieth century vainly attempted to establish by force a formal empire stretching from the Atlantic coast to the Ural Mountains and beyond, now at the end of this century finds herself on the verge of acquiring an informal empire of similar dimensions without having fired a shot.'[3]

That seemed a far-fetched scenario when Germany was first reunified in the 1990s, but now Germany appears much more dominant. If we follow the Pan-Germans plans for Mitteleuropa before the First World War, we have already got a customs union, which has prepared the way for community-wide legal and political institutions. Finally, we are at the stage where the Pan-Germans believed that force might have to be used to complete the process.

Military warfare was discredited after the Second World War but there is another means of securing one's ambitions, by economic manipulation. After the fall of the Berlin Wall, the D-Mark was too strong a currency for all the nations of Europe to adopt without going bankrupt; so the Economic Community decided to create a new currency called the euro.

President Kohl regarded the project as a 'castle in the air' because the countries in the European Union were so different in size and economic power, but the feat had been accomplished before by Bismarck.

After the Franco/Prussian war, Bismarck had almost the same number of large and small German-speaking states in what he called the 'Second Reich', as the European Union has today. He decided to adopt gold for his new Reich, but kept silver as well for the first three years. A stock market bubble ensued. Then Bismarck raised interest rates to quell it. The rise in interest rates and the imminent removal of silver from the German currency caused a collapse in the value of all the currencies that used silver, including the Austrian gulden and the American dollar. In the view of the Professor David Blanke the adoption of gold by Bismarck's Reich, and the resulting belief in America that it would have to abandon silver to stop the dollar's fall in the value, was the major cause of the 1873 American stock market collapse,[4] but Austria's stock market was the first to crash.

The Austrian gulden was entirely backed by silver. Naturally when money became tight people preferred Bismarck's gold mark to Austria's silver gulden. Bismarck blamed the Austrian Emperor's economic mismanagement for Austria's disastrous stock market crash but it came in handy for him because it occurred at the very moment when he introduced his infamous May Laws, which would result in over 100 influential Catholics being sent to prison.[5] The Catholic states in the south of Germany had disliked the Prussians and looked to Catholic Austria for leadership. After the crash Austria was impoverished and Prussia became dominant throughout Bismarck's Reich.

It is probable that Bismarck was unaware of the extent of the economic carnage that he would cause with his rises in interest rates and precipitous adoption of the Gold Standard although he would certainly have been happy with the extra power it gave him over his new Reich.

One can be more censorious over the former founder of the notorious Pan-German League, Alfred Hugenberg's part in causing the Wall Street Crash in 1929. The Pan-German League had actively advocated an aggressive 'defensive war' like Bismarck's in 1912 and pressurised the government to increase the size of the army to ensure its success. In the 1920s Alfred Hugenberg became the most powerful newspaper magnate in Germany. In 1929 he put Hitler on the committee of his petition stating that Germany should pay no more reparations at all as it was guiltless of starting the First World War and then gave prominence to the petition in his 500 newspapers. Its projected success in triggering a national referendum in Germany was crucial in also triggering America's disastrous 1929 Wall Street Crash and in giving Hitler the publicity, which started him on the road to power.

One could say that Germany was the major cause of both the 1873 and the 1929 stock market crashes. In 1950 the author of the *Madrid Circular Letter* wrote:

'Economic difficulties will one day plunge the United States down from its present dizzy heights. Such a catastrophe can be brought about through crafty manipulations and through artificially engendered crises. Such manoeuvres are routine measures which have already been employed in international power struggles.'

Did anyone in Germany toy with the idea of causing a stock market crash after the arrival of the euro, in order to further the cherished ideal of the United States of Europe? Like the 1873 and the 1929 crashes, the Lehman crash was associated with the arrival of a large new currency. The prosecuting side uncovers the fact that the German press instilled into the German people such alarm at the thought of losing their beloved D-Mark that there was a mass exodus of money when the euro arrived. A large part of the funds which fuelled the bubble in America after the euro's arrival was German. Then when the sub-prime sector of the American mortgage market was starting to overheat, Bundesbank President Axel Weber pushed ECB President Jean-Claude Trichet to raise the admittedly much lower European Central Bank interest rates with a spurious claim that German inflation was getting out of control, despite the fact that his action in raising VAT had actually been the trigger for the German workers asking for higher wages.

By the autumn of 2007, it was apparent that the American economy was in trouble. Central bankers usually help each other out in times of emergency. But not in this case. The Fed rapidly reduced its previous high interest rates to 5 per cent in April 2008 to resolve its sub-prime mortgage crisis. However, the ECB raised its interest rates to 4.25 per cent in July 2008, stating that the soaring price of oil was causing inflation in the European Union, even though a substantial part of the reason for the spike in price of oil must have been due to the soaring value of the euro against the dollar.

The difference between European interest rates and beleaguered America's was too small. European money came rushing home, Lehman Brothers collapsed and Wall Street suffered a devastating crash, followed by a crisis in the European Union, which Germany had also deluged with cash.

After the crash Germany's *Die Welt* newspaper declared: 'Greed and stupidity have plunged the market into chaos ... Any economics student in his first semester could have concluded that the American model is not tenable' as though the economic system adopted by coal-rich Germany before the First World War, consisting of a massively high tariff wall, cartels and syndicates, would be acceptable in a modern world without immediate counter sanctions; the economic system adopted after Hitler came to power is not tenable either because trade with Germany was reduced to barter because Hitler's Finance Minister Schacht not only defrauded governments but also all Germany's commercial creditors.

Before condemning the Americans, readers will have to look again at the historical parallels. Germany's policy of 'austerity' after the Lehman crash is so similar to *Hungerkanzler* Brüning's in the 1930s – but Brüning's deflation was imposed for political ends. It produced a banking crash and ultimately Hitler!

Was the German economic policy of austerity imposed for political reasons too after the stock market crash of 2008? If so the squeeze is continuing. 'From 2016, it will be illegal for the federal German government to run a deficit of more than 0.35 per cent of gross domestic product. From 2020, the federal states will not be allowed to run any deficit at all.'[6] As Germany is the strongest country in the European Union, its deflationary policy will have a dire impact on the rest of the European Union economy, and as the European Union is the largest trading bloc in the world, it will have repercussions world wide.

In May 2010 Angela Merkel declared: 'We have a shared currency but no real economic or political union. This must change. If we were to change this, therein lies the opportunity of this crisis ... And beyond the economic, after the shared currency, we will perhaps dare to take further steps, for example a European army.'[7]

We love the European Union because our feeling of kinship and belief in its respect for democracy, justice and the rule of law. However, it is totally wrong to say that we need it in order to ensure that we don't start fighting one another again. Indeed in order to ensure peace and prosperity in the European Union, the historical narrative accepted by America and the Allies after the Second World War that we all 'slithered into war' in 1914 and that Germany was given an 'iniquitous' Treaty at Versailles afterwards, must be abandoned.

However painful, it has to be disclosed that Bismarck was not a unifier but a deceitful conqueror, whose success in invading all his European neighbours, prompted his successors to copy him and try to get away with murder too. Germany was responsible for the First World War and emerged stronger from it than the Allies. The Treaty of Versailles was unenforceable as America did not ratify it and the economist Maynard Keynes further undermined it with his inflammatory and unfair depiction of President Woodrow Wilson and his encouragement to the German hierarchy to renege on payments.[8] No sizeable sums in reparations were ever paid, and Marshall Foch was farsighted in 1919 when he predicted another war in twenty years. The former Pan-Germans, who now called themselves the Nationalists, caused the 1929 stock market crash and the Great Depression in order to persuade the embittered and deluded German people to vote for dictatorship and return to war.

At the present time the European Union bears no resemblance to Bismarck's autocratic Second Reich, let alone the Reich that Hitler presided over. However, there are unnerving parallels. Only by smashing the myth of a weak and innocent post-First World War Germany can we begin to right the wrongs of the past one hundred years. Inside or outside the European Union is not the question. Rather an honest assessment of ourselves and Germany is what is needed. The truth is always a good place to begin.

Notes

CHAPTER 1

[1] Frederick the Great 'Political Testament' 1752, quoted in J Ellis Barker, *Foundations of Germany* (1916), 37

[2] Frederick the Great 'Political Testament' 1752, quoted in J Ellis Barker, *Foundations of Germany* (1916), 33

[3] General Morgan, *Assize of Arms,* 101

[4] General Morgan, *Assize of Arms,* 97–98

[5] S H Steinberg, *A Short History of Germany,* 207

[6] William Manchester, *The Arms of Krupp,* 103

[7] Frederick the Great 'Political Testament' 1752, quoted in J Ellis Barker, *Foundations of Germany* (1916), 88

[8] S H Steinberg, *A Short History of Germany,* 216

[9] S H Steinberg, *A Short History of Germany,* 217

[10] Frederick the Great in his *Guerre de Sept Ans'* quoted in J Ellis Barker, *Foundations of Germany,* (1916), 75

[11] Wilhelm Stieber, *The Chancellor's Spy*, 97–101

[12] Wilhelm Stieber, *The Chancellor's Spy*, 102

[13] Wilhelm Stieber, *The Chancellor's Spy*, 103–104

[14] Jonathan Steinberg, *Bismarck, A Life,* 239

[15] Jonathan Steinberg, *Bismarck, A Life,* 244–246

[16] Jonathan Steinberg. *Bismarck, A Life,* 246

[17] S H Steinberg, *A Short History of Germany,* 218

[18] Wilhelm Stieber, *The Chancellor's Spy*, 109

[19] Frederick the Great 'Political Testament' 1752, quoted in J Ellis Barker, *Foundations of Germany* (1916), 99

[20] Wilhelm Stieber, *The Chancellor's Spy*, 126

[21] Terry Crowdy, *The Enemy Within, A History of Spires, Spymasters and Espionage,* 184

22 Geoffrey Wawro, *The Franco-Prussian War, The Great German Conquest of France in 1870–1871,* (2003), 17

23 Terry Crowdy, *The Enemy Within, A History of Spies, Spymasters and Espionage,* 184–186

24 Wilhelm Stieber, *The Chancellor's Spy,* 134–5

25 Wilhelm Stieber, *The Chancellor's Spy,* 136

26 Jonathan Steinberg, *Bismarck A Life,* 285–86

27 Jonathan Steinberg, *Bismarck A Life,* 287

28 Wilhelm Stieber, *The Chancellor's Spy,* 140

29 Wilhelm Stieber, *The Chancellor's Spy,* 141

30 Wilhelm Stieber, *The Chancellor's Spy,* 216–17

31 Terry Crowdy, *The Enemy Within,* 186–87

32 *Wikipedia*

33 Wilhelm Stieber, *The Chancellor's Spy,* 204

34 S H Steinberg, *A Short History of Germany,* 231

35 Wikipedia *German gold mark*

36 Jonathan Steinberg, *Bismarck A Life,* 329: 'but all these conversions understate the actual value at the time, for these were gold francs'

37 Martin Kitchen, *The Political Economy of Germany 1815–1914,* 132

38 Jonathan Steinberg, *Bismarck, A Life,* 329

39 Martin Kitchen, *The Political Economy of Germany 1815–1914,* 139

40 National (American) History Education Clearing House, *The Panic of 1873*

41 E Eyck, *Bismarck and the German Empire,* 205

42 Jonathan Steinberg, *Bismarck, A Life,* 334–335

43 Jonathan Steinberg *Bismarck, A Life,* 330

44 Martin Kitchin, *The Political Economy of Germany 1815–1914* (2006), 170–71

45 Erich Eyck, *Bismarck and the German Empire,* (1950), 200

46 Erich Eyck, *Bismarck and the German Empire,* 219

47 S H Steinberg *A Short History of Germany,* (1944), 221

48 Description of coal pollution from Catherine Bailey, *Black Diamonds,* 71

49 Volker R Berghahn, *Imperial Germany 1871–1914,* (1994), 58, 302

50 Martin Kitchen, *A History of Modern Germany 1800–2000,* (2006), 200

51 Erich Eyck, *Bismarck and the German Empire,* (1945), 294–5

52 *Annual Register, 1888,* 268

53 J Ellis Barker, *Modern Germany,* (1919), 377

54 Martin Kitchen, *The Political Economy of Germany 1815–1915,* 196

55 S H Steinberg, *A Short History of Germany,* (1944), 235

CHAPTER 2

1 Seitz, Henning, *Die Zeit,* (2002). See Imperial Plans for the Invasion of the United States, *Wikipedia*

2 William Roscoe Thayer, *Theodore Roosevelt*, (1919), XIV, 'The President and the Kaiser'

3 Seitz, Henning, (8 May 2002), 'In New York wird die größte Panik ausbrechen: Wie Kaiser Wilhehlm II die USA mit einem Militärschlag niederzwingen'

4 William Roscoe Thayer, (1859–1923) *Theodore Roosevelt (1919)* XIV The President and the Kaiser (Bartleby.com)

5 First World War.com Who's who *Otto Liman von Sanders*

6 Notes by Hans Adolf con Bülow, 30 December 1904, printed in Rich and Fisher, *The Holstein Papers, IV*, no 904. enclosure

7 John C G Röhl, *Into the Abyss of War and Exile*, 310f.

8 Martin Kitchen, *A History of Modern Germany, 1800–2000*, 193

9 John C G Röhl, *Kaiser Wilhelm II*, 88–89

10 Volker R Berghahn, *Imperial Germany*, 1871–1914, Table 17, 303, 4,762,312 to 5,321,400 marks a year (20.43 to £)

11 Fritz Fischer, *War of Illusions*, 86

12 Roger Chicherinng, *We men who feel most German*, (1984), 79

13 Heinrich Class, *If I were the Kaiser*, (1912)

14 Henry Ashby Turner Jr, *Hitler's Thirty Days to Power: January 1933*, (1996), 137

15 Sebastian Conrad, *Globalisation and the Nations in Imperial Germany*, 175

16 Volker R Berghahn, *Imperial Germany 1817–1914*, 32

17 William Manchester, *The Arms of Krupp*, 16

18 *Zentrales Staatsarchiv, Bestand 19Alldeutscher Verband*, File 197.

19 In *We Men who feel most German* Chichering comments that Class lied in his memoirs about the extent of the industrialists' support, 173

20 Fritz Fischer, *Germany's Aims in the First World War* (paperback ed), 29,36

21 Fritz Fischer *War of Illusions*, (1975), 190–192

22 Fritz Fischer, *War of Illusions*, 210

23 Fritz Fischer *War of Illusions*, 209–210

24 *Annual Register 1913*, 318–320

25 Brigadier-General J H Morgan, *Assize of Arms*, 95

26 *Annual Register 1914*, 306

27 Fischer, *Germany's Aims in the First World War* (paperback ed), 47

28 Fritz Fischer, *War of Illusions*, 325, 326

29 4,664 million tons as opposed to Germany's 14,836 million tons.

30 First World War.com Who's who *Otto Liman von Sanders*

31 Fritz Fischer *War of Illusions*, 427–28

32 Terry Crowdy, *The War Within*, 190

33 Fritz Fischer *War of Illusions*, 372, quoted from Conrad *Aus meiner Dienst*, 626

34 Fritz Fischer, *War of Illusions*, 448

35 Fritz Fischer, *War of Illusions*, 453

CHAPTER 3

[1] Fritz Fischer, *War of Illusions*, (1975), 412
[2] Michael Waterhouse, *Edwardian Requiem*, 324
[3] Fritz Fischer, *Germany's Aims in the First World War*, (1967) (paperback ed), 55
[4] W Manchester, *The Arms of Krupp 1587–1968*, (1969) 288, 317, 318
[5] *Arms of Krupp*, 318
[6] *Germany's Aims*, 53
[7] *Germany's Aims*, 56
[8] *Germany's Aims*, 58
[9] *Germany's Aims,* 56
[10] *Germany's Aims,* 58
[11] *Arms of Krupp*, 312–13
[12] *Arms of Krupp*, 318
[13] *Germany's Aims*, 59
[14] *Germany's Aims*, 60
[15] *The Arms of Krupp*, 328
[16] *Germany's Aims*, 64
[17] *Germany's Aims*, 61
[18] *Germany's Aims*, 64
[19] *Germany's Aims*, 61
[20] *Edwardian Requiem*, 293, 296
[21] *Edwardian Requiem*, 293
[22] *Germany's Aims*, 65
[23] *Europe's Last Summer*, 195
[24] Norman Stone, *A Short World War II History,* 2013 (paperback ed), xiv
[25] *War of Illusions*, 427
[26] *Germany's Aims*, 66
[27] *Germany's Aims*, 66
[28] *Germany's Aims*, 67
[29] Sisley Huddleston, *Poincaré*, extract from Poincaré's *Les Origins de la Guerre* 63–64
[30] *Germany's Aims*, 68
[31] *Germany's Aims*, 37
[32] Butler, David Allen, *The Burden of Guilt, How Germany shattered the Last Days of Peace, Summer 1914*, 103
[33] Sir Eyre Crowe, memo to Sir Edward Grey, 27th July 1914
[34] *Germany's Aims*, 68
[35] *Germany's Aims*, 69
[36] *Germany's Aims*, 70 (author's italics)
[37] *Germany's Aims*, 71
[38] *Germany's Aims*, 71
[39] *Germany's Aims*, 71

40 *Germany's Aims*, 65
41 *War of Illusions*, 487–8
42 *Germany's Aims*, 72
43 *Germany's Aims*, 84
44 *Germany's Aims*, 73
45 *Germany's Aims*, 74
46 *Germany's Aims*, 75–76. The demand had been drafted on 26th July
47 *Germany's Aims*, 76
48 *War of Illusions*, 491
49 Poincaré, *Les Origines de la Guerre*, reproduced in Sisley Huddleston, *Poincaré*, A biographical Portrait, (1924), 65
50 *Germany's Aims*, 79
51 *Germany's Aims*, 77
52 Spartacus Educational, Edward Grey
53 *War of Illusions*, 137
54 *Germany's Aims*, 47
55 Douglas Haig, *Architect of Victory*, (2006), 136–7
56 *Germany's Aims*, 78
57 *Germany's Aims*, 78–79
58 *Germany's Aims*, 82
59 *Germany's Aims*, 82
60 *Germany's Aims*, 85
61 *Germany's Aims*, 83
62 *Germany's Aims*, 85
63 Sean McMeekin, July 1914, 301
64 *Annual Register*, 282
65 *Annual Register*, 282
66 *Germany's Aims*, 86
67 *Germany's Aims*, 86
68 *War of Illusions*, 504
69 *Germany's Aims*, 86
70 S H Steinberg, *Short History of Germany*, 254
71 Peter Frankopan, *The Silk Roads, A New History of the World*, 315
72 *The Times*, 1 August 1914
73 *Annual Register*, 168
74 *Germany's Aims*, 86
75 *Germany's Aims*, 84
76 *War of Illusions*, 508–9
77 *War of Illusions*, 390

CHAPTER 4
1 *Wikipedia*
2 *Germany's Aims in the First World War* (paperback ed) , 109

3 *Germany's Aims*, 104

4 *Germany's Aims*, 257

5 Martin Kitchen, *Political Economy of Germany 1815–1914,* (1978), 278t

6 *Germany's Aims*, 257–59

7 *The Times, 10 October 1923*, Stinnes Conditions 'eight and half hours under-
    ground and ten hours above ground'. Not only did they have to work longer
    hours but their wages were 20% lower than they had been in 1913. Feldman
    The Great Disorder, Table 49, 850

8 Peter Claughton, *New techniques, new sources: The British Steel industry and
    its ore supply 1850–1950*

9 *Germany's Aims*, 119

10 *The Times* 2 December 1914

11 *Germany's Aims*, 436–7 ft.

12 *Germany's Aims*, 167–8

13 *Germany's Aims*, 270–71

14 Miles, W, *Military Operations France and Belgium, 1916 Vol II: 2ⁿᵈ July to
    the End of the Battle of the Somme* (1992)

15 *Germany's Aims*, 121, 127–8

16 *Germany's Aims*, 292

17 Arthur S Link, *Woodrow Wilson, Revolution War and Peace*, 52

18 *Germany's Aims*, 294

19 Skiddelsky, *John Maynard Keynes*, vol 1, (paper-back ed), 335–36

20 *Germany's Aims*, 303

21 Barbara W Tuchman, *The Zimmerman Telegram*, (1959), 162

22 *Zimmermann Telegram*, 149

23 *Zimmerman Telegram*, 146

24 *Zimmerman Telegram*, 183

25 Arthur S Link, *Woodrow Wilson, Revolution, War and Peace*, 55

26 *Germany's Aims*, 308

27 *Zimmermann Telegram*, 185

28 John W Wheeler-Bennett, *Brest-Litovsk, the forgotten Peace, March 1918*, 16

29 *Germany's Aims*, 147–154

30 *Germany's Aims*, 367

31 *Germany's Aims*, 383

32 *Germany's Aims*, 385

33 *Germany's Aims*, 391

34 *Germany's Aims*, 396

35 *Germany's Aims*, 397

36 *Germany's Aims*, 396–8

37 *Germany's Aims*, 404

38 R J Unstead, *A Century of Change,* 129

39 *Germany's Aims*, 432

40 *Germany's Aims*, 493

41 *Germany's Aims*, 479

42 *Germany's Aims*, 500

43 *Germany's Aims*, 542

44 *Germany's Aims*, 483–5

45 *Germany's Aims*, 508, taken from Gottfried Mehnert, *Evangelische Kirche und Politik*, 64 ff

46 *Germany's Aims*, 507

47 Arthur S Link, *Revolution, War and Peace*, 86

48 *Germany's Aims*, 521

49 *Germany's Aims*, 535

50 *Germany's Aims*, 579

51 John Terraine, author of *Douglas Haig the Educated Soldier* estimated that Germany had over 500,000 troops on the victorious Eastern Front in 1918. Niall Ferguson in *The Pity of War 1914–1918* estimated the number to be almost 1,000,000, 285

52 Ray Stannard Baker, *Woodrow Wilson Life and Letters,* vol 8. (1972)

53 His 14 points include open covenants, openly arrived at, freedom of the seas in war and peace, a free-minded and absolutely impartial adjustment of all colonial claims, a free Poland with access to the sea, the autonomy of all the nations making up the Austrian and the Turkish empires, Germany to evacuate France and Belgium and its eastern empire, and a League of Nations.

54 Foreign Policy Research Institute, Michael S Neiberg, *Battle of Meuse-Argonne*

55 Etienne Mantoux, *The Carthaginian Peace,* 91

56 *The New York Times,* 12 December 1918

57 R S Baker, *Woodrow Wilson, Life and Letters*, vol. 8, 530–31

58 Smythe, *Pershing,* 233–234

59 Peter Frankopan, *The Silk Roads, A New History of the World*, 320

60 *Annual Register 1918, 25, Annual Register 1919;* A committee was set up which recommended amongst other things, no employment until the age of 14, a weekly day of rest and an 8 hour day.

61 Blake, *Private Papers of Douglas Haig*, 334

62 Blake, *Private Papers of Douglas Haig*, 329

63 *The Papers of Woodrow Wilson*, 51, 1918, 523–4

CHAPTER 5

1 J Ellis Barker, *The Foundations of Germany,* 101–2

2 Fritz Fischer, *From Kaiserreich to Third Reich,* (1986), 72

3 John A Leopold, *Alfred Hugenberg and the Radical Nationalist Campaign against the Weimar Republic,* (1978)

4 Ray Stannard Baker *Woodrow Wilson Life and Letters* 8, (1939), 533

[5] Sebastien Haffner, *Failure of a Revolution*, 72

[6] Sebastien Haffner, *Failure of a revolution*, 74–5

[7] David Fromkin, *In the Time of the Americans,* (1995), 258

[8] Wheeler-Bennet, *Nemesis of Power*, 25–31

[9] R S Baker, *Woodrow Wilson & World Settlement*, (1923) vol.2, 60

[10] *The New York Times,* 12 December 1918

[11] Sally Marks, 'Smoke and Mirrors' in Boemeke, Feldman and Glazer (eds) *The Treaty of Versailles, A Reassessment after 75 years,* 359

[12] J M Keynes, *Dr Melchior, A defeated Enemy,* 61–2

[13] J H Morgan, *Assize of Arms,* (1945), 188

[14] *Statesman's Yearbook 1923,* France's population actually fell in 1919 while the German population increased.

[15] Etienne Mantoux, *The Carthaginian Peace,* (1946), 156–7

[16] Robert Blake, *The Private Papers of Douglas Haig,* (1952), 351

[17] Morgan, *Assize of Arms,* 96

[18] Morgan, *Assize of Arms,* 19

[19] E Mantoux, *The Carthaginian Peace,* 156–7

[20] Erich Eyck, *A History of the Weimar Republic,* vol. 1, 102

[21] Address at St Louis, E Mantoux, *The Carthaginian Peace,* 59

[22] *Sun & New York Herald,* 24 January 1920

[23] *Sun & New York Herald,* 8 February 1920

[24] *Annual Register 1920,* 177–8

[25] *The New York Times,* 2 December 1918

[26] John A Leopold, *Alfred Hugenberg, The Radical Campaign against the Weimar Republic,* (New Haven Conn, and London, 1977) 11–13

[27] J H Morgan, *Assize of Arms,* 19

[28] Ian Kershaw *Hitler 1889–1936: Hubris,* (1999), 101

[29] *The New York Times,* 3 February 1920

[30] Erich Eyck, *History of the Weimar Republic,* vol 1, 167

[31] Guttman & Meehan, *The Great Inflation,* 112–3

[32] *Lloyd George Papers*, Baldwin File. c/8 F/3/1/13

[33] *The New York Times,* 1 February 1920

[34] Erich Eyck, *A History of the Weimar Republic,* vol 1, 168

[35] Etienne Mantoux, *The Carthaginian Peace, or the Economic Consequences of Mr Keynes* 5

[36] J M Keynes, *The Economic Consequences of the Peace*, 40: 'There can seldom have been a statesman more inept in the agilities of the Council Chamber.'

[37] Etienne Mantoux, *The Carthaginian Peace,* 134–137

[38] Niall Ferguson, *The Pity of War,* (paperback ed), 419

[39] Etienne Mantoux, *The Carthaginian Peace,* 139

CHAPTER 6

[1] William Manchester, *The Arms of Krupp,* 390

2 Terms laid down in a letter from Vladikavkaz to Lenin, 25 March 1922, *Foreign Policy Archives Moscow*

3 Erich Eyck, *History of the Weimar Republic,* vol 1, 212

4 Niall Ferguson *The Pity of War* 421

5 Lloyd George Papers, F/1/2/17, no 37

6 Lloyd George Papers, (Report No.40 dated 11 July 1922) referred to in Note on the German Chemical Industry and the possibility of its employment for the production of poisonous gases F/26/2 Q/8 (t28)

7 Lloyd George Papers, Sir Maurice Hankey to Lloyd George, 7 July 1922, F 1/2/17

8 Fritz Thyssen, *I paid Hitler,* 98

9 *The New York Times,* 18 January 1923

10 *Daily Mail* 3 August 1923, reported Poincaré's speech: 'Germany ought to restore its credit, stabilise its currency, balance its budget and encourage its production ... But Germany ... has ... disdained all advice.'

11 *Smythe,* Pershing, 233

12 *Annual Register 1922,* 79

13 In 1922 Germany became the second largest shipbuilder in the world, *Annual Register 1922,* 92, Finance & Commerce

14 *Annual Register 1921,* 79; Finance & Commerce, 1922, 91–92

15 Kershaw, *Hitler 1889–1936: Hubris* (paper-back ed, 1999), 248

16 *The Times,* 10 October 1923

17 *The New York Times,* 8 November 1923

18 G D Feldman, *The Great Disorder, Politics, Economics and Society in the German Inflation, 1914–1923,* (1993), Table 49, 850

19 Harold James, *A German Identity,* 126

20 Quoted in E Mantoux ,*The Carthaginian Peace or The Economic Consequences of Mr Keynes,* (1946), 5

21 Sarah Gertrude, Millin *General Smuts,* vol 2, 262

22 *The New York Times,* 11 October 1923

23 Hjalmar Schacht, *My First 76 Years,* (1955), 191–206

24 (Although Germany has, of course, given itself a get-out clause in the shape of transfer protection). See Stephen A Schuker, *American 'Reparations' to Germany,* 87: 'When the Germans accepted the Dawes Plan, they fully intended to ask for another reduction in reparations within three to four years. The outcome of London, by tying France's hands in the event of default, made it virtually certain that the next German bid for downward revision would meet with success.'

25 The American Federal Reserve agreed to consider certain trade bills, payable in the United States, as eligible for their open market purchases 'if Germany agreed to stabilise its currency on the basis of a 'gold exchange' in effect'. *The New York Times,* 17 May 1924

26 G Borsky, *The Greatest Swindle in the World, Table of Payments,* 45–6

27 Stephen A Schuker, *The End of French Predominance in Europe*, 386

28 Excerpt from C. Bresciani-Turroni, *The Economics of Inflation*, in ed. Capie, Forrest, *Major Inflations in History,* (Edward Elgar, 1991) 477

29 *Royal Institute Survey 1929*

30 Liaquat Ahamed, *Lords of Finance*, 229

31 *The Times* 20 April 1925, 'the Bank of England must use the weapon of the rate in the event of a persistent export of gold'

32 Liaquat Ahamed, *Lords of Finance,* 59

33 Liaquat Ahamed, *Lords of Finance,* 235

34 In the autumn of 1923 the French and Belgian engineers tried to argue that the price of German coal was so cheap that it would undercut British coal, even after 20% had been given in reparations. But the industrialist Hugo Stinnes argued that although this was true for the consumer it was not true for the producer who could only take the 'pithead price into account in making his calculations'. *The New York Times,* 18 October 1923

35 Gerald D Feldman, *Politics, Economics & Society in the German Inflation, 1914–1924*, Table 49, 850

36 *Annual Register 1919*

37 A M Newman, *Economic Organisation of the British Coal Industry,* (1934), Appendix A p.475. After the coal strike 'Most of the districts made arrangements on the basis of an eight hours working day: only Yorkshire, Nottinghamshire, Derbyshire and Kent agreed on a 7½ hour basis, whilst the North East introduced 7½ hours for hewers only'.

38 Catherine Bailey, *Black Diamonds,* 274, Recollections of a miner from Sheffied

39 Adam Fergusson, *When Money Dies* (2010), 246–47

40 9% 1925, 6.5% 1926, 7% 1927, 6.5% until 25 April 1929, 7.5% from April 1929

41 Clay, *Lord Norman*, 223

42 Stresemann's Diary (1/591) G Borsky, *The Greatest Swindle in the World,* 63

43 Barnett, Correlli, *The Audit of War*, 92; Carr and Taplin, *British Steel Industry*, 410. 1929 is a record year with coal output up in the Ruhr district by 23% and coke and briquette output up by 50%, *Economist 18.1.30*

44 The treaty was signed on 24 April 1926. E Eyck, *History of the Weimar Republic, vol 2*, 61

45 *Germany's Aims*, 78–79

46 *Germany's Aims*, 77

47 *Germany's Aims*, 85

48 W M Knight-Patterson, *Germany from Defeat to Conquest*, (1945), 400

49 *Central State Military Archives, Moscow*: Taken from a report from Chief of the Chemical Department, Fischmann to the Deputy Minister of the Red Army, Unchlicht (29 April 1927)

50 Royal Institute of International Affairs, *Survey 1929*, 115

[51] Royal Institute of International Affairs, *Survey 1929*, 115–116
[52] Borsky, *The Greatest Swindle in the World,* 57

CHAPTER 7

[1] Theo Balderston, *Origins and Causes of the German Economic Crisis, 1923–1931,* (1993), 250–251
[2] *The New York Times,* 15 July 1928
[3] Liaquat Ahamed, *Lords of Finance,* 282
[4] *Royal Institute of International Affairs, Survey 1929* and is harming world trade, 126
[5] *Royal Institute of International Affairs, Survey 1929,* 116, at no time did actual cash transfers exceed 35.8% of Germany's total payments. 65 million, 2nd year, 876 million (20.43 £) fifth year. G Borsky, Of the total of 3,834 million gold marks entered by the Reparations' agent as 'payment in gold and foreign currency only 1,737 million was paid in cash (including the Dawes Loan). The remaining 1,510 was revenue from tariffs and deliveries in kind.
[6] *Stresemann Papers,* 7439, Erich Eyck, *The Weimar Republic,* vol 2, 175
[7] *New York Times,* 26 September 1931
[8] David Fromkin, *In the Time of the Americans,* 257
[9] Erich Eyck, *History of the Weimar Republic, Vol 2,* 167–8
[10] *The New York Times,* 8 March 1929
[11] *Annual Register 1929,* 193
[12] *The New York Times, 26 September 1931*
[13] *The New York Times, 21 April 1929*
[14] *Survey of International Affairs, 1930,* 148
[15] Harold James, *The German Slump,* (1986), 284. For figures 298–300 *Statistiches Reichsamt* estimated capital flight at.3.9 billion RM short-term money and 4.9 billion RM long term
[16] Borsky, *The Greatest Swindle in the World,* (1942), 60
[17] Eyck, *The Weimar Republic,* vol.2, 207
[18] *The Times,* 27 June 1929, reported £3,414,000 gold bought by Germany over two days. Continued purchases thereafter prompted France and other countries to buy gold. Further heavy purchases in mid-September prompted the British government to put interest rates up.
See howhitlercametopower.com
[19] *The Times,* 25 September 1929
[20] *The Times,* 20 April 1925
[21] *The Times,* June 11,26,27,28, July 3,4,17,27, Aug, 28, Sep 11, 25. The announcement of a further large export of bar gold, £1,289,000 of which £700,000 was understood to be for France and most of the balance for Germany, naturally strengthened expectations of an early rise in the bank rate.

[22] Social Democrat Carl Severing, in June 1930, estimated Germany's capital flight to Switzerland at 7 billion RM. *The New York Times* also said that it was going to Paris, despite its low interest rates.

[23] Harold James, *A German Indentity,* (paper ed), 132

CHAPTER 8

[1] Erich Eyck, *The Weimar Republic II*, 212

[2] Young Report, 22

[3] Erich Eyck, *The Weimar Republic II*, 230–232

[4] Documents on British Foreign Policy, (1930), 1, 486.

[5] William L Patch Jnr, *Heinrich Brüning and the Dissolution of the Weimar Republic,* (Cambridge University Press, 1996) 77

[6] Eyck, *A History of the Weimar Republic*, vol 2, 267

[7] Hermann Kantorowitz, *The Spirit of British Policy, and the Myth of the Encirclement of Germany* (1931), 482–96

[8] *The New York Times*, 18 August 1930

[9] Michal Reiman, *The Birth of Stalinism*, 75: 'The national economy has almost no reserves at its disposal, either financial or material.'

[10] Foreign Policy Archives, Moscow, no. 390.

[11] Dyck, *Weimar Germany and Soviet Russia*, 147–8

[12] *Foreign Policy Archives, Moscow, Protocol 22. File 694. No 37*

[13] R W Davies, Mark Harrison, S G Wheatcroft, eds., *The Economic Transformation of the Soviet Union, 1913–1945*, 319, Table 52 gives Sources of Soviet Imports between 1921 and 1940. In 1931 over 50% of all Soviet imports came from Germany. 'The large new tractor factories under construction at Stalingrad, Khar'kov and Chelyanbinsk were designed for rapid conversaion to tank production'. 144

[14] Nekrich, *Pariahs, Partners and Predators*, 24, 61,

[15] A A Akhtamzyan, *New and Latest History* no 4 *Istoriya vtoroi mirovoi voinv*, vol 1, 270

[16] William L Patch Jnr, *Heinrich Brüning and the Dissolution of the Weimar Republic,* (1998), 103

[17] Erich Eyck, *The Weimar Republic Vol 2*, 332–3, 228, 314, 298, Hamilton, *Who Voted for Hitler*,278

[18] 1930 Documents on British Foreign Policy 2, 220–221

[19] Billion Reichsmarks in long term German bonds and 7 billion Reichsmarks in German short-term bonds

[20] Dinner discussion between John Foster Dulles and Dr Schacht 20 October 1930

[21] *Times,* 24 January 1931

[22] *Financial Times,* 17 June 1930

[23] *Annual Register* 1931, p.189

[24] *The Times,* 10 June 1931

[25] *Royal Institute of International Affairs, Survey, 1931*, 32

26 *Royal Institute of International Affairs, Survey , 1936*, gives figures for the trade between the two countries:
In 1931 German exports to USSR 762.7 million Reichsmarks. Imports from USSR 303.5 m Reichsmarks.
In 1932 German exports to USSR 625.8 million Reichsmarks. Imports from USSR 207.9 m Reichsmarks

27 Robert Boyce, *'Business as usual' in French Foreign and domestic policy, 1918–1940* (1998), 120

28 *Economist,* 7 December 1929 (after the payment of reparations and subtracting the net increase in foreign indebtedness)

29 David Marquand, *Ramsay MacDonald* (1977), 57

30 *Annual Register 1931*, 187

31 J M Keynes, *Two Memoirs,* 50

32 Carl Melchior to Hans Schäffer, State secretary to the Minister of Finance, Erich Eyck, *Weimar Republic, II,* 323–324

33 'The Young Plan in relation to the world economy' 14 (at Foreign Policy Association, 18 East 41 st, N.Y.)

34 Eichengreen, *Golden Fetters,* 289

35 Guido Giacomo Preparata, *Conjuring Hitler: How Britain and America made the Third Reich,* (2006), 182–185

36 *The New York Times,* 22 September 1931

37 Liaquat Ahamed, *Lords of Finance,* (hard-backed copy), 435–436

38 J Adam Tooze, *Statistics in the German State, 1900–1945,* 168

39 *September 26, 1931* Also gives data on Reichsbank reserves

40 *The New York Times,* 28 September 1931.

41 Eberhard Kolb, *The Weimar Republic* 181–184.

42 Report on Germany's war potential, July 28, 1945, given by Senator Kilgore of the Subcommittee on War Mobilisation, quoted in T H Tetens, *Germany Plots with the Kremlin,* 269

43 Stephen A Schuker, *American 'Reparations' to Germany,* 46

44 Simon Reich 'Fascism and the Structure of German capitalism' in Volker R Berghahn, *Quest for Economic Empire,* 83 & 87

45 Quoted in T H Tetens, *Germany plots with the Kremlin,* 159

46 Erich Eyck, *Weimar Republic, II,* 374, 409.

47 Nekrich, *Pariahs, Partners, and Predators,* 64

48 Robert Boyce, 'Business as usual' in Robert Boyce (ed.), *French Foreign and Defence Policy, 1918–1940,* 125

49 William L Shirer, *The Rise and Fall of the Third Reich,* 145

50 W Manchester, *The Arms of Krupp,* 385, 413

51 W Manchester, *The Arms of Krupp,* 429

52 David Fromkin, *In the Time of the Americans,* (paperback ed), 295

53 David Fromkin, *In the Time of the Americans,* 300

54 'GERMANY PAID NO REPARATIONS' letter between Amos J Peaslee of

the American Courier Service and Admiral Sir Reginald Hall who directed British Naval Intelligence from 1914–1919, 4th January 1940

55 T H Tetens, *Germany Plots with the Kremlin*, 30
56 *Survey of International Affairs 1934*, 40*
57 *Annual Register 1932*, 300 American exports of raw cotton had shrunk to 340 million dollars in 1932 compared with the average yearly exports of 611 million dollars for the previous five years.
58 *Survey of International Affairs 1934*, 37
59 *Survey of International Affairs 1934*, 38
60 Borsky, *The Greatest Swindle in the World*, 11. He estimated cash payments to be £253 million, but took £100 million off because the Dawes and Young Plan loans were not repaid before the Second World War.
61 Stephen A Schuker: This equates in price-adjusted terms, to 'four times the total assistance that the United States government will provide to West Germany from 1948 to 1952 under the much-heralded Marshall Plan', *American 'Reparations' to Germany*, 119
62 H James, *the German Slump*, Schwerin on Krosigle-Overy figures represent a reliable minimum spent on rearmament, 383
63 Dulles, *Vargas of Brazil*, 175
64 Dulles, *Vargas of Brazil*, 206
65 David Blaazer (2005) 'Finance and the end of Appeasement: The Bank of England, the National Government and the Czech Gold', *Journal of Contemporary History* 40 (1), 25–39

CHAPTER 9

1 *Annual Register* 1933, 186; *The Times, 19 06 1933* 14a: The incriminating text is alleged to be part of the notes of an undelivered speech.
2 Mark Harrison and R W Davies, 'The Soviet Military-Economic Effort during the Second Five-Year Plan (1933–7)' in *Europe-Asia Studies, Vol 49, No 3* 369–406
3 Ian Kershaw, *Hitler Nemesis*, (paperback ed), 239
4 Adam Tooze, *Wages of Destruction*, 363–66
5 Heinrich Brüning, *Memoiren, 1918–1934* DVA, Suttgart 1970, S.531
6 Robert Boyce, *French Foreign and Domestic Policy, 1918–1940*, 125: 'With Hitler's advent to power in January 1933 ... A new flight from the franc began'.
7 *Royal Institute of International Affairs*, Survey, 1936
8 Adam Tooze, *Wages of Destruction*, 368–9
9 Adam Tooze, *Wages of Destruction*, 385
10 Adam Tooze, *Wages of Destruction*, 389
11 Adam Tooze, *Wages of Destruction*, 385
12 Adam Tooze, *Wages of Destruction*, 382–3
13 Adam Tooze, *Wages of Destruction*, 387–8
14 John C Beyer & Stephen A Schneider, *Forced Labour under the German Reich*, parts 1 and 2

15 Raeder, memorandum, Sept 16, 1939, ND, D-804, ibid., 527.

16 Saul Friedlander, *Prelude to Downfall*, 57

17 Quoted in Saul Friedlander, *Prelude to Downfall, Hitler and the United States, 1939–41*, 60

18 Adam Tooze, *The Wages of Destruction* 399

19 Adam Tooze, *Wages of Destruction*, 394

20 Hillgruber, *Hitler's Strategy*, 159–162

21 Saul Friedlander, *Prelude to Downfall, Hitler and the United States, 1939–41*, 125

22 Saul Friedlander, *Prelude to Downfall, Hitler and the United States, 1939–1941*, (1967), 200

23 Tooze, *Wages of Destruction*, 394

24 Kenneth S Davies, *FDR: Into the Storm 1937–1940*, (1993), 621

25 Saul Friedlander, *Prelude to Downfall*, 136,

26 Fischer, *Germany's aims in the First World War*, 547 map

27 Shirer, *The Rise and Fall of the Third Reich*, (paperback), 84, *Mein Kampf*: 'The giant empire in the East is ripe for collapse'.

28 R W Davies, Mark Harrison, S G Wheatcroft, *The Economic Transformation of the Soviet Union, 1913–1945*, (hard-copy ed), 145

29 Aleksandr Nekrich, *Pariahs, Partners and Predators 1922–1941*, 24, 61

30 Istoriya vtoroi op.cit.Vol.Ip.270. quoted in Stephen M Tupper, *The Red Army and Soviet Defence* (Birmingham University, March 1982)

31 Lauran Paine, *The Abwehr*, (1984), 157–160

32 Lauren Paine, *The Abwehr*, 150

33 Timothy Snyder, (2010), *Bloodlands: Europe between Hitler and Stalin* 416

34 Brigadier-General Morgan, *Assize of Arms*, 261, Appendix 1V

35 W Manchester, *The Arms of Krupp 1587–1968*, 465

36 W Manchester, *The Arms of Krupp 1587–1986*, 541

37 W Manchester, *The Arms of Krupp 1587–1968*, 554

38 W Manchester, *The Arms of Krupp 1587–1968*, 513

39 March 1945, US State Dept. quoted in T H Tetens, *Germany Plots with the Kremlin*, 259

40 Burleigh, *The Third Reich: A New History*, (paper ed), 786

41 David K Yelton, *'Ein Volk Steht Auf', The German Volkssturm and Nazi Strategy, 1944–1945*, *Journal of Military History*, (2000), 1069

42 Michael H Kater, *Hitler Youth*, (2004), 238

43 *Weapons and Warfare, History and Hardware of Warfare* 24 February 2015, 25 03 2015 Article 'Volkssturm casualties'

44 US Military Intelligence report EW-Pa, 128

45 Nova Science magazine, (Kid Zone) Mark Walker, *Nazis and the Bomb* 11 August 2006

46 W Manchester, *The Arms of Krupp 1587–1968*, 635–7

47 Michael Dobbs, *Six Months in 1945*, 190

48 Michael Dobbs, *Six Months in 1945*, 198

CHAPTER 10

[1] OKW – Abwehr, 15th March 1944. Directive from Admiral Canaris, Chief of the Intelligence Division of the German High Command. Tetens, *Germany plots with the Kremlin,* 233–235

[2] William L Clayton to US Senate June 1945, Senator Kilgore report to Senate Military Affairs Committee, in T H Tetens, *Germany Plots with the Kremlin,* 261, 267

[3] Directive issued by the Chief of the Intelligence Division of the German High Command, Admiral Walter Wilhelm Canaris, on 15 March 1944.

[4] Volker Berghahn, 'Resisting the Pax Americana?' in Michael Ermath, *America and the Shaping of German Society, 1945–1955,* 91–92

[5] Victor Sebestyen, *1946, The Making of the Modern World,* 19–21

[6] Victor Sebastien *1946, The Making of the Modern World,* (paperback), 73

[7] 'The President was not a hero or a prophet … but a generously intentioned man, with many of the weaknesses of other human beings and lacking that dominating intellectual equipment which would have been necessary … What chance could such a man have against Mt. Lloyd George's unerring, almost medium-like sensibility to everyone immediately around him? John Maynard Keynes, *The Economic Consequences of the Peace,* quoted in Viereck's *American Monthly,* 1920

[8] *The New York Times, December 1945*

[9] Victor Sebastien, *1946, The Making of the Modern World,* 30

[10] Bark & Gress, *A History of West Germany, 1, From Shadow to Substance* 55–56

[11] Victor Sebestien, *1946 The Making of the Modern World,* 167

[12] Amos Yoder, 'The Ruhr Authority and the German Problem' in *The Review of Politics* Vol 17, No 3, 346

[13] Bark & Gress, *A History of West Germany 1, From Shadow to Substance,* 54

[14] Victor Sebestyen, *1946, The Making of the Modern World,* 192

[15] Bark & Gress, *A History of West Germany,1, From Shadow to Substance,* 178

[16] Volker Berghahn, 'Resisting the Pax Americana?' in Michael Ermath *America and the Shaping of German Society, 1945–1955,* 94

[17] From Senator Kilgore's report to the Senate Subcommittee, on War Mobilisation 10 July 1945, Statement by William L Clayton to the Subcommittee on Military Affairs, 25 June 1945

[18] Volker Berghahn, 'Resisting the Pax Americana?' in Michael Ermath *America and the Shaping of German Society, 1945–1955,* 88

[19] Simon Reich, 'Fascism and the Structure of German Capitalism, The Case of the Automobile Industry' in Volker R Berghahn, *Quest for Economic Empire,* (1996), 74–75

[20] Rudolf Augustein, *Konrad Adenauer* 14–15 (reproduced from *Daily Express* 15 October 1963)

[21] Victor Sebastyen, *1946 The Making of the Modern World,* (paperback ed), 91

22 Michael J Hogan, *Marshall Plan, America, Britain and the Reconstruction of Western Europe*, 415

23 The 'Marshall Plan' speech at Harvard University, 5 June 1947, OECD

24 Victor Sebastyen, *1946, The Making of the Modern World*, 68–72

25 Bark & Gress, *A History of West Germany, 1,From Shadow to Substance* 131

26 Sydney Morning Herald 12 March 1946

27 Bark & Gress, *A History of West Germany 1,From Shadow to Substance*, 201

28 Secret Memorandum issued by the Geo-Political Centre in Madrid.

29 D M Giangreco, D M Griffin, *Airbridge to Berlin: The Berlin Crisis of 1948, Its Origins and Aftermath,* (paperback ed), Chapter 11

30 Gary B Nash, 'Wars averted, Chanak, 1922, Burma 1945–7, Berlin 1948' *Journal of Strategic Studies* (1996) 343–3.63

31 Bark & Gress, *A History of West Germany, 1,From Shadow to Substance,* 128–9

32 Bark & Gress, *A History of West Germany, 1, From Shadow to Substance*, 184

33 Victor Sebastyen, *1946, The Making of the Modern World*, 48

34 Fritz, Stephen G, *Endkampf:* Soldiers, Civilians and the Death of the Third Reich, (2004), 191

35 R Overy, *The Bombers and the Bombed: Allied Air War over Europe 1940–1945,* (2014), 304–307

36 *Der Spiegel*, 'How many died in the Bombing of Dresden?' 10 February 2008

37 J L Gaddis, *The Cold War,* (paperback ed), 40–42

38 Townsend Hoopes, *The Devil and John Foster Dulles,* 92–97

39 Jung Chang & Jon Halliday, *Mao The Unknown Story,* (paper ed), 447–458

40 Rudolf Augustein, *Konrad Adenauer,* 24–25

41 Minutes of the foreign ministers' meeting, Sep 12–13, 1950. Quoted in Marc Trachtenberg and Christopher Gehrz, *America, Europe, and German Rearmament, August–September 1950*

42 Michael Ermath, *America and the Shaping of German Society 1945–1955,* 89

43 Deutsche Auslandsschulden, 1951, p 7 quoted in Eric Toussaint, *The Marshall Plan and the Debt Agreement on German Debt* 6

44 Eric Toussaint, *The Marshall Plan and the Debt Agreement on German Debt*

45 CADTM Eric Toussaint, *The Marshall Plan and the Debt Agreement on German Debt,* 24 October 2006

46 Until after Germany is reunified.

47 Charles Williams, *Adenauer, The father of the New Germany,* 364

48 Reichelt, *Das Erbe der IG Farben,* (1956), 74. In his speech supporting Germany's cartels Indiana Republican Homer Capehart even blames former Secretary to the Treasury Henry Morgenthau in Congress for the 'mass starvation' of the German people (in Germany's 1947 Great Inflation).

[49] Madrid Circular Letter, quoted in T H Tetens, *Germany Plots with the Kremlin*, 227–228

[50] W Manchester, *The Arms of Krupp*, 759

[51] Simon Reich in 'Fascism and the Structure of German capitalism' in Volker R Berghahn, *Quest for Economic Empire*, 86

[52] T H Tetens, *Germany plots with the Kremlin*, 167

[53] Annual Register, *1953*, 209

[54] T H Tetens, *New Germany and the old Nazis*, (1962), 24–27

CHAPTER 11

[1] Robert Mark Spaulding, Jr, Chapter 5, *Reconquering our old Position, West German Osthandel Strategies of the 1950s* in Volker Berghahn, *Quest for Economic Empire, European Strategies of German Big Business in the Twentieth Century*

[2] Charles Williams, *Adenauer*, 411

[3] Charles Williams, *Adenauer*, 412–18

[4] Hoopes, Tounsend, *The Devil and J F Dulles*, 301–2

[5] G B Foreign Office, selected docs. 188–9

[6] Charles Williams, *Adenauer*, 442–3

[7] J L Gaddis, *The Cold War*, (paperback ed), 69

[8] Charles Williams, *Adenauer*, 465–67

[9] Andrew Alexander, *America and the Imperialism of Ignorance*, (2011), 170

[10] Miguel A Faria, (2002) *Cuba in Revolution: Escape from a lost Paradise*, 93–98

[11] *Der Spiegel*, 10 April 2011

[12] *The New York Times*, 18 May 1963

[13] UN Doc ENDC/84, 8 April 1963

[14] For treaties made under Johnson and Nixon see Dennis L Bark & David R Gress, *A History of West Germany 2*, 162

[15] Mark Walker in *Nova*, 11 August 2005

[16] Friedrich Georg, *Hitlera Siegeswaffen Band 1; Luftaffe und Marine Geheim Nuclearwffen des Dritten Reich und ihre Traegersysteme*, (2000); Henry Stevens, *Hitler's Suppressed and Still-Secret Weapons, Science and Technology*, 76, 232

[17] Dennis Piskiewicz, *The Nazi Rocketeers, Dreams of Space and Crimes of War*, 184, 195

[18] Beate Klarsfeld, *Wherever They May Be*, (1975), 55–56

[19] Weimer Lippert, *Economic Diplomacy of Ostpolitik, The Origins of NATO's Energy Dilemma*, (2010), 174

[20] Stephen A Schuker, *American 'Reparations' to Germany, Implications for the Latin American debt crisis*, (1988), 131

[21] *Economist*, 10 July 1972

[22] Peter Uwe Schliemann, *The Strategy of British and German investors in Brazil*, (1981), 106

[23] On 27 June 1975, the Kraftwerk Union company (KWU) of Germany, owned by Siemens and AEG, concluded a giant order with Brazil for the *purchase* of up to eight nuclear reactors. A fuel fabrication plant was to be built by the KWU Nukem General Electric subsidiary Reaktor Brennelment Union. A nozzle separation enrichment plant was to be built by the Steag utility and a reprocessing plant was to be built by Kewa-Kernbrennstoff-Wiederaufarbeitungs-Gesellschaft mbH – which is a joint subsidiary of Bayer, Hoeschst, Gelsenberg and Nukem. The equipment and technology package was said to be worth $4.5 billion, *Nucleonics Week*, 20.12.1975. *Nucleonics Week*, 16.11.1976 reported that AEG was leaving the consortium, leaving Siemens as the sole owner of Kraftwerk Union, AG, effective from 1 January 1977.

[24] *Nucleonics Week*, 1 January 1976: 'since nations like Brazil would clandestinely protect themselves from the possibility of attack by their neighbours'.

[25] *Nucleonics Week*, 10 February1977

[26] Charles Williams, *Adenauer*, 507

[27] Cited in Wilharm (ed.), *Deutsche Geschichte 1962–1983*, 2: 200 also in Bark & Gress, 313.

[28] *The Times*, Obituary of Helmut Schmidt, material taken from Jonathan Carr's biography of Schmidt

[29] D. L. Bark & David R. Gress, *A History of West Germany*, 2, 'Democracy and its Discontents', 309.

[30] Andrew Alexander, *America and the Imperialism of Ignorance*, 196

[31] Bark & Gress, *A History of West Germany*, 2, 313–14

[32] Bark & Gress, *A History of West Germany*, 2, 315

[33] *Nucleonics Week*, 31 May 1979. Brazil declared that it wished to export her nuclear technology (just before the signing of the SALT II Treaty). *Nucleonics Week* reassured its readers, however, that the Germans still held effective control of Nuclen through key technological and commercial directors, although KWU held only 25% of the stock to Nuclebras's 75%.

[34] On 15 November 1979

[35] *Neucleonics Week*, 29 November 1979

[36] *Annual Register*, 85.

[37] John Lewis Geddes, *The Cold War*, (paperback ed), 84

[38] Bark & Gress, *A History of West Germany*, 2, 316–317.

[39] At the end of December an estimated 50,000 Russian troops invaded Afghanistan (24–26 December) and installed a puppet dictator (27 December).

[40] *The Times*, Overseas News

CHAPTER 12

[1] *Daily Express*, 13 October 2014 [2]

[3] T W Carr, lecture 'German and US involvement in the Balkans'

[4] T W Carr, 'German and US involvement in the Balkans.'

[5] *Der Spiegel,* 30 September 2010 'Was the deutsche Mark Sacrificed for Reunification?'

[6] David Marsh *The Bundesbank, The Bank that rules Europe,* (1992), 18

[7] T W Carr, 'German and US involvement in the Balkans'

[8] *The Guardian*

[9] *Guardian, 3 February 2005*

[10] Major Coleman 1V, Michael LaCour-Little, Kerry D Vandell, *Subprime lending and the Housing Bubble, Tail Wags Dog?* 4–5

[11] *Financial Post,* 'Bank Fiasco began with Northern Rock', 18 December 12

[12] *The New York Times* 21 August 2011 Gordon Brown 'The Euro Zone's Cure starts with Germany'

[13] *Daily Telegraph,* Ambrose Evens-Pritchard, May 2007, 'France and Germany clash over inflation as north-south divide widens'

[14] Micky Levy, 19 January 2012

[15] *Daily Telegraph,* 18 May 2007, Ambrose Evans-Pritchard, 'France and Germany clash over inflation as north-south divide widens'

[16] *Daily Telegraph,* Ambrose Evens-Pritchard, 19 October 2007, 'Dollar dives as US slump spreads'

[17] *Daily Telegraph,* Ambrose Evans-Pritchard, 9 November 2007, 'Eurozone at Loggerheads over interest rates'

[18] *Economist Intelligence Unit,* January 2008

[19] *Economist Intelligence Unit,* June 2008

[20] *Wikipedia World Oil Price chronology*

[21] *The Guardian,* 30 June 2008

[22] Wikipedia. World oil market chronology from 2003. Footnote 23. (http://newsvote:bbc,co,uk?1/hi/business/7052071.stm) Oil prices above $90 level, BBC News

[23] *The New York Times*, 21 August 2011, Gordon Brown, 'The Euro Zone Cure Starts with Germany'

[24] Paul Krugman, *End this Depression Now!,* (paperback ed), 19

[25] *Die Welt,* 7 February 2009: 'Under the pressure of the economic crisis the government and Länder have given themselves until 2020 to reduce their borrowings to nothing ... For the government the new regulations will reduce in stages to the whole country borrowing only 0.35% of gross national product in the budgetary year of 2011 till 2016. That is about 8.5 billion euros a year. The Länder must reduce their net borrowings between 2011 and 2020 to zero'.

[26] Information from The Local de, Feb 17th 2014

[27] Journal of Economic Perspectives, vol 28, Number 1, Winter 2014 see especially Fig 1, p,170 Comparison with UK Italy France Spain and US from 1994–2012 when German labour costs reduced substantially compared to all the other countries.

[28] *Le Journal International,* 13 December 2014, 'The rising Germanophobia in Europe'

[29] *Spiegel,* 6 November 2012, 'How the Euro Zone ignored its own rules'

[30] *Spiegel,* 30 September 2010, 'The Price of Unity. Was the Deutsche Mark sacrificed for Reunification'.

[31] John Laughland *Spectator,* 19 February 14, 'Ukraine: It's not about Europe vs Russia'

[32] January 2014, Thom Hartmann Program, 'Ukrainian Left-wing activists' appeal to UN, EU and USA: Don't back civil war and Fascist Coup in Ukraine! 2 February 2014, Executive Intelligence Review, 'Western Powers back Neo-Nazi Coup in Ukraine'.

[33] *Trumpet,* 26 March 2015

[34] *Spiegel,* 21 March 2014, '*Is* Germany a Country of Russia Apologists?'

[35] *German Foreign Policy.com* 'Renaissance of the West (1) 07 05 and (11) and 13 05 2015

[36] *Small Wars Journal,* Tony Corn, *Towards a Gentler, Kinder German Reich?* 13

[37] *German Foreign Policy.com* 'Steinmeier and the Oligarchs' 01 06 2015

[38] Wikipedia 1,650,500 military deaths. 3,700,000 civilian deaths due to military and crimes against humanity. 1,500,000 due to famine and disease.

[39] German Foreign Policy.com. 2 March 2016

CONCLUSIONS

[1] Robert Skiddeslky, John Maynard Keynes, *Hopes Betrayed,* (hardback ed), 55

[2] Secret Memorandum issued by the German Geo-Political Centre in Madrid.

[3] Volker R Berghahn, 'German Big Business and the Quest for a European Economic Empire in the Twentieth Century' in Volker R Berghahn, *Quest for Economic Empire,* (1996)

[4] Professor David Blanke, Teaching History.org. Panic of 1873. 'In 1871 Germany ended the use of silver as a monetary metal'. This 'instantly increased the value of Germany's money relative to other currencies'. The 'deflation' of silver backed currencies cascaded throughout the world'.

[5] Jonathan Steinberg, *Bismarck A life,* 334–335

[6] Wolfgang Manchau, *Berlin waves a deficit hair-shirt for us all,* 21 June 2009

[7] Karlspreis speech, May 2010

[8] Stephen A Schuker, 'J M Keynes and the Personal Politics of Reparations' August 1922 Keynes declared that the Reich could not spare a pfennig for reparations and would require a minimum eight year moratorium.

Bibliography

American Documents:

Dinner discussion between John Foster Dulles and Dr Hjalmar Schacht 'The Young Plan in relation to the World Economy' 20 October 1930 at Foreign Policy Association, 18 East 41 St. New York

US Military Intelligence Report EW-pa 128 (1944)

Statement by William L Clayton, Assistant Secretary of State, 25 June 1945

Report by Senator Kilgore to the Senate Affairs Committee on Germany's war potential 10 July 1945

British Documents:

Lloyd George Papers, House of Lords,

Baldwin File c/8 F/3/1

Churchill to Lloyd George, 7 July 1922 F/1/2/17

(Report No.40 dated 11 July 1922) referred to in Note on the German Chemical Industry and the possibility of its employment for the production of poisonous gases F/26/2 Q/8 (t28)

Lloyd George Papers, Sir Maurice Hankey to Lloyd George, 7 July 1922, F 1/2/17

Documents on British Foreign Policy, (1930)

German Documents:

Directive issued by the Chief of the Intelligence Division of the German High Command, Admiral Walter Wilhelm Canaris, 15 March 1944

Madrid Circular Letter 1950, Secret memorandum from the German Geo-political centre in Madrid (1950)

Russian Documents:

Central State Military Archives, Fischmann to Unchlicht, 29 April 27

Foreign Policy Archives, Moscow including

327

Protocol 22 File 694 No 37, 21 March 1922 on negotiations for Krupp's 50,000 hectare agricultural concession

No 36, August 2nd 1928 (no 698) on negotiations for setting up a joint agriculture venture with Krupp

No 701, 25 August 1928 and No 390 re: Communists regarding Social Democrats as Enemies.

Fund 79, Op 1. Case 785, 1930 on Krupp's training of Soviet engineers

Ahamed, Liaquat *Lords of Finance* (2009)

Akhtamzyan, A A, *New and Latest History*

No. 4 *Soviet and German economic relations between 1922 and 1932*, (1988) and No. 5 *Military Cooperation between the USSR and Germany 1920–1933* (1990) (information taken from extracts translated by the archivist at the Foreign Policy Archives, Moscow)

Alexander, Andrew, *America and the Imperialism of Ignorance* (paper ed) (2012)

Annual Register 1888–1952

Barker, J Ellis, *Foundations of Germany* (quoted from hardback ed 1916 (paper ed 2008) *Modern Germany* 1818

Baker, Ray Stannard, *Woodrow Wilson, Life and Letters*, Vol 8 (Garden City, New York, 1939)

Woodrow Wilson and World Settlement (1923)

Balderston, Theo, *The Origins and Causes of the German Economic Crisis, 1923–1931* (1993)

Barker, J Ellis, *Foundations of Germany* (1916)

Barnett, Correlli, *The Audit of War* (paper ed 1996)

Bark, Dennis L, & Gress, David R, *A History of West Germany Vol: 1, From Shadow to Substance,*

Vol: 2, Democracy and its Discontents, 1963–1988 (1989)

Berghahn, Volker R, *Imperial Germany 1871–1914* (1994)

'Resisting the Pax Americana?' West German Industry and the United States, 1945–55' in M Ermath *America and the Shaping of German Society* (1993) *Quest for Economic Empire, European Strategies of German Big Business in the Twentieth Century* (paper ed 1996)

Blaazer, David, 'Finance and the End of Appeasement: The Bank of England, the National Government and the Czech Gold' *Journal of Contemporary History* 40, (1)

Blake, Robert, *The Private Papers of Douglas Haig*, (1952)

Blanke, David, *Panic of 1873*, in Teaching History.org

Boemeke, Feldman and Glazer, *The Treaty of Versailles, a Reassessment after 75 Years* (2006)

Borsky, G, *The Greatest Swindle in the World, the Story of the German Reparations, with a Preface by the Rt. Hon Lord Vansittart* (1942)

Boyce, Robert, *French Foreign and Domestic Policy, 1918–1940, the Decline and Fall of a Great Power* (1998)

Bresciani-Turroni, C, *The Economics of Inflation*, in Ed. Capie, Forrest, *Major Inflations in History* (Edward Elgar 1991)

Brown, Gordon, 'The Euro Zone's cure starts with Germany' article in *The New York Times*, 21 August 2011

Burleigh, Michael, *The Third Reich: A New History* (paper ed 2001)

Butler, David Allen, *The Burden of Guilt, How Germany shattered the last few days of Peace, Summer 1914* (2010)

Carr, J.C, and Walter Taplin, *British Steel Industry* (1962)

Carr, T. W., *German and US involvement in the Balkans: A Careful Coincidence of National Policies?* (1995) (Presented at the Symposium on the Balkan War, Yugoslavia: Past and Present, Chicago, August 31-September 1, 1995)

Chang, Jung and Jon Halliday, *Mao: The Unknown Story* (2005) (paper ed)

Chichering, Roger, *We men who feel most German* (1984)

Clay, Sir Henry, *Lord Norman* (1957)

Claughton, Peter, *New Techniques, new sources: the British steel industry and its ore supply 1850–1950*

Class, Heinrich, *If I were the Kaiser,* pamphlet quoted in *Oxford Book of Fascism* (2010) and The Nazi Germany Sourcebook (2002)

Coleman, Major 1V, Michael le Cour-Little, Kerry D Vandell, *Subprime lending and the Housing Bubble, Tail Wags Dog?* (April 2008)

Conrad, Sebastian, *Globalisation and the Nations in Imperial Germany* (2014)

Crowdy, Terry, *The Enemy within, A History of Spies, Spymasters and Espionage* (2008)

Davies, Kenneth S, *FDR: Into the Storm 1937–1940* (1993)

Davies, R W, Harrison, Mark, Wheatcroft, SG eds., *The Economic Transformation of the Soviet Union* (1993)

Dobbs, Michael, *Six Months in 1945, FDR, Stalin, Churchill and Truman, from World War to Cold War* (paper ed 2013)

Dulles, John W F, *Vargas of Brazil,* (2012)

Dyck, Harvey L, *Weimar Germany and Soviet Russia 1926–1933* (1984)

Economist The, 1929

Eichengreen, Barry, *Golden Fetters, The Gold Standard and the Great Depression,* (paper ed 1992)

Ermath, Michael, *America and the Shaping of German Society, 1945–1955* (1994)

Evans-Pritchard, Ambrose, in *The Daily Telegraph*:

'France and Germany clash over Inflation as north-south divide widens' (2007)
'Dollar dives as US slump spreads' (2007)

'Eurozone at Loggerheads over interest rates' (2007)

Eyck, Erich, *Bismarck and the German Empire,* (hardback 1950)

The Weimar Republic, vol 1, (1962) vol 2, (1964) (both volumes \ translated by Harlan P Hanson and Robert G L Waite)

Faria, Miguel A, *Cuba in Revolution: Escape from a lost Paradise*, 93–98 (2002)

Feldman, G. D, *The Great Disorder, Politics, Economics and Society in the Great Inflation, 1914–1923* (1993)

Ferguson, Niall, *The Pity of War* (2009)

Fergusson, Adam, *When Money Dies: The Nightmare of the Weimar Hyperinflation* (paperback ed 2015)

Fischer, Fritz, *Germany's Aims in the First World War* (translated by Hajo Holborn and James Joll 1968)

War of Illusions, German Policies from 1911 to 1914 (translated by Marian Jackson and Alan Bullock 1975)

Financial Times, 1931

Frankopan, Peter, *The Silk Road, A New History of the World* (hard copy, paperback ed due 2016)

Fritz, Stephen G, *Endkampf: Soldiers, Civilians and the Death of the Third Reich,* (paperback ed 2015)

Friedlander, Saul, *Prelude to Downfall, Hitler and the United States, 1939–1941* (1967)

Fromkin, David, *Europe's last Summer Why the world went to war in 1914* (2005)

In the time of the Americans (1995)

Gaddis, John Lewis, *The Cold War* (2007) (paperback ed)

Georg, Freidrich, *Hitler Siegeswaffen Band 1; Luftaffe und Marine Geheim Nuclearwaffen des Dritten Reich und ihre Traegersysteme* (2000) quoted in Henry Stevens *Hitler's Suppressed and Still-Secret Weapons*

German Foreign Policy *newsletter@german-foreign-policy.com*

Giangreco, D M, Griffin, Robert E Griffin, *Airbridge to Berlin, The Berlin Crisis of 1948, its Origins and Aftermath* (paper ed 1988)

Guardian, The

Haffner, Sebastien, *Failure of a Revolution* (1973)

Harrison, Mark, and R W Davies, *The Economic Transformation of the Soviet Union 1915–1945* (December 1993)

The Soviet-Military-Economic Effort during the Second five-year Plan (1933–37) article (postprint)

Hogan, Michael J, *The Marshall Plan, America, Britain and the Reconstruction of Western Europe* (1998)

Hoopes, Tounsend, *The Devil and John Foster Dulles: The Diplomacy of the Eisenhower Era* (1973)

James, Harold, *The German Slump: Politics and Economics 1924–1936* (1986)
A German Identity, 1770–1990 (1989)

Journal of Economic Perspectives Vol 28, no 1 (2014)

Kantorowitz, Hermann, *The Spirit of British Policy and the Myth of the Encirclement of Germany* (London, 1931)

Kater, Michael H, *Hitler Youth* (2004)

Kershaw, Ian, *Hitler 1889–1936: Hubris* (1999), *Nemesis,* (paperback 2001)

Keynes, John Maynard, *Two Memoirs, Dr. Melchior, A Defeated Enemy and My Early Beliefs* (1949)

The Economic Consequences of the Peace (1919)

Kitchen, Martin, *The Political Economy of Germany 1815–1914* (1978)

A History of Modern Germany 1800–2000 (December 2005)

Klarsfeld, Beate, *Wherever they may be* (1975)

Knight-Patterson, W M, *Germany from defeat to Conquest* (1945)

Krugman, Paul, *End this Depression Now* (paper ed 2013)

Laughland, John, article in *The Spectator,* 14 February 2014 'It's not about Europe vs. Russia'

Leopold, John A, *Alfred Hugenberg, The Radical Campaign against the Weimar Republic* (1977)

Link, Authur S, *Woodrow Wilson, Revolution War and Peace* (paperback ed. 1979)

Lippert, W, *Economic Policy of Ostpolitik, The Origins of NATO's energy dilemma* (Berghahn Books 2010)

Local, The (Germany's news in English)

Manchau, Wolfgang, article 'Berlin Waves a Deficit hair-shirt for us all' *Financial Times,* 2009

Manchester, William, *The Arms of Krupp* (1968)

Mantoux, Étienne, *The Carthaginian Peace or the Economic Consequences of Mr. Keynes* (1946)

Marks, Sally, 'Smoke and Mirrors' Contributor in Boemeke, Feldman and Glazer (eds) *The Treaty of Versailles, A Reassessment after 75 Years* (2006)

Marquand, David, *Ramsay Macdonald* (1977)

Marsh, David, *The Bundesbank, the Bank that Rules Europe* (1992)

Millin, Sarah Gertrude, *General Smuts,* vol 2 (1936)

Morgan, Brigadier General J H Morgan, *Assize of Arms, The Disarmament of Germany and her Rearmament 1919–1939*

Nash, Gary B, 'Wars averted, Chanak, 1922, Burma 1945–7, Berlin 1948' *Journal of Strategic Studies* (1996)

Nekrich, Alexander, *Pariahs, Partners and Predators: German-Soviet relations 1922–1941* (1997)

Newman, A.M, *Economic Organisation of the British Coal Industry* (1933)

New York Times, 1923, 1929, Dec, 1945,

Nucleonics Week (Platts)

Overy, Richard, *The Bombers and the Bombed: Allied Air War over Europe 1940–1945* (2014)

Paine, Lauran, *The Abwehr, German Military Intelligence in World War Two* (1984)

Patch, William L Jnr, *Heinrich Brüning and the Dissolution of the Weimar Republic* (1988)

Piszkiewicz, Dennis, *The Nazi Racketeers, Dreams of Space and Crimes of War* (2007)

Reich, Simon, 'Fascism and the Structure of German Capitalism', in Volker R Berghahn, *Quest for Economic Empire* (1994)

Reid, Walter, *Douglas Haig, Architect of Victory* (2006)

Reiman, Michael, *The Birth of Stalinism: The USSR on the Eve of the Second Revolution* (1987)

Röhl, John C G, *Kaiser Wilhelm 11, A Concise Life* (2014)

Royal Institute of International Affairs, *Survey of International Affairs, 1929, 1930, 1931, 1936*

Royal Institute of International Affairs, Papers

Schacht, Hjalmar, *My First 76 Years* (1955)

Schliemann, Peter-Uwe, *The Strategy of British and German Investors in Brazil* (1981)

Schuker, Stephen A, *The End of French Predominance in Europe: the Financial Crisis of 1924 and the Adoption of the Dawes Plan* (1976)
American 'Reparations' to Germany 1919–1933, Implications for the Third World Debt Crisis (Princeton Studies in International Finance, No 61 (1988)
J M Keynes and the Personal Politics of Reparations (2014)

Sebestyen, Victor, *1946, The Making of the Modern World* (2015)

Shirer, William L, *The Rise and Fall of the Third Reich* (paperback ed) (1998)

Snyder, Timothy *Bloodlands: Europe between Hitler and Stalin* (2010)

Steinberg, Jonathan, *Bismarck, A Life*

Steinberg, S H, *A Short History of Germany*

Stevens, Henry, *Hitler's Suppressed and Still-Secret Weapons, Science and Technology* (2007)

Stieber, Wilhelm, J. C. E *The Chancellor's Spy* (translated by Jan can Heurck)

Skiddelsky, Lord Robert, *John Maynard Keynes, Hopes Betrayed 1883–1920* (1983)

Smythe, Donald, *General of the Armies* (1986)

Spiegel, der

Snyder, Timothy, *Bloodlands: Europe between Hitler and Stalin* (2010)

Soviet Studies Research Centre, The RMA, Sandhurst

Spaulding, Robert Mark, Jr., 'Recovering our position, West German Osthandel Strategies of the 1950s' in Volker Berghahn *Quest for Economic Empire*

Stevens, Henry, *Hitler's Suppressed and Still-Secret Weapons, Science and Technology* (2007)

Stone, Norman, *World War Two, A Short History* (2014)

Tarpley, Webster G. *British Financial Warfare: How the City of London created the Great Depression* (1996)

Tetens, T H, *Germany plots with the Kremlin* (1953)

Terraine, John, *Douglas Haig the Educated Soldier* (1968)

Thayer, William Roscoe, *Theodore Roosevelt, An Intimate Biography* (1919)

Thyssen, Fritz, *I paid Hitler* (1941)

The Times 1925, 1929

Toland, J.W, *Adolf Hitler,* (1991)

Tooze, J Adam, *Statistics and the German State, 1900–1945: The Making of Modern Knowledge* (2001)

Wages of Destruction, the Making and Breaking of the Nazi Economy (2007)

Trachtenberg, Marc and Christopher Gehr, article, America, Europe and German Rearmament, August-September 1950, Critique of a Myth

Toussaint, Éric, *The Marshall Plan and the Debt Agreement on German Debt* 24 October 2006 (CADTM)

Tuchman Barbara W, *The Zimmerman Telegram* (1959)

Turner, Henry Ashby Jr., *Hitler's Thirty Days to Power: January 1933* (1996)

UN Doc ENDC/84 8 April 1963

Walker, Mark, *Nazi Science: Myth, Truth and the Atom Bomb* (paper ed 2001)

Waterhouse, Michael, *Edwardian Requiem, A Life of Sir Edward Grey* (2013)

Wheeler-Bennett, *Brest-Litovsk, the forgotten Peace, March 1918* (1938)

Williams, Charles, *Adenauer, The Father of the New Germany* (2001)

Yelton, David K, *Ein Volk Steht Auf:* 'The German Volkssturm and the Nazi Strategy, 1944–1945' in *Journal of Military History* (2000)

Yoder, Amos, 'The Ruhr Authority and the German Problem' in *The Review of Politics*

Index

Acheson, Dean, 222, 237,
Abdul Hamid II, 37,
Abs, Hermann, 240, 259,
Adenauer, Chancellor Konrad,
  Burgomaster of Cologne again and sacked, 225-226,
  Chairman of CDU, 226,
  elected Chancellor,232,
  attitude to former Nazis, 233,
  chose Walter Hallstein to draw up Schuman Plan, 240,
  announced US nuclear weapons essential for Germany, 247,
  drew up 'Hallstein Doctrine', 249-250,
  failure of hard line over East Germany, 250-1,
  retired, 254,

Aehrenthal, Graf von, 39,
Alexander, Serbian Crown Prince, 63,
Angell, Norman, 76, 79
Anti-Semitism,
  under Bismarck 28-29,
  Hitler's in *Mein Kampf* 135

Anton, Prince, 20,
Asquith, Herbert, Henry, 54,
Baker, James, 269
Balfour, Arthur,
  Defended American fleet against Germany, 35

Baldwin, Stanley, 133

Barraclough, Brigadier John (Later Sir) 225-6

Beaverbrook, 221-222

Benedetti, Count, 21-22

Bernhardi, General, 47

Bernhard, Georg, 161

Bernstorff, Count, Johann von, 88-89

Beruch, Bernard, 133,138

Bethmann Hollweg, Theobald von,
  appointed Chancellor, 44-45,
  and the British, 48, 53,
  Zabern incident, 49,
  threatened to mobilise if Russian call-up of reservists confirmed, 64,
  deceived the Kaiser, 65,
  passed on Grey's message to Austria without final sentence, 66,
  changed the wording of Kaiser's 'Halt in Belgrade', 67-68,
  offered Turkey an alliance, 68,
  summoned Russia not to provoke Austria, 70
  egged Austria to provoke Russia into 'general mobilisation,' 69-70,
  told Grey via Goschen that he was going to war with France, 71-72, told that would mean war, tried to stop Austria, 73,
  agreed imminent war be proclaimed on 31st July, 75,
  to ensure socialist support postponed date till 1st August, 76,
  insisted the military advance had to go on 'for technical reasons, 77, offer over Belgium, 78-79,
  called Britain's Treaty with Belgium 'a mere scrap of paper', 79, September 1914 notes on war aims in Belgium and France, 82,
  1916 'appeal for peace' prior to renewing unrestricted submarine warfare, 88-90,
  downfall, 94

Bismarck, Prince Otto,
  youth, 10-11,
  description, 13,
  support for Russia, 13,
  employed spy, Wilhelm Stieber, 14,
  manipulated Austria into declaring war, 16-17,
  Peace with Austria and German states,18,
  manipulated accession of a Hohenzollern prince on the Spanish throne, 20-21,
  Ems telegram, 22,
  starved France into surrender, 23-24,
  Treaty with France, 25,
  similarities between Bismarck's Reich and the EU, 25-26,
  adopted the gold mark, 26,

kulturkampf, 27,
blamed Austria for stock exchange collapse, 27-28,
fought to retain large army, 29-30,
fought against Social Democracy, 30-31,
health and accident insurance and old age pensions, 31,
lost affection for Russia, 32-33

Blücher, General Gebhard von, 8,
Bock, General von,
   Put Guderian's proposal to March to Moscow to Field Marshall, von
   Brauchitsch, 208

Bockelmann, Horst, 268
Bosse, Dr, 213
Brandt, Willy, 254, 258-259,
Brauchitsch, Field Marshall von,
   Hitler flew to von Bock's headquarters and agreed that they could attack
   Moscow 208-209

Brentano, Heinrich von, 252
Briand, Aristide, 129, 151
Brest-Litovsk, Treaty of, 97-98,
   Supplementary Treaty with Romania
   Supplementary Treaty with Russia, 27th August, 99

Briey, iron ore basin in Lorraine, 51-52, 81-83, 86, 198-199, 240
   Map on page 52
   Thyssen declared that the acquisition of Longwy-Briey would help Germany
   overtake America and dominate the world iron market, 82

Brockdorff-Rantzau, Count, 93, 121
Brüning, hungerkanzler,
   character, 171-172,
   advocated 'austerity' for political reasons, 172,
   lowered wages and raised taxes, 172, 179, 181,
   visited England, 181,
   aim to return monarchy, 185,
   lost office, 187

Brusilov, General, 86, 93
Byrnes, James F, 224,
Caillaux, Henriette, 57, 70
Caillaux, Joseph, 49, 57

Calmette, journalist with le Figaro, 57-58
Campbell-Bannerman, Sir Henry, 54
Canaris, Admiral, 219
Carter, Jimmy, American President, 261-264
Casement, Sir Roger, 87-88
Castro, Fidel, 254
Churchill, Winston,
  alarm at Austria's Ultimatum, 62,
  alarm at Germany's predatory trading, 131-132,
  disregarded Keynes advice, 145,
  said that the U-boat peril frightened him worst in World War II, 203

Class, Heinrich,
  defined 'Pan Germans' aims to gain a larger empire 40-43, instrumental in
    gaining popular support for army bills, 44,
  outlined Germany's War Aims, 85,
  advocated blaming 'Jewry' for the loss of the war, 112,
  captivated Hitler with his ideas, 125,
  at Bad Harzburg, 186,
  became member of Hitler's administration, 196

Clayton, William I, 225
Clauswitz, von, 12,
Clemenceau, Georges, 102, 128
Clinton, Bill, 274-275
Coal (German)
  After World War I, 125, 132, 135-138, 146, 148, 294
  After World War II, 224
Conrad von Hötzendorf, Baron Franz, 57, 74
Cotton,
  1923, Germany America's best customer, importing 'double' the amount of
    France and England, 139,
  1933, only offered German beer or wine in payment for America's cotton,
    191

Crowe, Sir Eyre, 65
Dalton, Hugh, 229
Derby, Lord, 29
Diebner, Kurt, 215
Dubcek, Alexander, Czechoslovak leader, 258
Dulles, John Foster,
  1930 dinner discussion with Dr. Schacht, 178,
  1950 reassurance to South Korea, 236,

Secretary of State, 247,
and European Defence Community, 247,
on Soviet Union, 248,
hard-liner dying of cancer, 250

Duisberg, Carl, 187
Ebert, Friedrich,
1916, called for unequal Prussian vote to be removed, 94,
Dec 1918 saluted Germany's 'unvanquished' army, 115,
and Kapp putsch, 124
tried for treason, 139

Ems telegram,
text of and Bismarck's alterations, 22,
Bethmann Hollweg copied Bismarck's Ems telegram by changing Kaiser's 'Halt in Belgrade', 67-68

Erhard, Ludwig,
stabilised currency, 229,
wanted to develop Siberia in exchange for German unification, 255, alternative plan to use America's nuclear arsenal to bring USSR to negotiating table, 255-256

Ehlers, Dr. Hermann, President of the Bundestag, 242
Elbrick, Charles, Burke, US Ambassador to Brazil, 260
Erzberger, Matthias, called for compromise peace, 94
Falkenhayn, General Erich von,
29th July 1914, not allowed to use Russia's partial mobilisation as an excuse to proclaim state of emergency, 69,
wanted a 'state of imminent war' proclaimed on 31st July, 75,
battles on the Western front, 83,
lost his job, 86

Favre, Jules, 23-24
Ferdinand, Franz, Archduke,
assassination, 56,
Kaiser's friendship with, 58,
affect of death on Franz Joseph, 59

Foch, General Ferdinand, 108,
stated of Treaty of Versailles, 'This ... is an Armistice for twenty years', 122

Forstner, Günter Freiherr von, 49-50

Franco, 200

Francois-Poncet, French Ambassador, 43-44

Franz Joseph, Austrian Emperor,
  Bismarck stated that coexistence with was impossible, 16,
  portrait of in 1914, 59,
  decided that Serbia's response to Ultimatum was inadequate, 64,

Frantz, Constantin, 30

Frederick Wilhelm (1620-88, Great Elector) 8,

Frederick Wilhelm I, (1688-1740) King in Prussia (1713),8

Frederick II (the Great)
  wrote on necessity of creating a war chest, 8
  necessity of army's blind obedience, 11
  advantages of friendship with Russia, 13
  Sovereign's right to declare war, 14
  advantages of employing spies, 13
  advantage of giving Austria moderate peace, 18

Frederick VII, of Denmark, (1808-63) 14,

French, Sir John, 84

Friedrich, Otto A, 220, 224

Funk, Walter, 217

Gallieni, General, 81,

Gallois, General Pierre Marie, 270

Galvéas, Ernane, Brazilian Finance Minister, 265

Genscher, Hans Dietrich, 269

Germany, economic strength,
  Autumn 1914, 82,
  1918, 97-99,
  destroyed French competition on army's retreat, 103,
  ready for a trade war, 124,
  more gold in 1918 than in 1914, 117,
  second largest shipbuilder in the world, 134,
  W. Wilson predicted would conquer the world industrially, 138, British coal
    miners could not compete with, 146-147,
  wealth of industrial cartels, 148,
  German coal industry in 1929, 293,
  armaments factories abroad, 150-151,
  1931 leading export country, 179,
  industrial capacity 11% higher in 1947 than 1936, 225

George V, King, 70, 77

Gerlach, Walther, 215

German Officers Corps, 11-12, 50-51, 121

Gilbert, Parker, 153-154

Globke, Hans, 233

Goebbels, Joseph, 257

Gollanz, Victor, 229

Gomulka, Wladyslaw, 250

Göring, Hermann, 187, 208

Goschen, Sir Edward, 70-71

Grey, Sir Edward, British Foreign Minister, 1914,

asked Germany to modify Austria's Ultimatum demands, 62, suggested 4
power mediation of powers not directly involved, 63, asked Berlin to put
pressure on Austria to say that it accepted Ultimatum, 64,

stated that Germany should stop Austria from pursuing a 'foolhardy policy', 66,
received a deceptive reply, 67,

threatened Britain would respond if Germany invaded France, 73,

on his moral justification for advising that Britain go to war in 1914, 79

Gröner, General,

told the king the army was no longer responsible to him, 114,

told the elected government that it must 'cooperate' with the Officers Corps, 115,

sacked for refusing to lift ban on Hitler's SA, 187

Guderian, General, 208,

Haeseler, General Graf von, 51

Haig, General Douglas,

permission to pierce the Hindenburg line, 100,

10th October, 'he is a beaten army', 102,

19th October after Wilson's intervention, declares that the enemy is 'not ready
for unconditional surrender.' 103

Lost confidence in the American army, 108,

advised against the French entering Germany to pay off old scores, 106,

worried about Allied disarmament, 121

Haldane, Visount, 46-47

Halder, General, 208-209

Hallstein, Walter, 240, Hallstein Doctrine, 249-250

Hankey, Sir Maurice, 132

Hatry, Clarence, 163-164

Helfferich, Karl, 51

Helphand, Alexander, more commonly known as 'Parvus' – see Parvus

Henderson, Arthur, British Foreign Secretary, 173

Hillferding, Dr, 164, 171

Himmler, 211

Hindenburg, Gen. Paul von,

Tannenberg, 81,

war supremo with Ludendorff, 87,

passed the odium for signing the Treaty of Versailles onto the politicians, 122,

should have been put on trial, 123,

forced Prussian authorities to revoke ban on war veterans association, the Stahlhelm, 171-172

Hohenlohe, Prince, 83

Hitler, Adolf,

Became a 'drummer' for the Nationalist cause 125,

his 1923 putsch, 134-135,

Pan-German themes in *Mein Kampf*, 135,

protested Germany's innocence of starting World War I, 150,

newspaper magnate Hugenberg interested in promoting a man of the people, 154,

put on the committee of Hugenberg's anti-reparations petition, 167, success in 1930 elections, 173,

Bad Harzburg, 186,

Stalin's help with 1932 elections, 188,

military success in Europe, 200,

U-boat warfare, 202-203,

threatened invasion of Britain, 204,

invasion of Russia, 208,

persuaded by the generals to allow them to march to Moscow, 208, announced the *Volkssturm* after the Red House meeting, 213

Hoffmann, General, 98

Holleben, Dr. von, 36

Hoover, Herbert,

Advises using 'expediency' over Versailles Treaty 122,

inauguration as President, 158,

sympathy with Germany at Versailles, 159,

offered one year moratorium on reparations and war debts, 182

Hötzendorf, Conrad von, 57, 74,

House, Col. Edward,

Wilson told him that he wanted to give Germany an armistice 100,

promised Wilson that he would use threats to persuade the Allies to accept peace on his terms, 105

Hugenberg, Alfred,

description, anti-Polish sentiment, 43-44

and Pan German League, 44,

1914 invited trade associations to outline their war aims, 85,

initiated newspaper war against Wilson for denying Germany victory in WW1, 112,

leader of DNVP party in 1928,

expressed a wish to promote a man of the people as dictator, 154,

sent letter to prominent businessmen, spring 1929, 160,

mounted pernicious petition against Young Plan, 165,

put Hitler on the petition's committee, 167,

its effects on Wall Street, 167,

and Social Democrats, 170-171,

fears over him and Hitler combining to form a party of revenge, 173, Bad Harzburg, 186,

member of Hitler's administration, sacked but kept his newspapers, 196

Hynd, John, 229

Iron, (see Briey)

Ismay, Lord, 248

Jagow, Gottlieb von,

warned Austria that she (and Germany) must appear provoked so that 'Britain can remain neutral,' 48,

saw the conflict as a fight between the 'Teuton and the Slav', 61, promised to stand by Austria (and its Ultimatum) 'unreservedly, 61 passed on Grey's peace initiative late and without full text, 66,

told by Moltke: 'We shall manage the 150,000 British, 79,

replaced by Zimmerman as Foreign Minister, 90

Jenninger, Philipp, 265-266

Jews,

blamed for 1873 crash, 28,

Endlösung called for 'world problem' of the Jews, 29,

Bismarck's expulsion of from Poland, 32,

Vilified by Pan German Heinrich Class, 41,

blamed for army's defeat in 1918, 112,

worker's sufferings in Great Inflation blamed on, 137,

starved after 1939 invasion of Poland, 197,

slaughter of Jews before Final Solution, 207-208,

on Kristallnacht 50th anniversary said that they deserved to be shown their place, 265-266

Johnson, Lyndon B, 255

Kapp, Wolfgang, 124

Kahr, von, 135

Klarsfeld, Beate, 258
Keglevich, Stephen, 28
Kellog-Briand Pact, 151
Kennedy, President John F, 251
Kesküla, Aleksander, 93
Keynes, John Maynard,
  impact of his book, 127-128,
  prediction that Germany would be reduced 'to servitude' by reparations seemed
    true in 1923,138,
  Britain's return to the Gold Standard, 145,
  and Hoover, 159,
  and Melchior, 183,
  seeks a loan after World War II, 221-222,
  influence of, 247

Kiesinger, Kurt Georg, 257-258
Kilgore, Senator Harley M, 225
Kim II-sung 235-236
Kirdorf, Emil, founder of the German coal syndicate, 44, 132
Kleist, General von, 203
Kluck, General von, 81
Koch-Weser, Dr, 165,
Kohl, Helmut,
  and Mrs Thatcher, 267,
  and East Germany, 268,
  on the 'euro', 273,

Krugman, Paul, 286
Krupp, firm of,
  made train wheels, 13,
  3 kg breech-loaded cast-steel cannons, 19,
  nearly went bankrupt after 1870, 30,
  employed 77,000 people by 2010,44,
  Big Bertha gun, 86,
  incident at factory 1923, 134,
  company's health in 1920s, 148-149,
  expansion after Hitler came to power, 189,
  exported know-how so that Soviets could protect tanks, 175,
  fed slaves less than I G Farben, 211,
  called a 'state within a state' 211,
  rep. at Red House meeting, 212,
  poised to export household goods after WW2, 225

344

Krupp, Alfried von,
  character, 209,
  expanded slave- empire, 210-211,
  exploitation of slave labour worst, 211,
  jettisoned his war bonds etc. and put cash abroad, 215,
  let out of prison and became EEC's richest man, 243

Krupp, Gustav von,
  description, 59,
  close links with government and member of Pan German League, 44, hold over the Kaiser, 58,
  took agricultural concession in Upper Caucasus in 1922, 130, banquet in middle of 1929 reparations negotiations, 161,
  agreed to help Stalin create more giant farms so that Stalin could buy German armaments, in return for forcing the German Communists to vote with Hitler and Hugenberg, 175,
  elected Chairman of the Board of Reich Federation of German industry, 185

Kühlmann, Richard von, 96-97
Lambach, Walter, 55
Leyen, Ursula, von der, 289
Laval, 201
Lewin, Brigadier-General Harry, 117
Lenin, V. J,
  Description 92,
  explained peace conditions, 93,
  arrived in Russia, 93,
  how Germany dealt with his principles of 'no annexations' etc, 97, Later assisted by Krupp, 130,
  in return for German army training on Russian steppes, 219

Leopold, Prince, 20-22
Lichnowsky, Ambassador Prince Karl von,
  brought back soothing German responses to increasingly anxious questions from Grey, 62, 67

Liggett, General Hunter, 102
Liman von Sanders, Gen. Otto, 37, 53
Litvinov, Maxim, 196
Lloyd George, David,
  Morocco, 39,
  end of the First World War, 106,
  behaviour at Peace Conference, 117,

claim for huge reparations prompted Wilson to ask for 'no indemnities',119,

promised to do something about Germany's predatory exports, 126, bribed German coal owners to send coal reparations to France, 127, and Rapallo, 130,

allowed miners a shorter working day post WW I, 146

Longwy-Brie, (see Briey)

Lucieto, Charles, spy, 54

Ludendorff, Gen. Erich,

Tannenberg, 81,

'The alliance with Austria must remain but the conflict is bound to come', 85,

ordered 400,000 Belgium workers pumped into German industry, 86, sacked Bethmann Hollweg, 94,

asked the Kaiser to seek peace, 101,

Allies too weak to be able to bring him to trial, 123,

Tries putsch with Hitler in 1923, 135,

Macdonald, Ramsay, British Prime Minister, 182

Maginot Line, 151

Mao Zedong, 236

Marshall, George C, 227-228

Matsuoka, Yosuke, 205

Max, Prince of Baden, 102, 111-112,

Prince Max declared 'The Emperor and King has decided to renounce his throne' 114

McCloy, 236-242

Melchior, Karl, 183

Merkel, Angela, 284, 287, 290, 302

Michaelis, Chancellor, 94-95

Milosevic, General, 269

Mitterrand, François, 267, 272, 288,

Molotov, 235

Moltke, General Helmuth von, the Elder, 23

Moltke, General Helmuth von, the Younger,

dismissed Austria's border disputes as a pretext for Germany to go to war, 46,

little respect for French armies, 65,

pressed Austria-Hungary to adopt general mobilisation (without actually declaring war on Russia), 74,

pressed for a 'state of imminent war' to be declared on 31st July, 75, when the Kaiser tried to stop the war, protested that the patrols had already penetrated Luxembourg, 77, told Foreign Minister Jagow, 'We shall manage the 150,000 British' 79

Monnet, Jean, 239,
Moreau, Emile, 145
Morocco, Crises over, 38, 39
Mussert, 201
Mussolini, 200
Naumann, Dr. Werner, 244
Napoleon III, Emperor of France, 20, 21
Nicholas II, Tsar of Russia, 69, 77,
Nicolson, Harold, 101
Nitti, Francesco, 52
Nollet, General, 132
Norman, Montagu,
  approached by Schacht, 139,
  pedigree, 140,
  spellbound by Schacht, 141,
  took Britain back onto Gold Standard at high level, 144-145,
  anti-French, 145,
  accused Germany of needlessly borrowing money, 147,
  raised interest rates in Autumn 1929 due to persistent exports of gold (primarily
    to Germany), 164,
  left the Gold Standard, 183-184,
  after invasion of Czechoslovakia authorised the transfer of the Czech gold
    from BIS no 2 account to no 17 account, managed by the Reichsbank, 195

Nozari, Gholam-Hossein, Iranian Oil Minister, 282
Noyer, Christian, France's Central Bank President, 281
Orlando, President, 117
Pan-German League,
  40, 43, 55, 59, 84-85, 112, 229

Pancho Villa, General, 90,
Parvus, also known as Alexander Helphand, 92,
Pershing, General, 106-108
Peters, Jürgen, I G Metall, 280
Podewils, Heinrich von, 18
Pohl, Karl Otto, 273
Poincaré, Raymond, President of France, 48, 61, 64, 70,
  pleads for France to ratify Young Plan, 162,
Poroshenko, President, 290
Pleven, René, French Prime Minister, 247
Powers, Francis Gary, 251

Prussian Officers Corps (see Officers Corps)

Putin, President Vladimir, 289

Quisling, 201

Raeder, Grand Admiral, 202-204

Rathenau, Walther, 131,

Reagan, Ronald, 264

Redmond, John, 54

Ridley, Nicholas, 268

Rhee, Syngman, 235

Roon von, General, 11, 12

Roosevelt, Theodore, President,

took strong line over German threat to projected Panama Canal, 36,

in Dec 1916 declared: 'I don't think that Wilson will go to war unless Germany literally kicks him into it', 90,

in October 1918 declared: 'At this point, if we make an Armistice, we have lost the war,' 102,

died, 109

Roosevelt, Franklin D, President,

and dust bowl in US cotton-growing areas, 191,

Nov 1939, announced America's neutrality, 203,

proposed construction of world's largest military-industrial complex in 1940, 203,

promised not to get involved in 'any foreign war', 205,

Then Hitler declared war on America, 205,

died, 220

Rumbold, Sir Horace, 173

Rust, Josef, Chairman of Volkswagen's supervisory board in the 1970s, 260

Sanio, Jochen, President of the German Financial Supervisory Authority, 284

Sarkozy, French President, Opposition to rises in ECB interest rates in 2007, 280-281

Sazonov, Sergei, Russian Foreign Minister,

declared that it was clear to everybody that Germany had decided to bring about a collision, urged Russia to adopt 'general mobilisation' 75

Schacht, Dr. Hjalmar,

new President of Reichsbank, offered Norman attractive proposition, 139,

high interest rates attracted American funds, 147,

promised to curb socialists spending, 154,

aim for Young Plan to remove all controls from Germany, 157,

tough negotiations, 160,

won acceptance that implementation of the Young Plan should be from 1ˢᵗ

    Sep 1929, 163,
    forced Finance Minister to resign, 171,
    dinner discussion with John Foster Dulles, 178,
    attended Bad Harzburg rally, 186,
    as Hitler's Minister of Economics, declared a moratorium on Germany's debts,
        192,
    Norman a god-father to grandchild, 195,
    'Drang nach Südostern' 198

Schlieffen, Gen. Alfred von, 35, 37-38
Schlotterer, 201
Schmidt, Helmut, 261-263, 289
Schmidt, Paul, 163
Schröder, Gerhard, 274
Schumacher, Kurt, 232
Schuman, Robert, 239-240
Shouvaloff, Peter, 29
Smuts, General, 159
Sprecher, Drexel A, 211
Stalin, Joseph,
  agreement with Krupp, 174-176,
  concerned by Hugenberg, 196,
  German help for Stalin's armaments industry, 207,
  after invasion moved factories beyond the Urals, 208,
  organised the home front into the Osoaviakhim, 209,
  encouraged soldiers to 'rape and pillage' Germany, 217,
  meeting with Truman, 222-223,
  stopped delivering goods to the West, 224,
  post war empire, 223,
  refused to allow satellite states to accept Marshall Aid, 230,
  approved of idea of America being dragged into war in Korea, 235-236, died
      in 1953, 248

Stieber Wilhelm, 14-16, 18-20, 22-24
Stinnes, Hugo,
  put in charge of Belgium's coal mines and industrial production during the
      1914 war, 83,
  defied Allied coal reparations demands, economic clout, 125,
  forced German miners to work longer hours for lower pay, 137

Stresemann, Gustav,
  encouraged Americans to lend Germany money, 147,
  told of Schacht's plans for negotiating the Young Plan, 157,

got his DVP party to oppose Hugenberg's petition,
died, 165

Strong, Benjamin,
and Britain's return to the Gold Standard, 143-145, 183

Thatcher, Margaret, 267-268
Thyssen, August,
first to buy iron ore concession in France, 51,
huge territorial ambitions in September 1914, 81-82,
declared that the acquisition of Longwy-Brie would help Germany to overtake America and dominate the world iron market, 82

Thyssen, Fritz,
And passive resistance propaganda campaign, 1923, 133,
remarked on how Krupp became a 'super Nazi' once Hitler had achieved power, 188

Tirpitz, Alfred von,
plan for grabbing America, 34-35,
met Haldane, 47,
formed Fatherland political movement declaring 'What is really at issue is the liberty of the continent of Europe … against the all-devouring tyranny of Anglo-Americanism.' 95

Tisza, Count Stephen, 60, 64
Trichet, Jean-Claude, European Central Bank President, 280-283
Tito, President of Yugoslavia, 269
Toussaint, Éric, 238
Trotsky, Leon, 96-98
Truman, Harry S,
came to power, personality, 220,
and Stalin 222-223,
signed occupation directive JCS, preserving unity of Reich and Germany's ownership of the Ruhr, 223,
told Secretary of State, James Byrnes to 'stop babying up to the Soviets,' 224,
pledged to stop Greece and Turkey falling to the Soviets, led to the Marshall Plan, 227,
dropped bombs on Hiroshima and Nagasaki, and ended war against Japan, 235,
not keen on becoming involved in Korea, 236

Tschirschky, Heinrich von,
poor opinion of Austria, 57,

conviction that Britain would not intervene in war, 60,

commented that Austrian resolve was wavering, 63,

promised the Austria's 'declaration of war' would go off on 28th or 29th July 'in order to elimination any possibility of intervention' 66,

told 'you must carefully avoid holding Austria back' 68,

only showed the Austrians the amended version of the Kaiser's 'Halt in Belgrade' after their declaration of war, 68,

after Grey threatened war if Germany invaded France, received two telegrams from Bethmann Hollweg, telling him to refuse to allow Austria 'to draw us into a world conflagration … without regard for our advice', 73

Utrecht, Prince, 134

Ultimatum (to Serbia) 62, Churchill's reaction to, 62

Viktor, Archduke Ludwig, 28

Viviani, René, French Prime Minister, 61, 70,

ordered the French troops to leave a 10 kilometre zone between the French army outposts and the border, 75

Vögler, Albert,

head of coal conglomerate United Steel, 148,

German negotiator on the Young Plan with Dr. Schacht, 156,

resigned from negotiations after attending a banquet at Krupp's palace, 161

member of coal cartel, which funded Hitler, 185-186

Waigel, Theo, German Finance Minister, 272

Waldersee, Alfred von, 21

Warburg, Paul, 159

Wauchope, General, 147

Weber, Axel, President of the Bundesbank, 281, 301

Wilhelm I, 11, 12, 13, 20-22, 24, 33

Wilhelm II ('Kaiser Bill')

ambitions for an empire in America, 34-36,

for a colonial empire at the expense of France, 38-39,

blamed for setbacks, 40,

After Franz Ferdinand's murder promised that he would declare war at once if Russia mobilised, 59,

arrived back from holiday on 26th July, 65,

on 28th July saw and was happy with Serbia's reply to Ultimatum and wrote 'Halt in Belgrade' telegram, 67,

altered by Bethmann Hollweg and not delivered until after Austria had delivered her declaration of war against Serbia, 67-68,

30th July declared: 'England alone is responsible for the war and peace, not we any more,' 74,

ordered Moltke to hold up the start of the war, (ignored) 77,
forced to abdicate, 114

Wilhelmina, Queen of the Belgians, 38
Wilson, President Woodrow,
  peace offer in 1914 rejected, 83,
  won re-election, 88,
  received 'peace offer' from Germany as a prerequisite of it recommencing submarine warfare, 88-90,
  declared war in 1917 as an 'associate power', 91,
  produced 14 point peace proposals in January 1918 rejected by Germany, 96,
  prejudice against the winning Allies, 100,
  offered Germany peace again on the basis of 14 points plus 'impartial justice', 101,
  told his negotiator, Col House, 'There are many things in it (the peace offer) which will displease the imperialists of Great Britain, France and Germany,' 103,
  forced the Kaiser to abdicate, 105, 112-113,
  said that he would ask for 'no indemnities' 119,
  changed his mind about Germany's guilt after meeting delegates at Versailles, 121,
  said in 1923 that unless Germany was made to pay adequate reparations it would conquer the world industrially, 138

Young, Dr. Owen Young, 156,
Zimmermann Arthur, 90-91